MINDING THE EARTH, MENDING THE WORLD

MINDING
THE EARTH,
MENDING
THE WORLD

ZEN AND THE ART OF PLANETARY CRISIS

SUSAN
MURPHY

COUNTERPOINT

BERKELEY

Quotations from Naomi Klein's 'Capitalism vs the Climate',
The Nation, 28 November 2011, reproduced with permission from the author.

The author and publisher have made every effort to contact copyright holders
for material used in this book. Any person or organisation that may
have been overlooked should contact the publisher.

First published 2012 in Picador by Pan Macmillan Australia
Typeset in 11.5/16 pt Minion by Post Pre-Press Australia

Cover design by Gopa & Ted2, Inc.

Library of Congress Cataloging-in-Publication Data is available
Murphy, Susan, 1950– author.
Minding the earth, mending the world : Zen and the
art of planetary crisis / Susan Murphy.
pages cm
ISBN 978-1-61902-304-8 (paperback)
1. Human ecology—Religious aspects—Zen Buddhism.
2. Zen Buddhism—Social aspects. I. Title.
BQ4570.E23M87 2014
294.3'377—DC23
2013047444

COUNTERPOINT
2560 Ninth Street, Suite 318
Berkeley, CA 94710
www.counterpointpress.com

Printed in the United States of America

For Michael, Jack and Maeve,
and, as time goes on,
for Maya.

Contents

Foreword
by John Tarrant

Humans were born to develop and understand consciousness; we are the creatures who want to know who we are. The marvel of having a consciousness is entangled with the marvel of the universe itself, and our interest in how well we are understanding ourselves and our place in things runs through all religion and philosophy.

This book begins with an awakening, a childhood epiphany that becomes a touchstone for other discoveries along the way. The way is all about learning how we can live in our world as if we were making art. Susan Murphy is an artist and a most genuine Zen teacher, and she has taken on the great topic of our time in a unique way. The question she explores is a kind of magic thread—at one end there is climate change and at the other end is the fundamental fact of our human awareness. In between are dreams, carbon balances, what we eat, the smell of summer rain, whether we respect living beings enough to form relationships with them. The questions that allow us to explore these many linked territories are ones like: *How will we survive? How will we survive ourselves? What is actually happening to the climate? What are we allowed to take from this world? What is too much to ask and what is the right amount? What stories are we telling ourselves? How might we change if we had different stories? What gates are there for us to walk through? Can we be friends with the animals? With each other? What, in the realms of art and thought and awe, can we draw on that will change the story we are living?* And underneath all these questions like a hidden river is this: *Do we love life enough to live it and preserve it?*

The issue of climate change is, as Susan points out, so large and so near that in filling the view finder, it can disappear from the mind. She has taken on the task of making it visible and making us want it to be visible and want to understand how we might relate to so challenging a confrontation. Hard times are the test of whether we love life, and in dark times that cause fear and looking away, just to look is itself an act of love for the planet and also for ourselves. Because her interests and her experience range so widely, she can take us through every kind of landscape. Susan Murphy is a great companion for such a journey.

We humans have carried an interest in our consciousness on our long migration to every corner of the earth, making bone flutes in caves, drawing on the walls and on our own bodies, making pots, burying the dead. At the same time we were also born with a kind of a pain, a separation between ourselves and the intricate, ever-flowing universe. This separation is in the stories we tell ourselves—Adam and Eve bit the apple and were evicted from the garden; we must die, we must labor and give birth in pain.

The pain of separation appears in the way we treat the natural world inside us and outside us. In terms of what is outside, we have a climate crisis—the thing so large it is hard to mention. In terms of what is inside we have our obsessions. But we also have the arts of attention, which offer a way out of the dilemma; we learn from dreams, Zen koans, Aboriginal myths, childhood epiphanies. Even the great story of science, the story of evolution, is itself a kind of myth to orient the mind.

How do we honour the joy of being human, the charged meaning we feel in merely breathing under the night sky so full of stars, and also be true to the temporariness of us, our temporariness appearing in our time in the particular and most poignant form of climate change? It is in the joining of the outer and inner points of view that this book excels.

Susan starts like a romantic poet, taking us on a long arc through the causes of despair and the mortal danger of our time and a conversation with the earth and with our own animal nature. She releases us in the end into practices—she offers us something real to do, a medicine kit she calls it, a way to change our minds so we can see a bigger view.

In the medicine kit she offers Zen koans, poetic and disturbing stories and devices. She actually knows about and loves them tenderly, and shows them as gate openers, a way to step into the inconceivable, to grow wise through our mistakes.

These practices come at a place in the journey where they arrive as a kindness and a release. When overwhelming strength is arrayed, softness and dreaming might lead the way. When the situation is impossible then we will be able to step outside of the possible. It is never too late.

John Tarrant, June 2012.
Dr John Tarrant is a Zen master, the founding teacher of the Pacific Zen Institute in California, and the author of *Bring Me the Rhinoceros* and *The Light Inside the Dark*.

The chair, the kitchen table

It is hard to say when this book began life. It seems at least as old as I am, but also far older.

Perhaps the origin of any book, like the source of a river, is finally impossible to separate from all that is and will be. For which of a dozen or more feeder springs do you choose; or earlier than that, which moss bank dripping over a rock ledge, which raindrop that fell in that catchment; and how to put a date to a raindrop which is really as old as the earth, and in fact even older, as old as the elements formed in the earliest supernovae explosions? Or back to the start of time itself, arriving together with matter and energy some trillionth of a second after whatever unimaginable occurrence marked the birth of the ongoing revelation that we call the universe?

Why not? For when we take that reference point to search for who we are, and where and when we came from, conventional reality is dramatically shaken out of its small-time habits. And that's useful because 'conventional reality' is not serving us well right now. Its frame is too small and very dated when it comes to addressing the nature of what is happening on our planet, and our extremely interesting part in that.

But going back to the more tangible sources of this book, one moment that stands out took place in my late childhood on an ordinary morning when I casually drew my chair out from under the kitchen table to sit down for breakfast.

It was the mid-sixties and I was twelve years old. The kitchen table was oak, old, round and honey coloured, probably about eighty years old, bought for a song from the St Vincent de Paul shop that had furnished most of our house. All our family meals were eaten around that table, and it was the scene of much talking, arguing, laughing, reading, homework, breaking of bread and drinking of wine—in short, it was our communion table.

My older brother and sister and I had sat around the kitchen table late into the previous night—our parents must have gone out somewhere—and talked our way deep into the intense environmental pressures that were already being felt in the world.

Paul Ehrlich and others were already portending what would become known as 'the limits to growth', predicting nightmarish overpopulation and mass starvation scenarios for the seventies and eighties, many of which were deferred, though not solved, for several decades by the short-term agricultural successes of the oil-fuelled Green Revolution. Rachel Carson was already under fierce attack from the chemical industry for daring to point to the stark early warning signs of far-reaching environmental degradation by pesticides, and the avalanche of extinctions that would form its wake. The incremental climb in global temperatures due to the hothouse effect of carbon emissions had been underway since 1950 but was not yet part of public discussion, despite having been clearly predicted a century earlier. The more pressing climate threat at that time was the Cold War nuclear winter that would potentially extinguish most life on earth following any extensive nuclear 'exchange'—the preferred way of referring to the release of hundreds of intercontinental ballistic missiles armed with hydrogen-bomb warheads.

Around the kitchen table that night our hearts were rapt in wonder as we consciously stared one by one at the spectres stalking our world—the mounting industrial assault on a shrinking and collapsing natural world; the effects of exploding human population upon environmental sustainability and biodiversity; and the deepening cycle of exploitation, injustice, poverty and hunger the 'undeveloped' world was apparently expected to bear in support of our own relatively easy lives. Our childhoods had been spent almost entirely barefoot, exploring lush Queensland rainforest, swimming in clear creeks, floating over brilliant coral reefs. The thought that we might be the last generation to live on a planet with seas full of fish, tigers roaming free, a vast intact Amazon forest, was intolerable. Even our sheer good luck in living lives less impacted than most by the slow avalanche of ruin was painful. All of this was caught up in an unstoppable rush of words and feelings that night.

We talked on and on in a state of terror curiously mixed with intensely alive excitement, weighing up the fate of the world during our lifetime and our possible part in that. I think each of us sensed that facing the terror together was an act of love, forming deeper bonds between us. When we finally went to bed around three or four in the morning, I felt flattened, crushed. My mind was reeling but also filled with new capacity. My whole being was large and alive with the thrilled sense of having taken on a little of the mantle of adult awareness.

I remember the next morning as very bright—perhaps a shade *too* bright after the latest night of my life thus far. I had heaped cereal into my bowl, and milk, and walked to the same high-backed chair of the night before. The extraordinary night lay inside me as a kaleidoscope of amazing pieces of knowledge, sharp to the touch and overwhelmingly complicated, but strangely precious. I set my bowl onto the table. I took hold of the back of the chair and pulled it out. I sat down and put my hands on the table.

That was the moment of the tidal wave.

It washed through me and left nothing as it had been before. I found myself swimming in a sea of marvellous awareness that all was well and completely at ease. This fact was utterly undisturbed by the equally plain fact that I chanced to be alive at a time of slow-burning catastrophe for the entire life system of the planet. 'All things are well,' was how the anchoress Julian of Norwich put the same realisation, 'And all manner of things shall be well.' The clear *knowing* of this flooded my body and seemed to live vibrantly right *inside* every terrifying complication of the rider, 'And so much is wrong.'

I was astonished, and yet it seemed more like the astonishment of remembering something I had always known, something very deep lying and fundamentally fearless even in the face of matters of overwhelming concern. In fact, it was intimately and completely at one *with* that concern, stirred to life by it.

I felt immensely reassured, without being pacified or soothed. Concern was never more clear and alive. Everything—the chair, the kitchen table, the sitting-down and the placing of my hands either side of my willow-pattern bowl of cereal—bestowed this blessing: that we must *rely* on what is happening in order to learn how to proceed, that we can dare to meet it fully just as it really is, and that what is so urgently being called up in us flows naturally from daring to welcome a hard reality.

'Just as it really is' cannot possibly hide the suffering and ruin and awfulness of things; and yet that is exactly what opens the way for the deep reassurance of all things to reach us; and with it the possibility—the *fact*—that we are not helpless at all, that we all actively make this mysterious and wondrous world, and that everything we do counts.

I was bruised by wonder. A course was set. *Don't miss anything. Everything, everyone counts. Find out what this means, do what it wants of you.* Emily Dickinson said, 'Life is so astonishing, it leaves very little time for anything else!' At that moment, I was Emily.

Wonder is perfectly aware that we are all caught in a ridiculous posture right now. The posture of living 'normally' as we destabilise climate, trash seas and earth and atmosphere and decimate species, while chanting a mantra of perpetual growth and unrestrained human population increase and watching all these accelerate in runaway chain reaction. It is ridiculous to pretend it is not happening, and almost equally ridiculous to mention it, since no one can personally hope to change its course, and no one much wants even to hear about it. Our position as a species is now so untenable that it verges on rudeness to mention it in polite company.

But wonder does not stop at ridiculousness. For a start, it's nothing new. Were we ever not at least partly ridiculous, we smallish, frightened, mortal, highly conscious mammals, with our opposable thumbs and opposable minds? And have we not always been at the mercy of forces—natural and human—that appear to lie far beyond the scale of any personal action in response? Wonder just uses that as an energising and even humorous prompt to wake up a little more imagination and awareness. 'Let's see!' it seems to suggest: 'Don't flee. What about discovering more of what you are, instead?'

We are all in this emergency together, all answerable to the terms of one great biosphere. And it has no boss. It just has each of us. Carl Jung addressed that fact, saying, 'Each of us must remember that we are the make-weight that shifts the scale.' Small acts mount up. Drops of water carve mountain ranges. Small is not powerless. William James said:

> I am done with great things and big things, great institutions and big success, and I am for those tiny invisible molecular moral forces that work from individual to individual, creeping through the crannies of the world like so many rootlets, or like the capillary oozing of water, yet which, if you give them time, will rend the hardest monuments of man's pride.

And he was writing a good hundred years before the Occupy and Indignado movements began to surge through a thousand global networks—at last!—as the second decade of the new century opened.

This book is an enquiry into why change has seemed so hard to initiate, why we have been stalled so long in senselessness, and what must move in us in order to break free of a too-narrow frame. It asks what might be a *whole* response to the telling signs of planetary emergency, given that not one of us can 'save the planet' like a Hollywood action hero straight out of central casting? Such a whole response must start with clearly seeing the nature of the frame our culture has created for conceiving of reality, then move to see beyond the frame.

We need to change the story. We need a story that is able to conceive of where and what we are right now, and encourage a practice of awareness that can rouse and recall the vastness within us, less easily clouded by fear and self-defeating views that would make us each too small to be of value.

The industrialising world set in motion by the West has no bedrock story to help explain the looming environmental crisis with climate change at its heart. The ancient stories that underpin our sense of reality held warnings—about a dualistic splitting of consciousness; about greed that consumes the world and our selves at the same time; about the danger of overreaching inherent in each ambitious new technology; and about apocalyptic collapse of the human world. But the deep imperative of industrialised civilisation—to 'go forth and multiply and subdue the earth'—remains founded in an unquestioning human-centred and human-entitled cosmology formed several thousand years ago as one small Semitic tribe in the Middle East coped with vulnerability of the transition from nomadic pastoralism to settlement in small city-states.

That world could not possibly conceive of the universe and earth in which we now come to understand ourselves. Born in fire thirteen and a half billion years ago, it gave birth to innumerable galaxies, including the minor but remarkable one we call the Milky

Way that eventually formed a small, finite but remarkably productive planet. That in turn gave birth to millions upon millions of life forms, including us—the strange creatures with a self-reflective consciousness. The mindset at the foundation of the West literally belongs to another planet and cosmos altogether. This has profound consequences for the shift we have to make to understand and take care of the planet where we find ourselves.

The 'new' story that can help usher in a healing consciousness to our world—healing meaning 'return to wholeness'—is as old as the universe itself. It *is* the Universe Story, and the story of the earth, available as a reasonably legible whole at the exact moment in human history in which we have to face the possibility that our actions may be bringing us to the circumstances of our own extinction as a species. The story of the earth is not one headed for an End Time any time soon. It will go on without us to slowly return to wholeness if we can't find the right shift of consciousness in time to join it rather than oppose it.

That invitation to join it comes with our bodies and first breath. It opens progressively to us as children in the adventure of crawling and then walking on the earth among its sights and sounds and smells, in the presence of trees and rocks and other creatures. And this engagement with the earth opens our minds. Childhood in contact with the natural world is a perfectly shaped crucible for a true meeting of earth, mind and imagination.

Thomas Berry called the Universe Story 'the quintessence of reality', since the universe is the one self-referential reality in the phenomenal world, the sole 'text' open to all and with no external, culturally relative context. There is no outside to the universe. This immense and ongoing revelation can ignite the imaginative capacity in human beings to take in what is being made painfully clear by the earth right now, and to respond by according in skilful ways with reality, instead of denying it and staying on course towards self-destruction. To deepen this capacity takes conscious intention and effort. It is a practice.

Practising full accord with reality is always, like the universe itself, a work in progress. It requires holding yourself and your consciousness open towards the unknown (in which we all dwell) in a curious rather than presuming way. Meditation is the act of paying reality the courtesy of wonder and friendly curiosity that is sometimes called non-judgmental attention, a process that never stops opening and revealing itself, and clarifying what is needed at this moment. The discipline and love required for this is its own reward—it eases what the novelist David Foster Wallace called 'the constant gnawing sense of having had and lost some infinite thing'.

From the Zen tradition comes a unique way of easing this gnawing sense of displacement or loss. It's called a *koan*. The word means 'public case', because while we seem remarkably able to hide it from our selves, the boundless reality a koan reveals is in fact in plain view for all from the beginning. It has always been so close that there's no gap whatsoever, and yet we have to break the frame of ordinary thought to see this and heal our subtle self-alienation. It takes all that we are, to come down to earth to the liberating truth of all that we really are. But that's also its gift. Koans trigger a healing of crisis in consciousness that closes the gap we had forced between self and all that is.

The crisis facing us all right now is a tremendous koan set for us by the earth, speaking to us plainly but in words we cannot yet fully comprehend, caught as we are in the frame of the past that cannot conceive of this emergency. To respond we need to free ourselves from a too narrow sense of self and an unquestioned assumption or self-entitled priority as a species.

So on every level, in every chapter, the intent of this book is to help break free of the old frame that has held us paralysed and silent in the face of the crisis: by listening to the earth and responding to the koan of this crisis; by looking at the way we have framed the earth and thus ourselves with the old stories that are still generating the thinking that created the problem; by exploring the implications of an infinitely older story that is now in all our hands, the Universe Story, which is also the story of earth and life; and by exploring a practice of full awareness that can bring our actions back from an alienated state into more full accord with the terms of the earth.

Do we have any choice but to fight our way to this? Are we not answerable to the life of the earth? At every moment of life, this extraordinary gift bestowed upon us by our magical planet, are we willing to welcome the difficulty as our great chance? Surely we have to live up to this unprecedented moment we are in, or else cover our faces and slink away into oblivion, deeply shamed.

When my family left the wilds of north Queensland and moved to inner-city Sydney, the extremely exclusive, 'Murphy Adventure Club'—which had been dedicated throughout my childhood to secret training and bravery tests of various kinds—was quietly retired from active duty. The orange MAC flag my brother, sister and I had made was left behind, along with the special orange scarves with boy-scout woggles. There were no more march-pasts down our street, designed to incite envy among the neighbouring children. And our handmade clubhouse built from scrap timber, which had withstood a cyclone that tore down houses all around it, was left to the slower ravages of sweet potato vines. But what we never put aside was the MAC motto, chanted together in full salute as the flag was raised on our flagpole; *'Never give up on an adventure.'*

The intention of this book is rooted in that motto. I see the great adventure of our time as not losing heart or going crazy but regaining humanity in the course of fighting for a planet where our children's children can safely flourish. There is no map for this wild adventure, no ten-point plan, no guarantees. In all respects, it is oddly like life itself: discovered in the act of living. But win or lose, it's the great adventure on offer, and I am here to urge that no human being worthy of the name can ever give up on it.

Humanity might not make the leap the earth has placed before us. This possibility, too, must be included in our reckoning. Nature writer Barry Lopez said, 'There are simply no answers to some of the great pressing questions. You continue to live them out, making your life a worthy expression of leaning into the light.' Going up again and again to the extraordinary circumstances of being alive in the light of courage and uncertainty is, as he says, just what happens when you open up. We have forgotten our reverence for the earth and put aside justice where it retards profitability. Well, the earth is bringing us back to our knees again, and back to each other, in one way and another.

The understanding that there is a world beyond human control, human invention, human understanding, says Lopez, is the virtue of reverence, and reverence may be rekindled in us by sharply waking up to how much has simply gone wrong and grown profoundly unacceptable. For as Lopez says, 'There is another response to horror besides self-destruction. There is a way to enter into the bleakness that human beings are capable of, and not allow it to define what it is to be human.'

Thoreau famously wrote in *The Winged Life*:

> The life in us is like the water in the river. It may rise this year higher than man has ever known it, and flood the parched uplands . . . Everyone has heard the story which has gone the rounds of New England, of a strong and beautiful bug which came out of the dry leaf of an old table of apple-tree wood, which had stood in a farmer's kitchen for sixty years . . . from an egg deposited in the living tree many years earlier still, as appeared by counting the annual layers beyond it; which was heard gnawing out for several weeks, hatched perchance by the heat of an urn.

The 'beautiful and winged life' can be buried for ages under the woodenness of 'the dead dry life' of a society whose imagination has become dry and dead to its living reality. Once deposited in the green and living tree that had become its tomb, the creature is imagined by Thoreau as obscurely gnawing its way out for years by 'the family of man' as they sit around their table, before it bursts forth so unexpectedly 'to enjoy its perfect summer life at last!'

That's the winged life of the whole earth, and of all who have eyes to see.

Every crisis is the chance to see what we have been missing. This great, slow-building global crisis is our tremendous chance to see ourselves more clearly. Mistakes are our way of enlightenment; difficulty hatches our intelligence. A problem is needed to tell us what is missing, what we have not been seeing.

What the kitchen-table moment makes clear to me is that this dilemma we are in together is exactly the right dilemma. As Naomi Klein has said, climate change is not the issue. It is instead the unmistakable message that many of our most cherished ideas are no longer viable. And if we look and listen without preconceived ideas, it is also telling us *exactly* which ones appear to have been dreamed up on some other planet than this one. Climate change is intimating that we have some wondrous but as yet *undiscovered* ideas to learn to cherish, ideas that can teach us a little more about cherishing.

And if human beings are here on earth for any good reason at all, it is surely to learn about love. That is the great adventure, always worth the price of admission.

Medicine and sickness heal each other. The whole world is medicine.
Where do you find your self?
Zen Master Yunmen, ninth-century China

The first time I heard this old Chinese Zen koan, I felt the night sky and the centre of the earth as my own bone marrow. Koans are like that anyway, but this one more than most. You will be gradually getting to know how to be around koans and, in that way, gaining some fellow feeling for what they are. But like black and white cats, spotted pardalotes, red kelpies, clumps of seaweed, river pebbles or perfectly humble potatoes, being with them in person is greatly more instructive than anything you could ever presume to know in advance about them. So let me go on without stopping to explain.

The first two parts produced the immediate feeling of 'I know!' followed by a fascinated wondering, 'But I don't know *how* I know, or what *kind* of knowing this is!' The first sentence excited my thinking: medicine and sickness, not only inseparable but mysteriously each other! The second cut right through thinking, like an exhilarating bodily plunge into understanding, as if the natural outcome of how wondrous and beloved I found the earth to be when I faced it without flinching.

And the last part—well, it is the question that a self-reflexive consciousness continually asks of every human being, posed to us in every detail of what we perceive and experience in this life.

This book is a humble and provisional attempt to respond to the great lightning strike of Yunmen, which for me perfectly illuminates the country we must travel through to heal the earth, and in healing the earth, heal ourselves.

Provisional, because life is not yet over, and no koan ever stops opening.

They never give up on the adventure.

PART I

A PLANET IN CRISIS

CHAPTER ONE

The koan of the earth

You cannot solve a problem with the thinking that created it.
attributed to Albert Einstein

'Earth is where we all live. Earth sustains us. Earth allows us to be here temporarily. Like a good guest, we respect our host and all the beauty and bounty we are lucky to experience. We do no harm. And then we leave.' This comment was posted as part of a website discussion, and it's pretty hard to argue with, actually.

However, our industrialised world constructs itself in reverse image to inarguable reality. We live walled off from the earth as far as possible, though we will pay a high price for views of water or mountains. Many of us would by now find it unnatural to lie down to sleep on the earth, gather and cook food where we are, drink water from a creek, defecate in a hole dug in the ground. Our airconditioned, plugged-in level of material comfort estranges us from the earth and even from the sense of what is natural. And it insulates us from the high cost of this intensely self-centred way of living, leaving that to be borne out of sight by other people, other species, the earth as a whole. We live at maximum distance from the fact that we are here only temporarily, that we will age and die. Not only do we not respect our host and acknowledge the bounty and beauty earth pours out for us, we comprehensively distract ourselves from that by any means available. If pushed to notice it, we reassure ourselves that the mounting tsunami of harm left in our wake is entirely unintentional, not under our control.

'Doing no harm' to the earth remains low on the agenda of an intensely industrialised, energy-hungry world. Seven billion of us are now transfixed by an impossible promise of all securing the extreme material and technological advantages presently lavished upon members of the industrialised world. The dense forms of energy harnessed first from coal and then so spectacularly from oil has lifted the material lives of a growing number of us to levels of physical ease undreamed of in earlier generations, and this has happened so rapidly it has been hard to catch up with all of the harsh implications—though they are certainly now catching up with us.

If human beings ever were 'entitled' to make such short-term expendable use of the earth, it follows that all are equally entitled to the carbon-fuelled dream of unending bounty once enjoyed only by the West. The paradigm of continual economic growth insists that this is realisable and good, and in fact that all human wellbeing depends upon indefinite expansion of the market.

The problem is that the price of this indefinite expansion turns out to be the forfeiture of climatic conditions hospitable to our species. And of course not only to *our* species. The great extinction spasm we are living through right now, which could well include us, is tearing down the intricately interlaced ecologies of the earth as mere collateral damage in the pursuit of a single-minded, self-entitled idea. Too bad that it is extinguishing all 'entitlement' to life forever, for hundreds of earth's life forms every single day. While we continue to add more than 220 new human lives to the planet every second, or more than 200,000 every day.

From a position of accustomed comfort it is hard to conceive of living in a way that would require greater personal skill, effort and care to manifest the necessities of life. Breaking our reliance on the oil that has shown signs of peaking and beginning an inexorable decline, at exactly the time it has become woven into every detail of our lifestyle, is seemingly impossible to contemplate. Yet any child can see through the magical thinking and selfishness that under-pins the economic imperatives of limitless material growth and mindless waste—that nevertheless will duly go on to shape their adult lives.

The dream of an infinitely expandable planet placed entirely at our disposal was always just that, a dream, and it's fast becoming a nightmare. Tumultuous change on a vast scale grows increasingly likely with every day of business as usual. The only question is what forms it will take, which order of climate shocks and political crises will start to shake our world apart, and how people will react, as the market collapses and the source of plenty evaporates.

The magic flow of plenty

An old Scottish fairytale told of a fortunate village to which the fairies had given a magic cask in return for some good turn. Any time there was something to celebrate the villagers just turned the tiny spigot and the wine and communal goodwill would flow, inexhaustible. Everything went along beautifully until the day a curious housemaid decided to see just exactly how it all worked. She unscrewed the tiny spigot and took a peek inside. Nothing there but dust and ancient spiderwebs. And from that time on, the fairy wine cask yielded not a single drop of magic wine.

There are many ways to read this story in the light of our time. One is that we must never look too closely at what produces the magic flow of plenty we dream will continue forever. Look inside at its dark workings and the happy dream of 'forever' will be shat-tered. Scarcity, dust and ruin are waiting to be discovered inside it.

Another is that the earth sustains our life with its magical weave of infinite relationships of mutual dependency between all life forms and the elements that sustain them—water, air, soil, minerals, sunlight . . . Some call this peerless magic 'ecology', or 'nature'. Others may see it as the grace that animates creation. Failing to trust and protect this perpetually self-renewing gift, attempting instead to exploit it as a bounty earmarked for our exclusive use, we tear the web of life apart.

Let's take a kind of quick housemaid's peek inside the industrialised version of the fairy barrel and trace the biography of a typical North American tomato, as Peter Bahouth has described it. A genetically patented hybrid tomato derived from a Mexican strain is grown on land originally farmed by Mexican farmers in agricultural cooperatives. The new strain has low tolerance for local conditions so the land is fumigated with an intensely ozone-depleting chemical, methyl bromide, then doused in pesticides. The toxic waste from production of these chemicals is shipped to one of the world's largest chemical dumps in Alabama which is situated in a poor black neighbourhood, with marked effects on local health. The Mexican farm workers, displaced from their cooperatives but permitted to apply the pesticide to the plants now grown on what was once their farmland, are given no protection or instructions in proper application of such dangerous substances. They are paid around $2.50 a day and offered no form of health care.

The tomatoes are placed on plastic-foam trays and covered in plastic wrap, then packed in cardboard boxes. The plastic wrap is manufactured in Texas, where local residents suffer exposure to the dioxins that are by-products to chlorine manufacture and highly hazardous to their health. The cardboard boxes, which were once three-hundred-year-old trees harvested from an old-growth forest in British Columbia, are manufactured thousands of miles distant in the Great Lakes district, then shipped by truck all the way back to Latin American farms using oil extracted and processed in Mexico.

The boxed tomatoes are artificially ripened with ether. Now watery, weary and nutritionally compromised, the tomatoes are sent by refrigerated trucks on vast freeway networks all over North

America. Ozone-depleting CFC cooling equipment is used at every stage of their delivery to the tables of 'consumers' (once called 'people') who are bound to wonder what on earth has happened to that delectable fruit that once went by the name 'tomato'.

While there is no evil master plan of ecological destruction in this story, and little *conscious* intent to destroy communities and life-ways, disfigure the countryside and ruin the climate, nevertheless it is one small part of an overarching system that effectively does evil by way of countless repetitive, cumulative failures of care and conscience, easily brushed aside in the process of maximising profit.

Nature always was and still is the real magic barrel. Its gift economy of ever-evolving life provided the original soil, water, seed and flowering plants, and eventually the small red fruit that could be coaxed by human ingenuity and toil into large juicy tomatoes. The industrial super-magic barrel took over from there, turning this cyclical flow of gifts into a one-way flow of profit into a few hands. The product was wrought from nature at extraordinary cost to natural systems, while its engineers refuse point-blank to register on its balance sheets the vast destruction of 'natural capital' that it involves. That's a 'magic' that fast wears out its welcome.

Incidentally, there's no report in the story of the fairy-barrel village ever sharing its great luck with any neighbouring villages. The village apparently felt secure in its superior fortune, and a sense of entitlement no doubt helped cover over its naked mean-spiritedness. But a fairy gift can be double-edged. Misuse exceptional good fortune and you become cold and alienated, poverty-stricken in ways you may not even notice. Until the next time you try to turn the tiny magic spigot and find the supply of all that really matters most has run out forever.

Minds and worlds

These days I can find myself in many worlds—or at least entertaining many propositions about what this world is and what its fate may be—in even a single day. A whole flicker of darting thought and retreat from thought like schools of fish, surging this way then that. News of gigantic Antarctic ice shelves breaking away; the Gulf of Mexico fast becoming a vast ocean dead spot; the Great Barrier Reef expected not to survive beyond two more decades; phytoplankton, the foundation of the entire marine food chain, reduced by 40% since 1950 due to warming seawater; island nations pleading eloquently and uselessly in Copenhagen and Cancun; global poverty set to skyrocket with climate collapse; the gap between rich and poor growing to obscene extreme . . . My thoughts dart this way and that, surging like schools of fish, and my emotions follow. In the never-ending avalanche of factoids, opinions, gossip, trivia, brands and sound bites, there is no space or sufficient quiet for sorrow, reflection and resolve.

Is it like this for you? How are you dealing with it?

When I walk out into the world well away from phones, i-gadgets, internet, radio, television or newsprint and walk on the earth and breathe the open air, I begin to recollect myself and come back to earth. I gradually become a humble, humorous, earthy human being again, who belongs here as thoroughly as every natural thing I can find around me. This may be easier in the green and flowing world that lies beyond the nearly perfect human trance we call a city, but even in the city the earth is always in reach, and when the earth is in reach, wonder is in spitting distance. The weed life taking root in the cracks of the pavement, a glimpse of a pelican moving above the buildings, a cat's cool stare from a warm brick wall, a puddle riffled by breeze disturbing its upside-down reflections, a tree root powering its slow way out of the asphalt and into a gutter . . .

Just as they draw my attention, my attention calls them back to vivid life. Consciousness is partner to the composing of a 'world'. Every sentient being creates an entire world according to its earth-given style of sentience and its experience of life. The world of the blowfly blundering into a room will be utterly unlike the world of the person trying to ignore its frantic buzzing, though both breathe the same air and drink the same water. The poet, Anne Carson, says, 'There is no person without a world'; equally, there is no 'world' in the fully human, conscious sense of that word, without a person. Every human death takes with it an entire and unrepeatable world, a whole realm of memories, dreams, reflections, beliefs and observations. We suffer this fact in the loss of each other, and in fear of our own imagined loss of ourselves. If we do finally swat that blundering blowfly with a tea towel, what can we really know of the world extinguished in a single swipe?

Although there are countless trillions of worlds alive on earth, in 1968 astronauts Lovell, Anders and Borman of the Apollo 8 space mission became the first human beings to leave earth's orbit and see our one entire blue-green planet swimming in black space. The depth of surprise and awe in those three men suggest they did not merely witness an amazing physical fact but a surpassing and singular miracle. They found themselves deeply stirred by this planet's luminous presence. Earth brought them to tears.

Until we can expand our scope beyond self-centred and purely human concerns to hold in mind the trillion worlds alive on this one earth at any moment, and to glimpse *ourselves* exactly in that vibrant, seamless web of interconnectedness, we are living in a kind of madness—which is to say, not living in reality. The great question of our time is whether or not we will prove able to wake into full awareness of the earth, and the geophysical changes now in play, in time to avert full-blown catastrophe.

Even beyond skilful crisis management and regaining the intelligence needed for survival, such a challenge actually offers the exhilarating chance to reawaken to our real nature, which has never departed one inch from reality. For what is realisation or enlightenment but the earth speaking to us directly, with our own noise no longer overwhelming the signal?

The unending call and response between human mind and Planet Earth can be dimmed but it cannot be turned off. It can be hard to hear over the avalanche of distractions, but the moment our resistance softens or just mysteriously gives way, it cannot be silenced. At that moment we have arrived at the place where truly *minding* the earth begins.

Our increasing impertinence (to use a word which originally meant not just rudeness but lack of relevance) is that we have, somewhere in the march of 'civilisation', lost the humble amazement of feeling the earth and ourselves to be a prodigious unearned gift from the universe. How did we make ourselves self-appointed lords of the earth and, like spoilt children, throw all gratitude and humility out the window?

A deeper chord of human-earth relatedness composes the very cells of our body and lies entirely undisturbed by all our puerile strutting, but while we cannot kill the fundamental relatedness, we have broken our accord with the earth, and that may have us ejected yet again from Eden—this time setting fire to the Ark on the way.

'The world', from our earliest emergence as a species, has always signified a human project entwined completely with nature. But the advent of human agency in shaping the earth has now reached a point where the fate of much of the biosphere of the planet is in the slippery, forgetful hands of human beings. And we have forgotten that our fate, too, is completely entwined with the fate of the earth.

Clear and present danger

And the earth is slowly cooking. The last time earth experienced such warming was about 55 million years ago, when temperatures rose by about 11°F over the course of around 20,000 years, at far slower rate than the current pace of warming.

And it's not just the way we're pouring carbon pollution and its by-products into the atmosphere, just as if it were an open sewer, that's destroying the balance of climate. It's the humidity that comes with the heat, holding more water, causing freak downpours, killer mudslides, massive flooding, lethal snowstorms. It's the carbon pollution killing the oceans, turning them too acid as well as too warm. It's the concatenating effects of extinctions of species and destruction of habitats, the demolition of rivers, mountains and forests, and the concreting-over of the fathomless beauty and diversity of the planet. It is the burden we are bearing of our own increasing moral squalor, in knowing we are living far too fat, by means of so much unending damage.

And for all the talk of decarbonising the economy, we know that the rate of damage is actually only changing into higher gear. The carbon stored in the Alberta tar sands that Canada is presently preparing to process and transport by the massive Keystone pipeline network to the USA is estimated to have the capacity to raise the median temperature by a catastrophic 4°C. The rise by 0.9°C since 1950 has been enough to set in train significant disruptive weather events, almost clear the Arctic waters of summer ice, and threaten to release the vast methane banks stored in the melting tundra subsoil. The planet is already heating to the point where major world cities face inundation and drought is becoming endemic to large areas of the world's 'bread basket'.

A world 4°C hotter has been estimated to have a carrying capacity no greater than one billion people. This remnant population will be enduring regular temperature highs of 42 to 52°C across most of the continents of Australia and India, as an example. To put this into perspective, the last time south-eastern Australia experienced 45°C temperatures was the day that came to be known as Black Saturday—7 February 2009, which saw the mountain ash forests of the high country ringing Melbourne explode in 400 separate fires that converged to devour townships, destroying more than 2000 houses, and killing 170 people. Even if the brakes to the juggernaut are found soon, the earth will take more than a thousand years to sequester even the *present* amount of carbon released thus far, and to ameliorate its harm.

A rise of 4°C will ensure our goose is thoroughly cooked, the goose that laid the golden egg—being the nearly 12,000-year long planetary niche we have enjoyed—the current interglacial referred to as the Holocene—that has provided climate settings favourable for the development of agriculture, urbanisation and what we optimistically refer to as civilisation.

Although this book is not going to be a compendium of climate data, the summary from the Global Carbon Project consortium of scientists and economists, published in the December 2011 edition of the journal *Nature Climate Change*, makes chilling nonsense of climate-change denial that rejects the possibility of human agency in global warming. Here is a summary of the bullet points they fired off—the only bullet points you will find in this book:

- The amount of man-made carbon dioxide released globally has increased by nearly 50% over the past two decades. In 2010 it reached a record 10 billion tonnes, nearly 6% higher than in 2009. The trend continued on the same trajectory in 2011.
- Global CO_2 emissions since 2000 are tracking the high end of the projections used by the Intergovernmental Panel on Climate Change (IPCC), which far exceed 2°C warming by 2100. We are more on course for a 4°C rise, and possibly as high as 6°C if carbon feedbacks begin.
- The past decade has seen an unprecedented increase in greenhouse gases released from fossil fuels, deforestation and the manufacture of cement, resulting in an average rise of 3.1% per year. This compares with an annual increase of just 1% per year during the 1990s.
- In the developed world, carbon dioxide emissions fell by 1.3% in 2008 and fell again by 7.6% in 2009, reflecting the economic slowdown of the global financial crisis, but rose again, by 3.4%, in 2010.
- In the developing world, dominated by China, emissions increased by 4.4% in 2008, increased by 3.9% in 2009 and 7.6% in 2010.

Overall, global carbon dioxide emissions from burning fossil fuels have increased 49% in the past two decades, the study found. That's the two decades of relatively intense awareness of the impact of fossil fuels upon global warming. The report delivers findings for 2010 of the largest single jump in global carbon emissions in any year since the start of the Industrial Revolution.

And this, perhaps the most alarming news of the century in terms of clear and present danger to human life, caused hardly a ripple in the mainstream news.

Facing the music

When the full scope of the damage we live by is fully taken in, it is undeniably crushing. I think we've all felt a terrible sense of being frozen in the headlights of an unstoppable juggernaut. That juggernaut is the globalised coal- and oil-based military-industrial-media economy, along with its vast web of national and corporate power relations, digital information, opinions and gossip. It is greased equally by foreign wars and the seamless collusion of all who enjoy the comfortable living conditions and infinite distractions of the industrially developed countries of the world. All of us on board the juggernaut have chosen to live obliviously towards its immense destruction of the earth's natural capital. We have deregulated ferociously unrestrained corporate entities, licensing them to exploit the earth's 'resources' without mercy, just as if they were limitless.

It is an unlovely and fearful sight.

And yet, have a look: the juggernaut is not separate from us. We are staring with growing fear and disgust at something that is not 'safely' outside ourselves but exists with our own full-blown participation. Cursing the drug dealer does not free us from being junkies. With the exception of those living entirely off the grid in every respect, by necessity or choice, there is not a man, woman or child in the industrialised world who does not lend themselves daily in some measure to the all-consuming appetite that is exhausting the earth's resources.

Wherever the juggernaut arrives, it devours rivers, mountains, forests, oceans, peoples, creatures, and every sign of the loveliness, benevolence and balance of the natural world, leaving nothing indigenous, wise, beautiful, various or whole in the debris of its wake. Just a flat, homogenised streak of so-called civilisation: strip malls, car parks, industrial 'parks', concrete, smog and endless high-rise. Or in a poor country, not even that— just black plastic bags in the wind, intensified poverty and rampant exploitation of people and natural resources. The juggernaut we all help create—by failing to resist its stream of 'things' and 'stuff', by turning a blind eye to its evils, by fearing it when it shows itself to be beyond moderating—is not driven by malevolence. It is powered by the usual array of human vices, but magnified exponentially by the speed and reach offered by oil and digitalised communication.

The juggernaut pushes a barbarous worldview that has, in the last three decades, gradually left all public forms of caretaking and altruism—towards each other and all life on earth—almost entirely to voluntarism and religion. It is a worldview that still understands 'we' and 'us' in national and sporting terms, but barely at all in societal terms.

I think we are all aware by now that the emperor of limitless consumption and economic growth has no shred of morality to cover the nakedness of its greed. But I think we also know that with the naming and exposure of the emperor, there goes 'the lifestyle'.

Is this why the moment that global warming began to make a strong moral, physical and practical claim on our attention, a blizzard of blinding denial was immediately unleashed? Public relations skills, honed on seeding doubt about the effects of Big Tobacco on public health, have been applied to a campaign aimed at seeding climate-change denial under the rubric of 'scepticism'—a handsomely funded snow job traceable back to Big Oil. At the same time all moves to decarbonise the economy have been branded a plot to destroy jobs and ruin the nation, despite the fact that a more comprehensive destroyer of jobs and nations than climate and environmental collapse is impossible to imagine.

We must find a liveable transition away from an economic system that is at war with the earth, but weighing up the harms between different courses of action and inaction will be extremely challenging. Yet if we manage to accept the challenge, the intense rigour of responding to this great question of our time can wake up forgotten parts of ourselves and usher in our maturity as a species. The shared peril of global warming is not just an economic and political matter but an overwhelming 'moral opportunity', as Al Gore has called it, to restore effective ethical brakes to a worldview religiously devoted to rapacious self-interest.

My tone of hope in this book is tempered by awareness of the grossly unequal material conditions of humanity—a gap in justice and sanity that has grown astronomically in the last fifty years, and promises to yawn ever more widely as climate change impacts on water and food security in the developing world (as we fondly call it from our padded sofas). I reflect on our shared emergency from a relatively easy first-world life; without that luxury, my chance to do so would be severly curtailed. I am also aware of how easily our comfort can insulate us for just a little bit longer from the sharp end of the emergency of climate change and global poverty already being endured by a majority of people on earth.

Any illusion that we can safely enjoy the present flow of costly abundance is its own catastrophe ahead of the train wreck. To the extent that we find it possible to delay responding and defer paying attention, we are suffering diminished ability to think and move in timely reaction to danger. Our equivocation and easy distractibility is a form of succumbing in advance to the disaster. It enables our present limp state of political leadership, permits the shameful discrediting of those who publish hard scientific findings, and retards the push towards a shared, cogent vision of the magnitude of change that must come.

How did we let ourselves fall so deeply asleep at the wheel?

The neoliberal economic 'rationalism' to which the global economy has been wedded for the past three decades has almost completely disengaged a political 'we' who can respond to serious threat. Margaret Thatcher's infamous 'there is no society, there are only individuals' has burgeoned into the extreme egotism of a materially driven individualism, and left us no longer very able to build solidarity around a coherent political position. For decades we have seemed unable to believe in or even perceive a threat that so directly addresses something called 'us all'; any threat that was not 'all about me' appeared to be undetectable.

Planetary crisis has so far been addressed purely in terms of 'the thinking that created the problem'. Take the longest and richest coral reef system on the planet that stretches for more than a thousand miles just off the coast of Queensland. In 2007, signs of coral bleaching in the Great Barrier Reef became impossible to ignore. It seems hard to believe now, but the then Prime Minister of Australia, John Howard, suggested that this could be 'solved' by simply erecting shade structures over the most tourist-accessible sections of the reef.

Such 'problem solving' glides serenely past the stark fact that, besides being one of the most prolific sites of biodiversity on the planet, the reef is a *whole*—a most intricately and delicately balanced ecology of fish, crustacean, shell and coral species—not a series of 'spots'. And that likewise the warming of seawater that is killing the reef is part of a *whole* ocean system of currents. Most of all, it entirely disavows the fact that the reef is being killed by a global economic system that can never afford to admit to the fundamental flaw of its logic of limitless expansion on a finite planet. As for the possibility of seeing that the highly heat-stressed state of the largest coral reef on earth beginning to suffer a degradation of its complexity that threatens its entire collapse presents something much deeper than a problem to be solved, that it poses a profoundly important moral and metaphysical question to every human being alive today—this does not even begin to dawn at the horizon of such severely compromised thinking.

An inescapable opportunity

We are living in what must surely be the most daunting and arresting moment we have ever faced as a species. We face a developing reality that can either condemn human beings to oblivion or inspire us to wake up to our lives in a dramatically more interesting way. A way that begins in living soberly and creatively towards the crisis of our planet—not as a problem to be solved by engineering an ever better, safer, human 'bubble', but as a constantly unfolding obligation to begin considering the remaking of ourselves as ecologically awake human beings.

It is possible to live straight on to our reality instead of hiding out from it in ten thousand different ways. To do so, first we have to see through the way our sense of the world has been framed by the stories that form the bedrock of our civilisation, stories that pose nature as a dubious force to be mastered and utilised, or put more bluntly, raped and pillaged for profit.

To the extent that these stories no longer explain the many things that urgently need explaining, they have become untrue. We can no longer adhere to 'truths' that we have depended on to steer civilisation in a trustworthy direction. At the same time, we have to recognise the need for a common story that can help us understand and engage with the new reality breaking upon our heads.

In the stories we tell, as one Kwaikutl elder said, we tell *ourselves*. What would we find ourselves to be, and how would we behave, if we were to live with all of our human ingenuity brought to bear upon living within the terms of the earth instead of despite them? If we were to recognise the rights of earth and other species in law, to mould agricultural and economic choices and the design of our technologies accordingly, discovering in the process a vast opportunity of learning and shared prosperity? This can be a huge and difficult adventure that will bring out the magnificence of human beings. It is also an act of love and compassion worthy of the earth—an unparalleled rousing of human minds in lifted awareness of our shared reality and shared planet. Transition away from the dream that we can live forever by massive damage to the earth is inevitable. We can do all we can to ensure that this transition is politic, able to take the great majority of us with it to a saner understanding of what a good life might be, in the little time available. We'll still have to pay every part of the price wrought by the changed climatic circumstances already incurred, but we can at least work to ameliorate them and avoid the truly unpayable price of continuing to pretend that this collective fantasy can endure.

A powerful rebellion of the heart

The transition begins in a rebellion of the heart and the waking up of awareness that is inherent in us all.

Perhaps it begins in noticing a growing repulsion towards the very excess itself. Do we really need more i-gadgets, apps, accessories, fashion items, short-lived toys, supersize serves, outsize cars, huge houses, and double garages bulging with all the things we have grown tired of? A rebellious refusal rises in the heart towards such a shallow, narrow and essentially *dull* idea of what a human being is.

Or it may start in fury at the growing gulf between rich and poor, the behaviour of the banks in privatising every cent of their massive profit while nationalising their trillion dollar losses through public bail-outs by the same taxpayers whose life savings and homes they gambled and profiteered away. Or in the despair of being young, educated, saddled with a huge education debt, but with no prospect of work. Or in the grief of seeing old growth forests clear-felled for disposable chopsticks and paper packaging, or burned to make way for palm oil plantations, dispossessing the last orang-utans of their remnant ecological niche.

One playful Zen koan, shaped to kickstart our startling left-of-field heartfelt intelligence, goes like this: 'Once, a woman raised a goose inside a bottle. When the goose was grown, she wanted to get it out. How do you free the goose without breaking the bottle?'

How *do* you break free of the human mindset that has trapped us, become toxic and begun eating the earth alive? Now that question is still too full of the thinking that created the problem. There's a self-imposed barrier in proposing a problem of breaking free, since original freedom might well be discoverable as the very nature of the one who asks. To get down to that you have to first let go of all you think you know about 'glass', 'bottles' and 'goose'. 'So where do you find your self?' asked Yunmen, so casually you might think he was not urging you to break out of prison.

How will we avoid shattering human life into post-apocalyptic shards of its former self? An immensely practical and important question, yet this koan is also asking us to rediscover our original undividedness, and the freedom it bestows, right there in the suffocating fear itself. It invites you to glimpse what the kitchen table moment revealed: that the crisis and salvation are inside each other. Or, as Yunmen put it, 'Medicine and sickness heal each other.'

Change like this doesn't come from a top-down approach. No living system has a boss. The boss is all of us, inextricably together, using the distributive wisdom of countless local actions occurring simultaneously.

At a practical level, ways of freeing the goose without breaking the bottle can be seen in some of the communal intelligence of nonviolent resistance emerging recently in the Occupy and Indignado movements. I have caught glimpses of the freed goose right there in the inventive energy of those recent uprisings. To be able to realise our real freedom within a sober, creative, playful awareness of reality is vital to get beyond the thinking that created the problem. Even if one in a hundred people begin to wake up to this degree, change ripples through, person to person, exactly like the Occupy Wall Street's 'people's microphone', created to pass words of a public address person to person when the right to using a public address system was denied.

As William James said, countless small acts wear down the mighty when they simply persist in going under, over or around every barrier placed in their path, or act from seeing right through them, in the spirit of the Zen koan. The ancient Taoist text, the *Daodejing*, which foreshadows and influences much of the character of Chinese Zen, says the same thing in the form of a fine koan for our time: 'The softest thing on earth overtakes the hardest thing on earth.'

It is almost as though we need to relearn the fundamentals that once were natural to us, like someone recovering from brain trauma: what it means to be a human being, a member of society, part of a family and a community, and of the great community of life, in literally remembering what *planet* we're on. Can we quiet our nerves and minds for a time, look deep inside our own humanity and our natures to rediscover the medicine to heal our collective madness? For we're not dead yet, and the world is still alive to sensitive human touch, so long as we extend it.

And when the stakes are life on earth, all else is a diversion.

Chapter Two

What if this was real?

A lie can travel halfway round the world while the truth is still putting on its shoes.

Mark Twain

Old King Canute has been made a laughing stock for centuries, for having placed his chair upon the beach in front of his people and commanding the rapidly incoming tide to turn back. In fact he was forcing his people to know something that they had wished not to know: that the alleged power of a king to save his people from any frightening eventuality was by nature limited. That he was an ordinary mortal human being.

A mighty king on his throne up to his neck in water: now there's an image for our times.

Canute would have appreciated something I glimpsed from a taxicab one afternoon in the mid-1990s on my way to LAX, the wonderfully well-named Los Angeles International Airport. Giant billboards lined the way, one after another in rapid succession. I was idly scanning them when I saw one that simply read, *What if this was real?* Delighted, I swung around to check if I had dreamed it, but wasn't quick enough. The next giant billboard had already replaced it.

Given LA's bent towards manufactured realities, it's possible someone had sought to pose aloud what turns out to be a nested set of pertinent questions. What if living inside this frenzied, unsustainable human-centred 'reality' we have avidly created for our endless consumption had real consequences? What if our current propositions about what is worthy of our attention had no relationship at all to anything we actually need to know to live and survive? What if we live inside thought worlds that have little risk of making any contact at all with the reality of our situation? What if beyond these thought worlds reality was coming to meet us headlong like a runaway Mack truck? Or worst and best of all—what if this unprecedented situation was real and worthy of deep attention, despite our lack thus far of formal recognition of its existence?

In the mid-1990s, it was still possible to ask 'What if this was real?' in an ironic, postmodern way. The internet was establishing its central place in everyday life but was not yet the ubiquitous echo chamber it has since become. We were becoming aware of how our greed- and carbon-fuelled way of life was polluting, stripping and despoiling the world. The World Trade Organisation meetings were being disrupted by fierce protests against the social injustice and galloping environmental destruction following in the wake of a radically deregulated marketplace. We were just starting to learn that greenhouse gases were warming the planet towards precipitous tipping points, and that there was only a twenty-year window of possibility to avert setting full-blown catastrophe in motion. We did not stir much beyond ironic fatalism.

What happened in the meantime, to so completely change the tenor of the question, 'What if this was real?'

The events of September 11, if anything, just made things more profoundly unreal. Instead of sobering us all to consider how blind-sided the West had grown to the extraordinary array of political grievances in the world, wars were launched. As a result, that precious first decade of the new century was lost to lies, ignorance, subterfuge, wars and ever more surreal mismatch between words and realities. Oh, and to vast military expenditure on the real goal of securing oil supplies, an expenditure that would have been more than adequate for commencing the decarbonising and retooling of industrial civilisation.

The Boxing Day Tsunami at the end of 2004, and Hurricane Katrina soon after in 2005, began to bring us to humble awareness of the implacable impartiality of geophysical events towards human beings. The first left us aware not only of the huge after-wave of public altruism, but also of the appalling idea that massive physical disaster can be a golden economic opportunity for corporate aid, reconstruction and seizure of foreign real estate. The second left an even more appalling smell behind it: not just a rotting city full of rotting corpses of the poor, but the moral stench of a government whose adherence to market ideology increasingly entailed indifference to its duty of care for its people.

By the global financial crisis of September 2008, that 'financialised' market supposedly taking care of the economic foundations on which so much depends had turned out to be little more than a fantastically profitable confidence trick played upon the public, who were never let fully into the secret that the stock exchange had become a casino and was no longer a trustworthy edifice guarded by such funny old ideas as probity, sobriety and frugality.

The discovery of what was really going on was not followed by punishment of the perpetrators but rewarded with a sixteen trillion dollar bail-out by government, paid from the taxes of its victims. The financial sector was permitted to continue unpunished for its crimes, unregulated in its business practices and unchecked in its naked greed.

All this set back progress on what Australia's former Prime Minister, Kevin Rudd, called 'the greatest moral challenge of our time'—climate change—only a year before caving in to populist fears and taking the greatest moral challenge back off the agenda. Although climate change had begun to make a significant dent on public conscience following Al Gore's 2006 documentary campaign, *An Inconvenient Truth,* when the economic seismic shockwaves of the global financial crisis hit, everything suddenly looked a bit of a luxury alongside pressing personal financial concerns. A whole new array of targets for moral outrage replaced irreparable damage to the environment. Suddenly the name of the devil was no longer 'Big Coal', 'Big Oil', and 'far too much of everything', but 'banker' (gradually morphing to 'bankster'), 'hedge-fund manager', 'short-seller' and 'bail-out'.

Nevertheless, despite the intensity of public disgust, the marketplace has barely skipped a beat. The fundamentalist 'free marketeer' can look upon natural disasters, unwinnable wars and sovereign debt crises and see golden opportunities, will continue leveraging gain from buying and selling toxic financial 'products', and gladly exploit the 'moral hazard' of the current situation in which governments both protect the vast profits of financial institutions and insure against their losses, which encourages further reckless risk-taking by those institutions.

It is no longer even surprising when financial buccaneering is rewarded not by penalty or imprisonment but by supersize bonuses. Nor that a man who robs a bank of the several thousand dollars he needs to pay his debts, but returns it next day mortified by his own actions, is given a seven-year jail term. *That* is where the moral compass is now set by our three-decade-long acceptance of the predatory behaviour of unrestrained forms of capitalism as if it were a species of fiscal virtue.

The greatest moral hazard of all has been that we have tolerated all this for so long without rebelling. I picture a fallen branch of a tree I once saw, heavily laden with cicadas that never paused in their unabashed shrilling as the branch made its way down a swollen creek in that strangely glassy stretch that comes just ahead of a thirty-metre plunge down a waterfall.

The unseeable hyper-object

Philosopher and artist Timothy Morton has suggested that something as huge as human-caused climate change, and all of the intellectual, political, social, cultural and economic change and adaptation to change that this entails, is an 'object' that is right in front of us but too big to see. He calls such phenomena 'hyper-objects'. The universe itself is one. Climate change and all that it entails, another. What does it take to learn to perceive a hyper-object?

The diary of Sir Joseph Banks, the botanist who accompanied James Cook on his voyage to the South Pacific that led to the 'discovery' and mapping of the east coast of Australia, records the moment of sailing into what would be named Botany Bay. The *Endeavour* sailed quite close to the shoreline where Aboriginal men and women were fishing on a headland. One world sailing right by another in astonishing close range. Banks described the people glancing up at the unparalleled sight of a large vessel under sail full of strange white people, and then almost pointedly looking away, back to the water and the fish. Is this how we deal with the inconceivable? Was the *Endeavour*, like global warming, a hyper-object, by nature unseeable?

Banks does not explore this, but it is the case that a subtle, robust, resilient oral culture, possessing millennia-deep knowledge of the continent and ritual protocols of rapport with the land, was equally unseeable to literate Europeans on their globe-circling craft equipped with the tools of astronomy, navigation and Enlightenment civilisation—including muskets.

Climate change may be hard to see with eyes that do not want to believe things are changing and will change even more drastically, but that there is such an object as climate change is unmistakeable. And what is coming towards us is already more here than it seems: the changes being experienced now reflect the volume of carbon emissions of twenty years ago; the impact of today's much higher levels of emissions are still to arrive.

Climate change is happening at hyper-speed by earth standards, and yet the sheer impossibility of continuing business as usual for any more than the next three seconds, geologically speaking, has entered no political agenda. Yet this may also be the first time in history that human beings have been able to see with awful clarity the unsustainability of their actions and an unliveable future of their own making coming towards them. Why, then, is the urgent conversation about this so hard to get started?

This is not happening

The wake-up call to the fact that global warming might be real had been a persistent, audible murmur from the 1980s, or actually from much earlier, going all the way back to the turn of the twentieth century if you cared to listen. But by midway through the first decade of this century, for many people it has become a steadily building warning siren nobody can dismiss or turn off.

And yet, how are we responding to it?

Blanket denial is often the first, and ultimately most painful, recourse of a terrified human being unable to consider reality—think of Eva Braun obliging everyone in the final Nazi bunker to join her feverish partying as Soviet mortar shells thumped directly above their heads in the streets of Berlin. In the face of such strenuous and fervid group denial of what is happening, it can feel dizzying and outlandish for a guest at such a party to say, 'What if this is not real? My bones are saying that we've all agreed to be true is not quite real. And I suddenly have grave fears for my unborn grandchildren.'

These days we have a robust set of safety standards for buildings, machines and infrastructure to encourage safe practices that will reduce accidents and try to forestall catastrophe. Where earthquakes, floods and fires threaten there are efforts to build to standards that will allow buildings, roads, bridges and people to survive the natural disaster. What is missing from this picture of intelligent public concern, both nationally and globally, is a genuine policy of safe practice for maintaining a climate friendly to life.

Science is beginning to warn it is likely that only a small fraction of the current population would survive the feedback consequences of a global temperature rise of 4°C. Our earth with a mean world temperature 4°C warmer, shorn of ice caps, with barely recognisable coastlines, and mean temperatures 6°C higher inland from those new coasts, would be barely liveable. Even with its deceptive twenty-year delay effect, global warming is already generating dangerously high temperatures that have placed our world on the slippery slope of possible tipping points. The delay is not a friendly offer of a little more time, but a dangerous invitation to let spin and self-deception and inane politicking flourish while Rome is knowingly set for burning. The hour is beyond 'late', and in our heart of hearts we know it.

Denial and scepticism

Denial takes many forms, including the misnamed 'scepticism' towards climate science. Climate science is already sceptical by nature. It is fundamental to scientific method to doubt and test assumptions, and to make them transparently open in the interests of continuing (sceptical) inquiry and replication of results by others.

So-called 'climate change scepticism' has largely moved from 'It's not happening' to 'Well, if it is, there's no proof it is caused by the burning of coal and oil', although there are still pockets of 'It's not warming, it's actually cooling', and a few remaining followers of solar flares and sunspots as providing the explanation of most things. Talk that might question the unbridled power and operation of Big Oil, and raise the spectre of things changing in the way we live our lives, produced a virulent backlash led by Fox television news, radio and internet shock jocks, and the Murdoch press throughout the world.

It is fair enough to entertain reasonable doubt and a genuinely open mind until convincing evidence arrives. It is quite another matter for lobbyists for Big Coal and Oil to spin the debate right off the axis of reason, carefully seeding the public discourse with memes and talking points for shock jocks and opportunistic politicians and undermining the reputation of science in general and attacking individual scientists, while parading the counter-opinion of their own highly paid scientific authorities. It has become clear that the backlash against the evidence of global warming has been driven by a skilfully mounted campaign to discredit climate science from every possible angle. Since the message climate science has been delivering is not good news, large numbers of the public have fallen into the spin with alacrity and relief.

The attack on the science of climate change—which openly acknowledges the vast fluidity of the parameters of climate and the corresponding limitations of even the most sophisticated models—has sought to undermine the very reputation of science by exposing its Achilles heel of perennially underfunded research and the competition for research patronage. The rivalry and competition for scarce research grants can subtly influence the agenda of even the most scrupulous research scientists, sometimes to the point of massaging data to dramatise trends, or suppressing results that disturb hypotheses. Avid, well-orchestrated press revelations of a very small number of incautious emails, mistakes in reports, or overly hasty predictions have been deployed to dent the entire credibility and authority of climate science at this critical moment in human history.

Exposing impropriety, dishonesty and untruths is the job of a functioning fourth estate in an open society. And good science never suffers, ultimately, from being held to account. However, the press has been by no means free of the political agendas of its proprietors. And the concerted attack upon scientific credibility has set back the attempt to convey urgent concern about climate change for more than half a decade.

Expert scientific findings have been treated with open contempt in the public discourse, denigrated as if they were merely one opinion among many and deserving of no particular credibility or respect for their rigour, restraint or evidence-based character. The indiscretions of a tiny handful of scientists, which have been held up as proof that the entire science of climate change must be held in doubt, are a mere hill of carefully arranged beans alongside the Himalayas of robust evidence from highly credentialed scientists that global warming is rapidly underway.

That fact has remained starved of publicity. Likewise, despite all the cries for balance in reporting on climate change, flagrantly distorted data and historical inaccuracies found in the publications and assertions of the small handful of handsomely rewarded scientists who signed on to the exercise to taint reports of global warming with extreme doubt have received no comparable media scorn. And there have been no comparable shocked headlines about the money trail leading back to Big Oil and energy interest groups in this relentless campaign to create misinformation and doubt as a game changer. 'Balance' appears to consist merely in saying that extreme weather events may not necessarily be evidence of marked climate change.

The global financial meltdown of September 2008 and revelations of the flood of toxic debt permeating the world market may have added to the collapse of a broad consensus about the need for urgent action on climate, environment and social justice, but the retaliatory campaigns of Big Oil to climate change awareness—such as its frantic, fine-toothcomb search for minor glitches to loudly expose in the voluminous 2009 United Nations International Panel on Climate Change report—have been tireless. The two errors, and not the momentous findings and warnings of the report, were what made mainstream headlines. At exactly the same time, a go-ahead for the obscenely expensive and destructive Canadian coal tar sands project, and the lifting of US restraints on offshore drilling, including in environmentally sensitive Arctic waters, provided the evidence, if required, that we are indeed entering the time of peak oil.

In an age of interminable opinionated internet chat and the proliferation of online 'facts' of unknown provenance, it seems that personal opinion ('I'm not convinced by all this talk of climate change! All this talk is just scientists trying to get grants.') can effortlessly trump actual physics. But this emphatic blather covers a fear of having to look seriously at our own actions and obligations in response to the serious deterioration in what has been our fortunate human ecological niche on this planet for 10,000 years.

But back in reality and away from all the blather, climate science is no witches' brew of one-eyed opinions about climate change. It is equally concerned with natural *and* anthropogenic (human-induced) sources of change, and must correspondingly attempt to model an extraordinarily complex spectrum of change. And while it publishes findings of changes in mean temperature, precipitation, frequency of storms, etc., the extremes of intensity and frequency of flood, storms and changes in temperature are equally important. We understandably focus with greatest interest on change that seems dramatic in the micro-phase horizon of our immediate lifetimes—a run of extra hot days, a colder than usual winter—but the extremes beginning to be discernible in macro-phase terms are where the telling signs appear. I am speaking of the signs of an emergent climate change that presents a looming emergency for so many of the settings, behaviours and expectations that have become customary and 'natural' to our global industrial and post-industrial order.

To fail to respond to what is taking place is to passively await collision at speed with an unyielding brick wall—an implacable physical reality of vastly altered global climate, one that is at the very least exacerbated by our choice to persist with a carbon-fuelled engine of 'limitless' economic growth. Big business is doing everything it can to make sure that the urgent message of climate scientists is as blurred as possible, and governments and the fourth estate of the press have been both passively and actively colluding with this desire to exonerate current economic behaviour from any charge of destroying hospitable climate settings. To permit or foster climate-change denial for short-term political or economic gain is a conscious act of criminal neglect of the biosphere on which all life—and thus all economic activity—fundamentally depends. It deliberately obfuscates a peril to all life, one that urgently needs clear minds and trenchant reform of our current global business model, and our taken-for-granted environmental recklessness that lies many thousand years deep in us. The warming of the climate may indeed also be influenced by other factors than human agency, but to fail to ease on the brake and turn our economic base away from the brick wall would be entirely an unforgivable result of human agency.

Natural or human-induced climate change?

I take the reality of at least some measure of anthropogenic climate change as read, while noting that climate 'change' itself is something of a weasel word to mask the harsher reality of viable climate and habitat destruction. Climate science studies both natural and anthropogenic drivers of climate change, and neither source is easily tracked or modelled. The sources of natural geophysical change are mainly understood, if imperfectly predictable. For example, oscillations in earth's orbit are reasonably predictable, whereas solar changes are less so, and vulcanism is relatively poorly understood and its influence difficult to predict. Some factors drive climate change, others amplify it. Some amplifying factors, such as the effect of the ice 'albedo' effect in reflecting rather than absorbing heat, are well known; but others, such as the ultimate effects of rising ocean temperatures upon ocean 'pumps' and current speed and patterns, for example, are far from predictable. It is very clear that at least some anthropogenic changes lie far outside the bounds of past natural changes—in particular, the rate of rise of atmospheric CO_2, as well as deforestation rates that affect the absorption of solar radiation and the cycling of water through plants into the atmosphere.

What is beyond doubt is that the present rate of increase in atmospheric CO_2 exceeds all past such events and the knock-on effect unleashes many other processes that feed back into greenhouse warming. For example, warming affects the photosynthesis rates of plants, the efficiency with which they can use water and their protein content. Likewise, the great mass of phytoplankton—which forms the base layer of all marine life, absorbs CO_2 in photosynthesis, and feeds the deep layers of oceans with the nutrients of its decay—is declining sharply in numbers in some areas and forming sudden vast ocean 'blooms' in others that decay fast and deplete oxygen, creating ocean dead zones. Warmer oceans become less graduated and more sharply stratified in terms of temperature. This slows down the biological carbon pump that both absorbs and transfers nutrients to the larger animal plankton populations on which the marine food chain relies, and which presently transfers around ten gigatonnes of carbon from the atmosphere to the deep ocean every year. Any significant slowing of the carbon pump will add to (by subtracting less from) the rising rate of CO_2 in the atmosphere, compounding the warming. Rising atmospheric carbon dioxide concentrations acidifies oceans as well as warms them, threatening the destruction of the world's great coral reefs and the rich marine life they support. And this is before the galloping desertification of the oceans by extreme overfishing has been factored into the equation.

As oceanographer Sylvia Earle has said, the most pressing concern about rapacious fishing activities is not loss of fish for people to eat but 'the dismemberment of the fine-tuned ocean ecosystems that are, in effect, our life-support system'. She explains how photosynthetic organisms in the sea like phytoplankton are not just the source of most of the oxygen in the atmosphere, but they also take up and store vast amounts of carbon dioxide, shape planetary chemistry and, as she puts it, 'hold the planet steady'. The earth's oceans not only originated life, they are 'a living system that makes our lives possible'. With every breath we breathe and drop of water that we drink, we are connected to the sea. Only the power of a human mind can achieve such a comprehensive remoteness from this reality as to treat the oceans as a dump, a sewer, a tank holding human food just waiting to be stripped out. But equally, it is in the power of a human mind to come back to its senses and to readmit the full power and beauty of the ocean into a wide-awake awareness of who we are, and what this is.

The impact of human beings upon the earth is undeniable, now visible from deep in space and measurable in such terms as earth displacement. For the first time in history, engineering and mining operations have displaced more earth than the great elemental earth-shaping forces of volcanoes, glaciers, frost and wind. Never before has the potential existed for a great multiplicity of changes caused by humans to markedly exceed the bounds of natural changes.

Simultaneously, we are not only pouring a rising concentration of greenhouse gas emissions into the atmosphere but clearing and burning forests, which further increases atmospheric aerosol concentrations, increasing ozone concentrations at the surface and in the stratosphere, and reactive nitrogen concentrations on land and in waters (such as fertiliser run-off in rivers, leading to algal blooms and further dead zones in coastal waters), and on and on.

It was famously cold in Copenhagen during the 2009 UN Climate Change Conference. Some climate-change scepticism and denial points to a recent spate of harsher winter extremes in Europe and North Asia as proof that warming cannot be underway. However, recent geophysical research is now pointing to the two to three times faster rate of warming temperatures in the Arctic compared to the global average, and the 20% loss of floating ice cover, as the source of sharply increased winter extremes in lower latitudes. Dark blue sea absorbs far more radiative sunlight than highly reflective ice and snow, accelerating the warming process. A warmer ocean creates a massive persisting source of heat that is no longer trapped under ice, and is much warmer than the overlying polar air in

45

winter months. In turn, this forms a strong high-pressure system over the newly exposed sea, sucking cold polar air counter-clockwise into Europe, Asia and North America. Exceptionally severe winters therefore supplement rather than conflict with the picture of global warming, and their probability is three times greater than it was before 1950.

Much climate-change denial turns upon doubt that the assault of the global economy upon the oceans, rivers, forests and atmosphere can have any possible significant effect on climate settings, insisting instead that any change is due to natural causes or cycles that fall entirely outside the frame of human activity. However, our knowledge of natural changes alone is dauntingly imperfect and demands urgent research into causes and possible ways of preparing for the effects of obvious climate change now underway.

Climate scientists study the entire range of immensely complex factors we must try to understand in order to have a chance of accurately predicting and preparing for both natural and man-made sources of global warming and related climate change. They do not cover up but openly factor in the imperfection of our present knowledge about both natural and anthropogenic effects, thereby admitting challenges that are far greater than any either/or approach. Their challenge is to communicate strong concerns about clear emerging signs of accelerating warming that are emerging from a picture of such complexity. They are up against a scientifically illiterate popular press unwilling to disturb the 'business as usual' on which it depends for revenue, as well as the whims of the instantaneously opinionated internet gossip chain that now constitutes so much of the public sphere (which is not to deride the passionate intelligence of at least some of the blogosphere).

Climate science, by the very nature of climate itself, can never offer complete certainty about the rate or sequence of events of climate change, let alone the exact mix of causative factors. Rather than a linear pathway of events, it is a dynamic, multi-factorial flow. Chaos theory grasps it better than anything else, but climate change remains always at the very limit of predictability. This is not a reason to hold the science in contemptuous doubt—rather, it can more sensibly inspire trust in the extreme caution and care shown by climate scientists in alerting the world to the very bad news they see lying ahead of us. It would be far wiser to err on the side of fearing that their professional conservatism may lead them to understate the danger rather than assuming they can be safely dismissed as overstating the likely contribution of greenhouse gases to an upward trend in median global temperatures, and so on.

In any case, in an emergency, once we accept it is an emergency, who wastes time in speculation about its exact array of causes? As the Buddha pointed out:

> It is as if a man had been wounded by an arrow thickly smeared with poison, and his friends and kinsmen were to get a surgeon to heal him, and he were to say, I will not have this arrow pulled out until I know by what man I was wounded, whether he is of the warrior caste, or a Brahmin, or of the agricultural, or the lowest caste. Or if he were to say, I will not have this arrow pulled out until I know of what name or family the man is—or whether he is tall, or short, or of middle height . . . Before knowing all this, that man would die.

The Precautionary Principle

The Precautionary Principle as defined in Principle 15 of the Rio Declaration (1992) states 'that where there are threats of serious or irreversible environmental damage, lack of full scientific certainty should not be used as a reason for postponing measures to prevent environmental degradation'.

Even if, by some miracle that subverted the laws of physics, the logarithmic spike in atmospheric carbon corresponding exactly to the rise of a carbon-based global economy had little or no impact upon climate, how does it make sense to burn all remaining fossil-fuel reserves just as though they were inexhaustible? Would it not be wiser to apply the brakes to a limitless carbon-based energy economy, even if the writing were not already on the wall? The remaining reserves of coal on earth, limitless as they may look to the rapacious eye, are in fact, just that—remaining reserves, critical for steel production, and surely worth reserving.

Whatever the mix of causes, putting ourselves out a little to conserve limited reserves of fossil fuels as much as humanly possible makes plain sense. It even makes economic sense to actively pay the nation with large coal reserves to keep so much runaway atmospheric warming sequestered safely in the ground—once you understand a viable biosphere to be the true economic bottom line.

The transformation wrought in the past one hundred and ten years by feeding the dense energy of oil into the economic bloodstream of change and 'development' has proceeded faster than prudent reflection can take place. Now we are hooked into oil in just about every capacity: defence, agriculture, medicine, communications, transport, building materials, clothing, furniture, cosmetics—all are massively geared to petroleum, and in grave danger of collapse if the fix should be withdrawn. It seems anything—*everything* in fact—is considered appropriate to put at stake to ensure supply. We have almost no system that can do without it now, so we are drilling and burning it as if there's no tomorrow, with a haste that will make sure that's true.

To the extent that a functioning 'we' still remains in a time of populist individualism, wouldn't we attempt to be as conservative as possible towards remaining stocks while doing all we can to propel and steer an urgent transition to a new energy economy, that must be significantly weaned from oil, coal and gas? To conserve oil for essential products that depend so heavily upon it, and to carefully conserve stocks of coal for the production of longer-term needs, rather than for the momentary generation of power?

The ferocious rise in coal-fired electricity generation in China, India, Brazil and across the globe, and its massive pollution of the air and acidification of the sea, may arguably be 'fair' in terms of everyone having a right to take their turn in living beyond the limits of the earth, but what remains of the principle of fairness if this damages the biosphere irreparably? I must own that my right to question the argument is made almost untenable by the living standard I currently enjoy by sheer accident of birth, but the argument of 'fairness' is actually not about broad equality at all. Such a principle is evidenced in no other political position of the rich countries of the world. Instead it is an expedient mask for the immense unwillingness of the wealthy and powerful of the earth to countenance any significant change to business (and vast profits) as usual.

And can a short-lived rise in the number and distribution of what will always be a minority of people who can briefly secure high material living standards for several decades—less than a split nanosecond of geological time—possibly be considered worth the cost, which is the precipitous collapse of climate and destruction of the intricate webs of life that enable human existence?

A crime on such a scale needs a new word, coined by necessity to embrace the reality of our time: geocide.

Population growth, economic growth

In 1968, Paul Ehrlich's *The Population Bomb* broke upon the reading public, making a huge impression with its grim Malthusian predictions of imminent population explosion that would cause world collapse within decades.

It didn't. Nothing is so surely set on clickety-clack train tracks that its course can be determined now and arrival accurately predicted then. This lack of certainty can be the very gag that stops our mouths and makes us feel foolish in speaking out about climate change. But the Precautionary Principle says that when so much is so profoundly at risk of irreversible damage, we can't risk *not* speaking and *not* acting.

Ehrlich's florid overestimation of the risks posed by population growth had high value in raising consciousness and sounding an alarm about overpopulation.

World population took a century to double between 1830 and 1930, but the acceleration after that (reflecting the impact of sewer construction and other advances in hygiene, and vaccination and other advances in medicine, upon life expectancy) has been astounding. My own generation has been the first to experience a doubling of world population in its own lifetime, and there are people alive today who have seen it triple. The seven billionth human being was born in 2011, and by 2045, demographers conservatively expect nine billion people to be alive, all things being equal (though they aren't, and won't be).

Ehrlich could not foresee the oil and chemical fertiliser-based Green Revolution of the seventies that boosted agricultural productivity in developing nations and staved off millions of deaths by starvation, for the short term. But while he was wrong in some of his predictions of global food shortages and starvation, he delivered a jolt to the consciousness of the affluent West, to the point of making it socially uncomfortable for a time to defy the 'Stop At Two' campaign and have more than two children per couple. But despite birth rates falling in the West, and the likelihood of affluence leading to a slowing in the current surge in world population, the world will still need to cope not just with all of the new souls now on earth in the current marked global 'bulge' of children, but with the net increase that will follow as they reach sexual maturity, even if they manage to stop at two or less children.

Eighty million new souls a year, in a world with water tables falling, soils eroding, glaciers disappearing, fish stocks collapsing, and one billion people going hungry every day . . . How is this going to work? Can our planet sustain, and our civilisation survive, such a massive human load, especially if it has to do so while weathering warming close to 4°C above current mean temperatures and the vast disturbances to cities and agriculture that would follow?

Natural and human-made catastrophes, plagues, food shortages and wars are the traditional pruners of populations of any species. Yet although the last hundred years have seen all of these writ grotesquely large, it has also seen unprecedented population increases due to a dramatic decline in infant mortality. It is impossible to avoid the fact that population pressures, essential to an economy geared to unending growth, are driving intractable damage to environmental integrity.

The value of scare scenarios like Ehrlich's is to rouse passionate awareness of what threatens us, but that does not necessarily lead to the formulation of sober choices. Especially if they pit us in an impossible fight describable as people versus planet. To pose the problem of global warming as an epic battle between irreconcilable opposites feeds the ambition of some to overpower the deadly enemy of planetary warming by heroic human geo-engineering—seeding algal blooms in the ocean to absorb carbon, for example, or browning the sky with clouds of iron particles to deflect radiation. It also invites a surge of species self-disgust that has people saying 'the planet will be better off without us'. Neither of these positions can think beyond 'the thinking that created the problem'. They only deepen it, and so fail more profoundly to really meet what is happening.

Melodramatic scenarios depend upon simplifying the play of forces down to two opposing ones, and suppressing all thought of a middle ground. To contemplate a subtle, skilful reconciliation of a whole field of opposing forces emasculates the heroic push for 'the solution'. The fact is already plain that a war against the earth or against 'nature' is a war waged against ourselves. Winning such a war offers the ultimate Pyrric victory: a burnt earth, an industrial civilisation that set fire to itself.

Consumers and citizens

Emergencies and horror scenarios can awaken dormant faculties of mind and spirit, as even Malthus conceded, but first we have to break out of our mental cocoon of consumerist distractions. But any interruption to the endless shopping ordained by globalised hyper-capitalism is itself regarded as a horror scenario. The national emergency posed by the events of September 11 inspired George W.

Bush not only to declare a 'war on terror' but also to piously intone in the name of patriotism that everyone should resume their duties as consumers and go shopping again with religious fervour.

Does shopping till dropping really exhaust your sense of what your life is for? How does *your* soul respond to the word 'consumer'? Mine shrinks. Has a less imaginative, more ignobly reductive and petty idea of human beings ever been dreamed up and foisted so completely upon the once large human spirit?

Right at the time in the early 1980s when 'consumers' began to replace 'citizens' as a way of identifying we, the people, I was passing through LAX airport when I became aware of dozens of little pay booths set up in the gate lounges so people could while away waiting time by playing computer games. Players sat transfixed by one of the few games available at that time, the newly launched Pac Man.

Pac-Man involved a screen filled with rows of dots that it was the job of the simple little Pac-Man figure, who was all mouth, to rush along and consume as fast as possible. There was nothing required of him but an ever-ready voracious appetite and undying devotion to eating up his world—comprised by dots upon the screen. All while evading the unexplained ghost that from time to time would appear, and attempt to consume *him*.

Eat up all the dots, avoid ghosts. What a poignant emblem of where we agree to find ourselves as 'consumers'.

I wonder what moral ground we still possess from which we can address the flagrant trashing of the biosphere happening in the world's biggest developing industrial economies (China, India, Brazil, South Africa). It is the same behaviour that developed nations in the post-industrial world have profited by for generations. Apparently all for nothing more noble than a limitless horizon of shopping. Can we possibly establish that moral ground while also scrambling after Canadian tar sands, the sudden possibility of Arctic Sea oil—any possibility, at whatever cost? It's sometimes said that an addict would sell their own grandmother for supply. As 'consumers' we are asked, effectively, to sacrifice our grandchildren in order to maintain our comforts, keep up supply, and maintain the illusion that nothing needs to change.

'Addiction' is a far too forgiving account for this behaviour. The ghost in this addled Pac-Man scenario who must be avoided at all costs may well be us.

Meanwhile, exactly as corporations openly honour no principle beyond maximising profit, and creatively massage balance sheets to give lip service to a 'triple bottom line' of environmental and social accountability, the earth's systems keep a meticulous ledger of every impact of every decision we make or promise we forget to honour. As Thomas Berry said, 'Whatever fictions exist in Wall Street book-keeping, the earth is a faithful scribe, a faultless calculator, a superb book-keeper; we will be held responsible for every bit of our economic folly.'

We are casually ending the Holocene era

Our current ways are foreclosing on the Holocene, that most fortunate, temperate, richly biodiverse geological epoch that endowed the planet with sufficiently moderate and stable conditions to permit the flowering of agriculture, technology, civilisation, art, music, the great religions—as well as the rise of warfare, pollution, subjugation of the weak and desecration of land and of other species. In other words, our emergence as a most remarkable, and remarkably dangerous, species.

Human beings do not live much in geological time, it beggars the scale of our human-sized imaginations; but when we do, we discover that the climates and corresponding agricultural practices to which huge human populations are now minutely adapted are merely the provisional, semi-stable climate settings of the latest in a series of geologically brief interglacials.

We are now recognising that human beings have caused an actual epochal shift in geological terms. Yet our geological imaginations lag behind. Responding is an imaginative move of the mind and heart; we need to bring forward the story that can wake that imagination.

It turns out that strongly and even stridently pointing out what our current behaviour is placing so spectacularly at risk, as scientists have been doing for longer than the last twenty critical years, does not shift consciousness into urgent response mode. Losing jobs, homes, food, water, living space, the stark disappearance of a future for our descendants—this might finally shift us from our stubborn comfort zones by dissolving them around us. But by the time such dire consequences have arrived, so many tipping points will have been reached and passed that an avalanche of climate and civilisation collapse may become irreversible.

The untellable story

We all half-know this and equally cannot quite let it in, feel too helpless before it.

We seem as humans strangely able to live both as if there is no tomorrow and as if we have a childish right to demand that tomorrow be guaranteed to arrive. We surely must do whatever we can to disturb this terrifying sleep and wake ourselves up. That's the first move of any kind of response to the emergency. But it has to be a waking-up to sobriety and coherence, not an arousing of panic or shame, which leads only to further dissociation.

At times it can be hard for the lucky few living in rich countries to remember there is a problem, with countless blessings as well as relentless diversions that involve consuming and being consumed by the trance that our restless, narcissistic, digital culture can induce. Especially hard while we still have a measure of clean wind blowing, leaves swaying, birds flitting, potable water in the taps, the sky still reassuringly blue . . .

Such a strong illusion of insulation from such an urgent problem is a critical part *of* the problem. The narrow breathing space afforded by the last two decades for clear thought and response has already been wasted. People can respond with magnificent bravery and self-sacrifice when an immediate danger strikes, but a slow-motion planetary meltdown is on a scale that is difficult to relate to. It seems that until it really sinks its teeth into our lives, it sets our minds to paralysis, flight or denial rather than action. We will seize upon any suggestion from opinion columns, blogs, gossip, chat sites, taxi-drivers—any source that suggests there's a simplistic way out of a situation that demands urgent deep thought.

Like the New Yorkers running from the toxic dust storm of the falling Twin Towers in 2001, our minds seek immediate refuge from reality. This cannot be happening. This can't be real. It's like a movie!

But what if this was real?

Just say it *is*

My sister and I played endless imaginary games as children. They could sprout from any idle moment, creating whole worlds, fascinating characters, magical powers, as well as opportunities to relieve the tension of being under even benevolent adult rule. The portal to another world was the words: 'Just say . . .' Whatever followed was instantly present, and malleable, open to almost any further elaboration that also branched from 'Just say . . .' A story began to play, and we entered the story. Wonderful things followed.

It's not so different for adults. A powerful story begins to play, we can enter it, and it makes a world that is different, leaves us open to seeing differently, reinventing us.

The short remaining time we may have before the slide becomes unstoppable affords a slender but real opportunity to rouse ourselves, to let the urgencies of the earth reach us and fashion how we think about sustainability, the economy, our local place, community, human rights and the rights of rivers, trees, all living beings . . . A great crisis calls up human spirit, ingenuity, imagination, mental discipline and technological sophistication. It is in fact an unparalleled opportunity that looms before us, as impossible to avoid as it is easy to bungle. Yet where is the political will among world leaders to turn and face the prospect of such a change, let alone think into it with the curiosity and imagination it deserves?

Why are the words so hard to find? And our legs so leaden, as if we are all wading through the treacle of a classic nightmare. Is it that the scale of what seems to have gone so wrong is so huge, our lives suddenly so small, that the only way to restore the scale appears to be to retreat to even smaller, more manageable concerns: a cup of tea, the pile of email, SMS, the immediate needs of the ones we love, the trouble at work, our personal doubts and problems?

Perhaps the silence is understandable when we remember the shame of knowing we contribute to a slow-motion disaster that is sweeping away our children's hopes and future. Much easier to turn away, or get pre-emptively angry and deny.

Painful numbness

The writing's on the wall. Graffiti on the blank wall opposite my local bus stop says simply, *A numbful painness*. That speaks to me of the present-day feeling of stifled distress that can barely get its words straight.

Any multi-layered intergenerational trauma—meaning one in which the children bear the burden of events too great for their parents to have digested—is hardest of all to address. The unconscious weight of denied or repressed suffering or failure is unwittingly passed on from one generation to the next. It is possible that some of our oblivious way of living is a sign of the mountain of undigested trauma of the century just ended—two world wars, countless smaller wars, holocausts, genocides, nuclear weapons, famines, dictatorships, the AIDS epidemic. Yet this intergenerational damage and trauma is different to any before it. Instead of trauma being handed unconsciously to the next generations, this trauma is being inflicted with foreknowledge of the unconscionable pain that our inaction will cause our unborn descendants. We are by no means unaware that our inaction is stealing their future.

So it is unsurprising to find ourselves tongue-tied in the face of the almost untellable trauma of loss of a human future. Where is the story that can imagine or make sense of that? Easier by far to turn back to relatively trivial concerns, secretly relieved of the burden. There is an understandable impulse to limit our sense of who we are to a most short-term, purely personal existence, in which we care just for this generation of family and friends as best we can, and turn away from all that we sense is being so grievously lost.

The geological, macro-phase dimension of what is happening is just too big, too indeterminate and too threatening. Even our steps in the right direction are timid—in Australia, a tax on carbon that recompenses consumers and heavy industry so generously that it loses any possibility of rapidly pricing carbon out of the energy marketplace. Its only remaining value is that it draws a line in the sand of ever-shifting opinion and doubt and says that climate change is real. What political steps are risked must never ruffle the lifestyle: limiting car use a little, recycling plastics, going back to hanging the washing out, banning incandescent light bulbs. With this view of how much reality we can stand, the greater part of political energy goes into massaging the avalanche of bad news, or squirming out of its reach with weasel words. The perspective on climate change from the micro-phase dimension of the average human life span does not seem to stir us to particularly brave acts or imaginative leaps. We dearly need to take possession of the macro-phase dimension of the human soul, the deeply imaginative understanding that we are between five billion and thirteen and a half billion years old, that we also belong to the immensity.

There is a gap in sanity between the long-term geophysical force of what is happening on our planet under human impact and the crippled policy response we have seen from elected governments with three- to five-year terms. It would seem that a global, inter-generational plan of action calling for a major transition away from living by damage is like anti-matter to elected governments. It confronts them with inadmissible realities and impossible demands. Best to file it under 'hyper-object', and order capsicum spray and excessively hard-handed policing for protesters occupying public spaces.

Yet the long-term and immediate dimensions of this reality meet in every moment. They meet in us. And any possibility of responding in a meaningful way in this strange and demanding period of human history begins with knowing we cannot separate the small from the vast, or ultimately hold apart the short-term from the long-term. We exist, are formed by and belong entirely in both, and must urgently discover a workable account of what that means.

In fact, among all the species, that may well be our peculiar destiny as human beings.

PART II

SEEING THE FRAME

CHAPTER THREE

How stories frame us

In the stories we tell ourselves, we tell ourselves.

Kwaikutl elder

Stories ignite imagination and give it a place to come alive. Places themselves are made of stories, layer upon layer of them. And in the end, the only objects that truly continue to matter to us are rarely the bright and shiny ones fresh out of their packaging, but the scuffed, bent and thumb-marked ones whose story we know and have shared for generations.

Stories tell us ourselves, and create the world. It is good to know what story we are living in, and vital that we know when that story has lost its power to create a world we can inhabit.

While it is easy to relate a litany of disasters that are forming the unprecedented crisis on our planet, it is desperately hard to find the story that can help us imagine where we really are and how we should proceed. The stories that make our world *frame* our collective reality in ways that give meaning and enable us to live in a shared world; but they also limit what we may be, what world we might realise. There is a dearth of viable story accounts that open the way to imagine our kinship with the whole earth that are influential in the industrialised world. No wonder we are letting the planet slowly die like one more disposable item our imaginations have abandoned.

There are, of course, alternative mythic shapes to the imagination, stemming from much older, pre-industrial layers of the human mind, that understand humans to exist in a deeply indigenous kinship with the earth. Take the words of Chang Tsai, for example, an eleventh-century administrator in China:

> Heaven is my father and earth is my mother and even such a small creature as I finds an intimate place in its midst. That which extends throughout the universe, I regard as my body and that which directs the universe I regard as my nature. All people are my brothers and sisters and all things are my companions.

Compare, too, St Francis of Assisi's canticle of affiliation with Brother Sun, Sister Moon, and all his fellow creatures.

But the mind formed by our civilisation's post-agricultural stories has generally framed the earth as separate from us—a somewhat beautiful but untrustworthy place that houses a collection of things for our use. Instead of provoking a deep and poignant love, these stories have allowed us to dare to imagine and to proceed in killing the earth, or at least letting it die. It is essential, in this moment of emergency, that we understand how we are confined by the thinking that shapes us. For the beginning of release from a deadly mindset lies in knowing we are not yet seeing beyond its confines.

Big stories

The universe is infinite and we are finite; it is vast and we are tiny; earth is home, but her scale and her wild might reduces us to 'poor bare forked animals' as King Lear saw it (in the madness of the storm that finally broke him back to sanity). There is a scale shift here, one that either defeats us or ignites a potency of imagination. What human beings have always used to make the vast and the personal intelligible to one another are stories of how we got here and what that means. Creation stories, myths, legends, wonder-tales, folk tales.

The overarching name for this depth of story-making that can plumb our souls is the Greek word 'mythos'. It refers to the body of enduring narratives that structure a whole cultural consciousness out of the profound mystery of the cosmos to make a consensual reality a community can share. They are not indifferent to our fate. They spring from a deep desire in human beings to share a sense of something more powerful than mere self-serving impulse, something worthy of effort and sacrifice, something bigger, more harmonious and satisfying than the indulgence of petty gratifications. Moreover, because they are stories, they are memorable and can be told and retold, so they are highly portable down through time and across space, carrying essential cultural DNA that has evolved and been passed on, not just for fun or for art, but for survival. This gives them a sacred force.

A myth is not some quaintly fanciful and untrue story but a story with an honourable purpose of moral and religious instruction, an exemplary tale addressing the whole of what a human being is. In fact, stories may be our strongest protection against forgetting who we are and how we intend to conduct ourselves in the world. They are windows or doorways into the largest of existential realms—birth, death, marriage, war, loyalty, sustenance, survival, and relationship with all that is. Thus they remain always on the edge of both mystery and making sense, which adds to their hold on the imagination. They both form and evoke the imagination, and some of the forms of their imagination are made more concrete and communal in ceremony, liturgy, music, chant and dance. These forms make a strong demand upon awareness. Every myth, every society's body of myth, creates different shaped windows and doors into the mystery of reality, a frame that at once offers both access and limits the angle of view.

Without a powerful myth in common to place us creatively and actively within the drama of the earth and universe, we are facing a planetary crisis that implicates us all, bereft of imagination. We literally cannot imagine what is happening on our planet, despite the ominous graphs, statistics, models, photographs of shrinking glaciers and ice caps, shrouds of carbon pollution, catastrophic weather events, and frighteningly sober scientific assessments of what the future looks likely to hold. Our imaginations have been framed in ways that cannot reach to this. We find it incredulous, impossible to quite believe.

The poet Muriel Rukeyser brought home the power of human myth-making by saying, 'The world is made of stories, not atoms.' Buddhist philosopher David Loy has glossed this to bring it further home: 'Not atoms? Of course it is made of atoms. That's one of our important stories.' So clearly, stories are not just stories, but ways we teach ourselves what is real, how things hold together, and what is possible. Stories give us a world and a self. Self is a story too, of course, a valuable and necessary one, but not the whole story. 'The whole story', as we say when speaking of a full account of reality, cannot ever be set out as one, but it can be glimpsed as one in a myth that addresses what this universe and wondrous planet may be. Such a myth will shape us in its image, its power to imagine the wholeness of reality.

Stories of such resonance are not created overnight or even thought up by someone in particular. They grow slowly from a deeper place than conscious intent, out of a process of many human beings making many mistakes, noticing them and then finding ways to wise up, in both conscious and less than fully conscious ways. They offer a way to make sense of forces that are, perhaps mercifully, infinitely bigger than us and beyond our powers of manipulation.

So the *mythos* of a civilisation is a treasury of stories carried forward by each generation, containing our best collective efforts thus far at wising up and grasping the nature of reality. The stories that endure gradually sink deeper into the cultural unconscious until the reality they frame for us is difficult to regard as anything but natural and obvious. It can be quite difficult to perceive what 'reality' our most potent and long-lasting *mythos* have guided us into, or when the account of reality that they proffer has ceased to be viable. Or when it has even begun to threaten our long-term survival by blinding us to powerful alternatives that may be right in front of us.

According to the 'boiling frog' theory, a creature may make so many infinitely small accommodations to a growing threat to its existence that it can no longer recognise when the critical threshold has been crossed. The frog that would naturally leap straight out of hot water may allow itself to be slowly boiled to death if the incremental increases in temperature that threaten him are subtle enough.

The analogy with the slow-motion crisis of climate collapse is plain and painful enough, but what is it that can so powerfully turn off a natural leap of commonsense and leave us conceding to be slowly 'cooked'? The big, influential stories—the ones that have laid down the more enduring planks on which reasoning has habitually depended—hold powerful clues to this mysterious inability to wrap our minds around the reality in which we find ourselves.

This is so despite the fact that these stories came into being as a way of passing on wisdom that may help us survive in the ongoing negotiation of fragile human bodies and sensitive human imaginations with elemental cosmic forces. Large predators, for example, volcanoes, the sun, the moon, the tides, the seasons, wind, snow, ice, fire . . . And also the human side of precarious and often painful existence—hatred, greed, jealousy, murder, illness, betrayal . . . But equally, birth, blood, milk, great love, for myth knows that birth and death, life and extinction, love and hate, violence and sacrifice, suffering and realisation, medicine and sickness—each contains the intimate, fruitful seeds of the other.

The big stories are set in motion by powerful sets of apparent opposites. But rather than 'resolve' them, they ultimately hold these opposites in precarious, semi-stable tension. In this way they actually nudge awake the dimension of mind and imagination that can reach for the always mysterious whole that lies beyond contradictions. To the extent that they allow this to be felt, they become worth passing down through the generations. But over time, they slowly descend like great blue whale bodies into deep ocean trenches, passing into the deepest recesses of mind, where thousands of other stories feed off them only semi-conscious of the source.

This persistence in ten thousand variant forms gives the most enduring stories truly powerful influence on our understanding of reality, even while the logic of such stories can remain strange and elusive, never completely open to being explained. For stories are a way in which the inexplicable can become approachable, and transmissible to others.

Thus myth, or big story, usually begins as a kind of best go at situating human consciousness within the unknown and uncontrollable whole of reality, in a way that opens up a space for human life to be able to proceed and flourish and come to know itself, without causing too much collateral damage to others in the community of life. Folklorist and poet Robert Bringhurst has said, of that folk offspring of myth, the orally transmitted wonder tale or fairy story: '[it] is a world where humans find and stretch their limits, establish their interdependence with their nonhuman neighbours, and make themselves at home within a universe they do not, cannot, need not, *must not* fully understand' (my italics). I am interested in that 'must not'. Bringhurst reminds us of a humble unknowing quality upon which all wisdom depends.

At least that humility was a good description of what prevailed before nature began to be seen as the unstable, unreliable partner to agricultural endeavours. At that point, our relatively intimate sense of kinship with nature, that unfolded by paying it keen attention as hunters and gatherers, began to get left behind. Our post-Neolithic (post-agricultural) big stories, which are the ones that remain extant with us today, were gradually shaped by a growing uncertainty and mistrust about the hospitality of this planet to human life.

It is important to remember that the big stories originate in a submerged, only half-conscious place in the collective awareness of a group, and they arise with an intent that is fundamentally altruistic and interested in the group's survival. Otherwise they would not endure: pernicious ideas or intimations are not deliberately carried forward, parent to child, time and again. But issues around survival are always shaped in part by fear, and fear does not always see clearly, nor does it remain up to date with changing circumstances. So enduring stories may actually cut us off from appropriate fear—such as the fear of losing our world!—while shipping inappropriate, no longer current sources of fear down through the centuries, distorting how we respond to what is confronting us right now.

The big stories—even when brought down into fairytales for children—pull no punches; they seem to know us all too well. (They should, they helped shape the 'us' we are.) And so in their dark images and bizarre twists, we trust them, expect them to secrete some form of wisdom that can save us from our worst selves. Or if not save us, then caution and guide us. They are imaginative deposits in our shared memory that prove to have a very long half-life, and no obvious authorial fingerprints on them. In many cases, they are in fact ascribed to gods, or to God.

Reason and wonder

To say, as Robert Bringhurst said, that we 'do not, cannot, need not, must not fully understand' these stories is not to say that we can't let them stretch us towards what they encompass, about a world and universe wondrously beyond any single lifetime's mind to grasp. Rather, it seems humble and proper to admit that a mind that expects to fully understand the universe will fail. And it will not be able to track between ordinary experience and the numinous depth of the whole, which is realised not in understanding but in wonder.

Or at least, not without reducing a great ox, rippling with the mystery of life, to a small, four-square ox-cube, packaged for easy human consumption (just add water). That whole ox can only walk into ordinary human-scale life with the aid of reason inspired by pure wonder. That's a good working definition of how wisdom makes its way into human cultural DNA.

Wonder and reason are two feet walking: no journey gets very far on one foot alone. Reason without the prompting of wonder is hobbled by received ideas. Wonder that is not transmuted into human understanding with the help of reason is condemned to blather.

Reason is usually reduced to rationalism, or a schooled ability to make plausible and logically defensible distinctions in sorting and judging the plethora of information coming in through the senses. Reason is more than rationalism, which is merely one of its significant and most often misused tools. It encompasses the ability of human minds to finely sort phenomena in service to establishing a greater access to truth, or ensuring the carriage of justice. It is the apt and essential partner to wonder and awe in wising us up in the service of life.

'Wonder' brings curiosity and humility to a strong sense of awe before the vast, mysterious and compelling unknown-ness of things. Wonder is impelled by love for this amazing phenomenal reality where we find ourselves, as living beings—as well as by a healthy fear of the many ways we have to limit and harm the extraordinary gift, of consciousness of being here. Not just anywhere, but *here*, and *now*! In the best sense, wonder is often mute; the words that can do some justice to what wonder sees, and bring its insights down to earth, do not always arrive easily and should not arrive too soon.

What arrives instead, in the minds of an image-forming species like us, is image and story, which feed each other. So apprehending the wholeness of reality depends on an innate and subterranean form of knowing, that finds its place in the ritual of a story that can hold it without necessarily naming it. And that then can carry it, make it memorable, lively, portable, transmissible person to person, parent to child, and priest or shaman or artist to community.

And so realisation, and the stories that carry a sense of it, always hover tantalisingly right at the very brink of understanding and not understanding—and of forgetting and then remembering and then often misremembering, sometimes creatively; of rediscovering, reinventing, uncovering and plumbing new deep layers. In a big, persistent mythic story, the unfolding of understanding never comes to an end. Like koans, they never stop opening.

Sometimes as a myth or big story ages it will go to seed, so to speak, in simpler forms such as children's fairytales or blockbuster films. But even then some residue remains of the power of myth to hook into memory and propagate itself, like a seed within a burr. A seed is a complex propensity of knowledge—the makings of a whole plant or creature—inside a discreet, chaste casing—egg-like, but dynamically pointed to securely enter the fertile earth of your imagination and mine.

In the case of a big story or its innumerable off-shoots, the seed is the implicate realisation the story contains, inexplicable in the end but nevertheless intended to be mysteriously useful in guiding, prompting, and saving us from the worst in ourselves. The burr will be found in the very strangeness of some detail or 'impossibility' that catches the attention and sticks with us, coming along with us as soon as we hear the story. The memorable nature of the story itself makes it likely the seed will be remembered, that is, lodged in us, until the sense has time to ripen. And so a story makes sure that we can pass not only the story but also its inherent wisdom on to another, even if we should fail to see it for ourselves at that point.

Thoreau famously wrote in *Walden* that 'in wildness is the preservation of the world'. The human world, of culture, meaning-making, rituals of living, forms of love and conflict, religious insight. Wendell Berry asks if the reverse is equally true: 'In human culture is the preservation of wildness.' Wildness includes the fantastically intricate web of life, the molten core of our dynamic planet, the infinitude of turning stars, and the minds open to this. Culture—how we cultivate our humanity, how we act in the world as a conscious species, the way we understand the 'domestication' of the wildness we share with all things—is what we have, perhaps all we have, with which to preserve nature from the worst tendencies of ourselves.

This partnership goes deeper than the fact that we can only live at the expense of—or by the good grace of—other lives. It goes deeper even than 'partnership'. We are not one hair's-breadth separate from all that is. That's where the crux lies. As poet Robert Hass put it so cogently, 'We are the only protectors, and we are the thing that needs to be protected, and we are what it needs to be protected from.'

How have our oldest and most enduring stories handled this? What kind of covenant have they established with the earth, what kind of warnings do we find laid down, what kind of mind bequeathed to industrial civilisation? If the stories we most repeatedly tell ourselves tell us *ourselves*, who do we find when we look into them?

Chapter Four

Stories we've been telling ourselves

And God said to them, 'Be fruitful and multiply and fill the earth and subdue it and have dominion over the fish of the sea and over the birds of the heavens and over every living thing that moves on the earth . . .'

Genesis 1:28 (English Standard Version)

The oldest traditional stories are our creation stories. Literally so, for they create how we think of ourselves. They are cosmologies, stories of the universe and the world, how it got here, how we got here, and who we turned out to be. As Thomas Berry put it, 'We awoke in the morning and knew where we were. We could answer the questions of our children, identify crime, punish transgressors. Everything was taken care of because the story was there.' They also shape what rights we give ourselves in carving a manageable human world out of a wild universe. They frame from earliest times the kind of thoughts we can have and confirm as a culture.

Until you catch sight of the frame that 'the thinking that created the problem' puts upon the world, you can be unaware there even is one. It is only when we see how we have thus far been 'framed' as a culture that we can start to judge how well or not it prepares us for our voyage into the unknown of climate change.

An entire worldview works its way into the very DNA of our cultural inheritance and is handed down within the stories that constitute 'us' until it becomes all but impossible to see objectively. The ruthless algebra of power relations over millennia that created a 'weaker' sex, 'darker' race, 'lower' class, 'traditional' poor, 'beastly' animals, 'savage' nature, etc., rests upon a functional blindness that keeps us unaware of our best interests. Our growing autism towards the earth and its great web of interrelated life forms is not merely reflected but actively engendered and transmitted in our traditional stories. We now have an urgent need to identify and reject what we find to be the most radically confining or destructive assumptions about the natural world perpetuated in ways of thinking that by now seem natural, three millennia deep as they are in post-industrial Western culture.

Fortunately, even now, in the second decade of the twenty-first century, the world still holds remnants of what has been the most enduring human lifestyle of all, stretching back almost unbroken for tens of thousands of years—that of semi-nomadic hunting and gathering. So we still have fragile access to taproots that reach back into a time when the conversation with the earth and the natural world was a more equal and respectful one. That remains as a fragile treasury of intelligence about some ways of understanding the terms of the earth and of living more intentionally within them but one that rarely receives more than passing notice or respect.

Between the two extremes—and across a span of the interglacial epoch that has been named the Holocene—lies a continuum. It stretches from forms of living in direct contact and communion with the natural world, through different degrees of removal with the gradual invention of agriculture and then the rise of industrialisation, until we reach a stage which retains only the most fleeting and superficial awareness of the earth that sustains us, and how it continues to speak with us and through us.

The emergency bearing down upon us demands we take a hard look at the images of human-earth relationship bred into our bones by the archetypal stories that underpin the Western—and now globally prevailing—version of that relationship. I take up some key examples of these in this chapter, not only because they are the ones around which I best know my way, but also because our present emergency is traceable to a consensual reality that first entered the imagination of the West, has been tacitly carried forward for thousands of generations by means of our most persistent stories, and now permeates the globalised 'thinking' that is laying waste to the earth.

A myth is a story that, evident in its very survival, manages to excite group recognition and adherence to the world it implies, which becomes our world, the one in which we both make our meaning and unconsciously live out the myth's prevailing worldview. Our immersion in myth is subtle, pervasive, almost imperceptible. It is far from easy to resist or even to clearly see what has formed our very language and fed our repertoire of imagination from the earliest years of life.

We need to be aware of what kind of world we have been unconsciously re-creating and perpetuating, and to see how powerful and almost imperceptible the implications of the narratives are that have brought an increasingly dangerous world into being. A drift of shared thought is so pervasive it becomes hard to see. When a mindset takes hold, it becomes what can be thought, and even the words to say it. And so it can accustom us to insanely destructive ways of doing things and 'thinking' of the world. Until we have a sea of boiled frogs, bobbing everywhere.

I turn first to the Hebrew scripture's account of creation in Genesis, before looking to the even older Sumerian story of Gilgamesh, and slightly later Greek myth of Erisychthon, to see how they helped usher us in to the destructive mindset we are labouring under now. I'll look also at some more recent stories that echo their themes, and look for whatever can be found of the premonitions and warning signs secreted in them as their vital freight of ambiguity. Above all, it is important to reflect on the old story that has framed our relationship with the earth, in order to realise the full power of the new to consecrate the massive transition we have to make.

Genesis: The alienation of the Tree of Life

The account in the first two chapters of Genesis of the origin of the world is neither the only nor the earliest creation narrative in the annals of the West, but is by far the most universally familiar. Its earliest extant written form is in fragments found in the Dead Sea Scrolls that date from 150 BCE to 70 CE, but it is believed to have reached the form in which we know it much earlier in the first millennium BCE, probably around the fifth century, when the Jewish community in exile was attempting to adapt to life in the Persian Empire.

'In the beginning', then, Western culture formed in a narrative of alienation and longing for a lost home—lost to us by our own actions. This story of creation, and the nature of the world in which we can make sense of ourselves, was adopted in the Christian West from the Hebrew scriptures as 'The Old Testament', then spread by way of European colonising and missionary activity throughout the world. The Muslim Koran also borrows the account to a considerable extent, and has spread that far and wide.

In light of what is now understood by the ongoing evolution of the earth and the universe, Genesis is easy to dismiss as a literal account of how life came into being. Theologians, however, have argued that the six days of creation are a poetic evocation of a long, nuanced unfolding of planetary and cosmological events that can be reconciled in spirit with scientific accounts.

To me, Genesis feels shrouded in that kind of dark light that the earliest events of our own lives seem half-lost in. We can see and recall a few intense moments, but how like half-remembered dreams they are. It is when we look back at them with love mixed with wonder (the world so vast, so strange!) that we can arrive at the kind of childlike yet deeply serious awe we sense in the mythic form of Genesis.

I have no desire to contest that awe on the grounds that it doesn't resemble the kind of account a scientifically informed adult would give. Nor am I setting out to judge or mock the deeply held tenets of faith of many millions of people in the world. I'm concerned with the *world* and the human *self* that this account of creation implies, understandings that we have been fleshed out in countless cultural forms down through the generations.

The Genesis account of the creation and first days of the cosmos and the earth grants human beings shared a likeness with God and regency over the earth, charging us to populate the earth and subdue it to human rule. Until the taboo against eating the fruits of the Tree of Knowledge of Good and Evil is broken by Adam and Eve, introducing sin into the world, the whole of creation, including animals and birds (leaving fish to their own devices), has a gentle and non-harming character. No creature eats another; all species mentioned, even predators, gather and eat only wild seeds, fruit and green leaves. Adam is given the privilege of naming them, confirming our possession of the powerful spell of naming rights over all other creatures, thus bringing them into a world of human meaning, which is something every myth does, but this one most pointedly and self-aware.

Before the Fall, birth and death are absented from the fact of life. Man has been created directly by God from the sacred dust of earth, and woman secondarily from his rib—an unashamedly blatant reversal of the primacy of the female of almost every species as bearers of life. It seeks to establish male priority on even this level, partly because patriarchal religion at that time still needed to suppress remnants of Neolithic fertility worship.

In this pointed upturning of the usual logic of biology we may also discern a sensitivity approaching aversion to the strange and danger-ous facts of sex and death, a refusal of the very force that has sculpted the evolution of all advanced forms of life on this planet. The facts of sex and death seem to jar our sense of being made in the image of God and to mar God's perfect creation. It is as though something needs to be found to account for their unsettling intrusion into the original innocence of the world, and the edge of harm and danger they bring with them, and in Genesis, the problem is resolved by seeing them to be the result of the temptation and fall of humanity.

Eden is a mysteriously beautiful pre-harm world, not unlike the experience of the very earliest stages of infancy. It proffers a gar-den of earthly delights that requires no labour—one in which you can stroll in the evening cool and talk with God—as the original ideal surrendered forever through human betrayal of God's trust. The once changeless Edenic world changes utterly; in fact, with the human fall from grace, change itself is seen as being set loose into the world. Birth (with labour pains), toil for a living and fateful death must be suffered as the wages of sin. Impermanence begins, causes suffering, must be endured.

Genesis finds human beings responsible for the harsh side of life on this planet. Or, to look from a subtler angle, so great is our shame at our persistent tendency to harm the bountiful earth and act towards it in bad faith that we cannot but see our guilty selves everywhere figured forth in 'nature red in tooth and claw'. All harm is our harm. But this narrative also confirms and sets in place a world in which harm and pain have been rendered both explicable and to be expected. Home has been lost. We are cast out of a sense of ease about belonging here. The world has fallen from grace. Merely surviving it is a feat. You have to fight for your place in it. From now on, 'shit happens'.

And in the broken-forever world Genesis presents, *transcending* rather than venerating earthly reality is seen as the only rectifica-tion on offer—for how far can we truly love what is seen as a fallen, blighted, savage world? Its dream of transcending the earthly realm seems to begin with distancing from ourselves the facts and appetites of bodily life, and the inescapability of death, which we accept as the lot of animals but not for ourselves.

The recoil from death

The later revision of the consequences of the Fall in the gospel of Jesus finds God inhabiting mortal human flesh and suffering, embracing death in one of its most agonising possible forms, thereby assuaging all guilt and forgiving all human failing. From that point on, the experience of the unknown that is found right inside the joy and horror of this life is no longer entirely 'outside God', but rather humans are reconfirmed and restored as 'universe-capable', to paraphrase St Augustine. However, this understanding has not been the prevailing wind blowing through the last thousand years or so of the West.

The act of God completely sharing human death with us has not led to death becoming more fully embraced by theology as intrinsic to life. Instead it has been seen as the overwhelming mark of sin, to be overcome by resurrection of a deathless body after death. Yet if God can inhabit a human body, is not a deathless body in some form being offered to us during life itself? So even though the incarnation blesses the human body—and its natural eventual death—by having God enter a mortal body and agreeing to die, the world bequeathed to us under the sway of Genesis remains categorically unwilling to embrace death as an equal part of the whole. Its idea of redemption remains fixed on an afterlife. But the afterlife will be too late to redeem the damage we have done to a world alive with intelligent sentience and beauty. And the idea that we have blighted it from earliest days and caused it to fall from grace, rather than stirring us to restore and love the earth, seems to leave us passive and accepting towards whatever horrors and indignities we continue to inflict upon it.

The bodily life and death of Jesus would seem to reconsecrate human suffering and mortality, and yet the Western mindset stops short of embracing the fullness of the sacrament of earth's great web of interconnected life, in which the gift of life must constantly change hands. And so the logic laid down in Genesis and revised in the gospel leaves us fundamentally inert towards atonement in the form of human beings making conscious, even sacred reparation to the creation we 'blight' by both unintentional and intentional activity, and salvation as an act of profound restorative justice to a world that has now become deeply harmed by human overreaching.

Where Genesis leaves human beings 'fallen', the Gospel revises that to 'salvageable'; and yet both leave the earth as fallen, a mere stage-set dressed for a completely human-centred drama focused on relief from guilt and from death. The massive collapse of biodiversity and the ecological destruction we are currently witnessing—an extraordinary crime against a truly wondrous creation *and* the generations that follow us—appears to have difficulty registering even as worthy of attention in this worldview, let alone the truly surpassing 'sin' that it is.

Dividedness

When Adam and Eve eat the fruit of the Tree of Knowledge of Good and Evil and fall from original grace, humanity falls out of wholeness—into a divided and contentious world in which men must labour hard at agriculture in order to eat, and painful pregnancy and birthing, as well as firm subjugation to men, are to be the lot of women. And not only human beings but all creatures are abruptly subject to mortality when Adam and Eve are expelled from Eden.

Eating of the fruit of this tree seems to leave us condemned to struggle in a world of right and wrong, good and evil. To the degree that we have fallen from a state of original grace by our very act of defiance of God in eating the fruit and attempting to take this weight (of arbiter of good and evil) upon ourselves, we are left floundering in an imperfect world of our own making, attempting to make judgments of right and wrong that can never be free of possible harm, bias, blind spots and error. This is a fair description of the ongoing human struggle; unfortunately, as Solzhenitsyn famously said, the line dividing good from evil lies not between one individual and another but passes right through every human being. And yet fortunately, as it is also true that the need to become as capable as we possibly can of discerning right and wrong within ourselves is the source of moral character, one of the best things about us.

Good and evil is inseparable from dualistic consciousness. From one point of view, Genesis is the story of how thoroughly that casts us out of (the original paradise of) wholeness. From here begins the splitting process that divides the self from the world, and goes on to fillet the world into unending sets of opposites: good/bad, man/woman, culture/nature . . . One term will be implicitly approved and superior; the other, implicitly inferior and open to being despised. Human dominance over the natural world begins not only in the power to walk on two legs and free up hands to grasp and wield objects, but with the extraordinary outcomes, both wonderful and terrible, of the power to categorically divide up the world this way.

A more subtle and inward fruit of this bifurcating mind is the pervading human sense of unsatisfactoriness, or '*dukkha*', the sense of being not quite at ease for long in any state of being, with its origin in a sense of self felt to be distinct and disjunct from all that is perceived. One Zen koan calls this constant itchiness, which undoes all calm contentment in simply being, 'picking and choosing'. 'The Great Way [of freedom and wellbeing] is not difficult,' it states (against the apparent evidence). 'It just avoids picking and choosing.' 'Nirvana is exactly what is happening, minus our *opinions* about it,' is the way someone else said much the same thing.

The problem is not so much seeing the possible pleasure of being free from endless picking and choosing—that's the relatively easy part (even though consumerism depends entirely upon it being our supposed greatest need and pleasure). The difficult part is the *realising* of this not picking and choosing, the embodying of it. '*Just* avoiding picking and choosing' may indeed restore an Edenic world, but it takes a lifetime of conscious practice to get near.

The *other* forbidden fruit

But what draws my attention even more strongly about the expulsion from Eden is that God orders human beings not to arrogate to ourselves the fruit of *two* trees in the garden. The other is the Tree of Life, which it seems we left roundly untouched. Some would see this as emblematic of eternal life—immortality—from which we alienated ourselves by our act of disobedience to God. But the nearly universal image of the branching streams of life on earth and the living world itself as a great tree bursting with fruit and sheltering all life is also present here, nudging us to reconsider what unending life may be. The ecology of evolution itself is present in this understanding, and with it the immortality that comes with participating in this never-ending life—'*zoe*', as the Greeks called it, distinguishing it from a single life, '*bios*'.

Can we understand that the burden of human consciousness leaves us one-sided and in a deeply compromised state because it cuts us off from the fruit of the Tree of Life? Instead of holding both great matters signified by the two trees in one mind—an original state of wholeness 'in the likeness of' God—we have a mind divided, and a self alienated from its original, whole self. We are closed to the presence of immortality in the moments of our mortal lives, and have huge difficulty seeing life and death as indivisible.

So Genesis seems to understand two tremendous pulls in us. One is towards unifying consciousness and sense of belonging and being at home on earth (Tree of Life). The other is towards analytic consciousness that can divide just about anything from anything and oppose one against the other, which both hones and burdens human consciousness, and dims our wholeness or access to God (Tree of Knowledge of Good and Evil). The Garden of Eden—our original self—was like a mind that could contain both in harmony, not choosing one over the other. This image suggests the power of thought not pitted against life, thus moderating and reconciling the dividedness of dualistic thinking.

But the moment we choose to eat from the Tree of Knowledge— or give way to the seduction of judgemental picking and choosing—it seems to become oddly hard to dream of exactly what that *other* marvellous tree held forth. Life becomes feared as deeply as it is loved. The human branch of the Tree of Life becomes severed from a unified perspective that knows life and death to be unopposed. And we are cut off from knowing the Tree of Life to be immanent in every detail of the experience of being here.

I sense much of the Genesis story to be 'reading back' from an existential anxiety about life and death, and expressing our distance from the unified mind that can, while not denying there is life and death, see through the dualism that seems endemic to the human mind shaped by language. Both trees, Genesis suggests, grow in the mind of God where we all originally played, naked. This suggests an originally perfect compatibility, lost to us when we appropriated and identified so fully with the mind of either/or, that gave us so many ways to manipulate the world while locking us into our sense of implacable mortality, and locking us out from the taste of immortality in the many fruits of the Tree of Life.

Not-knowing and wholeness

Eating of the fruit of the Tree of Knowledge seems to mean forgetting how to *not know*—how to wait, patient and quiet, paying attention, allowing things to show themselves in their own time, carefully not putting knowing and preferences in front of things, while attending to them closely just as they are. Does this give a clue about how to regain the fruit of the Tree of Life? Is it relearning how to 'not know'—for example, to allow our faculties of judgment and discernment to rest for the time it takes to allow ourselves once more to *not* know our selves as separate from all that is? This describes meditation—reasonably well in fact.

Perhaps Genesis tracks the millennia-long movement in humanity from a more participatory consciousness in which we knew ourselves intimately through immersion in the natural world and cosmos, into an increasingly walled-off human-made world that leaves us split from the sanity of an ecological mind. The intense push for security from nature and mortality wreaks havoc upon the ecosystem of the earth while narrowing our lives to a kind of glorified padded cell.

And perhaps the story also finds a poignant thorn of an image for what happens when we 'grow up', which seems to mean grow increasingly *away* from what we knew as a child about a more embodied wholeness of mind and being. You can still spot Eden alive and well on earth any time you see a small child asleep, or someone alight with laughter or joy, for example. But it's also not far off when the mind grows deliberately still, and thoughts soften, and nothing is wanted; then it is enough that you feel the air on your face and your weight on the earth, and re-enter the continuing conversation with the earth, that preoccupied thought can dim but nothing can extinguish.

In the Garden of Eden, or the original nature of human beings, both trees grew from the beginning, and in the deepest sense, both *already* constituted us and our 'likeness to God', or our fundamental rightness, joy, completeness. There was no need to eat the fruit of one or other; both were already our deepest substance.

Perhaps the real breach with God was doubting that fullness and perfection and taking for ourselves the most powerful-seeming fruit in the garden. Putting aside questions of why human beings were thus set up to be tested by God, in Genesis, this act is seen to inaugurate all human suffering: not just the unavoidable suffering of sickness, old age and death that comes with the gift of life, but the additional avoidable suffering created by anticipation, fear, loathing or rejection of these and other inevitable aspects of experience in a body.

And so with the fruit of that tree came instant shame *for* the body and, by implication, ambivalence and shame towards sex and reproduction, and towards women for so obviously embodying these great facts of life. It is as though we are witnessing in Genesis the way we have turned sickness, old age and death and the prospect of loss of the self, which sex and birth fully imply, into an enduring wound of consciousness, a stigma of shame no human can avoid or be rid of. It is hard to imagine what else but shame could cut us off so thoroughly, and expel us more comprehensively, from an original fundamental sense of being at home in our circumstances here on earth.

And it doesn't take long after that expulsion for all hell to break loose.

The first murder follows soon after the expulsion—fratricide, to be exact, when Cain kills Abel. To the horror of the God who created them, tainted by their now poisoned consciousness, his people proceed not only to multiply but to act out the worst things imaginable, unrestrained by care for the earth or each other. In short order the Flood is sent to wipe out all but the very few good enough and wise enough—Noah's family—who are needed to carefully count the animals two by two and ensure the barest survival of God's creation, brought so close to ruin by humans, whose inability to restrain themselves is what brings on the torrential deluge that sweeps away all the creatures on earth.

It is in the moment after the flood that Genesis sees God instructing Noah in what has been taken in Western thought to be the God-ordained status quo on earth, and duly carried out: to 'Be fruitful and multiply and fill the earth and subdue it and have dominion over the fish of the sea and over the birds of the heavens and over every living thing that moves on the earth . . .' To have dominion over something is to make it subject entirely to your need and will, and to begin to lose the intelligence, sensitivity and care involved in being a subject among other subjects. The outcome of such an idea of human exceptionalism is vividly expressed in the current state of the planet: groaning under our numbers and suffering a terrifying crash in the biodiversity of life. The naturalness of birth and death, sickness and old age, and being also part of the food chain, is lost to Genesis, and this has greatly helped it become largely lost on us. Genesis implies that we were once immune from the fact that life has no fixed state but is an experience of constant change, including the most final change, which is death and disappearance from the world. The story carries with it an implicit rejection of the very essence of life, which is not some small, private endowment to be successfully hoarded against 'moths and rust', but a great, shared and ongoing sacramental event in which 'your life is my life' and 'my life is your life'.

Genesis has endowed the post-agricultural Western world with an hereditary bundle of cultural 'givens' and intellectual 'DNA' that can become the lethal mix of vast entitlement and narrow self-interest that fuels industrial civilisation. It is evident in our capacity to live far beyond the means of the earth while maintaining a state of oblivion towards that fact; and to regard the surpassingly beautiful earth as a mere inventory of resources not yet seized for immediate human consumption.

That we know we must die is one of the heaviest facts we are ever obliged to learn to bear; and such knowledge seems to divide us from the other species of life, which quite naturally struggle to live and not die prematurely but appear to live unburdened by explicit concern about death. The Fall, as with any great mythic account of reality, will always remain a mystery to be gradually penetrated by experience, but in 'the knowledge of good and evil' it seems to identify the flaw in us as our lapse into a grasping kind of 'knowing' that structures the world by perceiving opposites pitched against each other. A world in which life opposes death; man opposes woman; humans oppose the other animals; humanity is split from God; paradise, from earth; 'good' is confined to being the opposite of 'evil'; spirit is defined as sundered from matter; and so forth.

The energy of all this combative splitting is very strong; it generates our forcefully manipulative world that fights so strenuously not to be subject to nature with its ruthless give and take. Beside it, the more altruistic and fertile energy of reconciliation, composting, return and renewal can look the weaker force. However, in the roundness of nature *everything* ultimately displays it. And we wouldn't be here at all, could not possibly have survived our species' predations upon its own members, if altruism had not quietly prevailed, or at least come along too, and actually endured in great measure.

The sin of exceptionalism

In summary, in this foundational story of our civilisation and where it has landed us, as I read it, we are to know ourselves to be marked by an indelible flaw so powerful that it flows back into all creation, or at least into our perception of the whole world. It tells us we are carved out from the seamless flow of creation by a quality of consciousness that is at once a wound and a deserved punishment, condemning us to exile right here in the midst of our lives—leaving each of us trying to find our own way home.

Closely associated with this sense of profound flaw in ourselves comes a whole set of Genesis understandings that bear heavily upon the earth and the other creatures we presently share it with. That we are so exceptional among the species that the rules of nature should not wholly apply to us. That we are to suffer but are not meant to be completely subject to 'brute nature', for the earth is given over to our regency, to populate, tame and use. That humanity is pitted against a natural world that we must suffer (for our sins) while striving to overcome (with God-given powers). The upshot of all this is that we may have ushered in a new human 'order' on earth, not by a godlike capacity to create and tend so much as a fearful desire to dominate and devour; and in so doing, irreparably altered our environment to settings decidedly hostile to human life.

The Genesis story of our fall from grace suggests that we go against the grain of our very best possibilities as a species by falling into a dualistic, universe-splitting consciousness. And in consequence, condemn ourselves to grief and homelessness on our own planet—to be born in pain, to toil, to deceive, to suffer, to inflict suffering, and to die, cut off from awareness of the fruit of the Tree of Life.

In balance, our foundational story of Genesis offers us a potent warning of our own remarkable powers of self-alienation, but at the same time, in its irreversible certainty of our fallen nature, it helps actively engender a shameful and ruinous attitude of a world-become-plunder. The shame of this is grindingly hard to acknowledge, which then unconsciously feeds the unstoppable cycle, like an ever-turning waterwheel in the darkness.

Gilgamesh: Death and the city

Even earlier than Genesis, lying at the foundation level of our civi-lisation in the Sumerian city-states of the Tigris-Euphrates valleys (later Babylon, then Mesopotamia and Persia; now Iraq and Iran), are the clay tablet fragments that make up what we can know of the *Epic of Gilgamesh*. Estimated to be 4000 years old, it is probably the oldest extant *written* story on earth, yet it offers a pitiless X-ray of the tensions composing the soul of the city-dwelling human being of today. And of the destruction of the natural capital of the earth entailed in catering for those tensions.

Gilgamesh is the overbearing king of the walled city-state of Uruk who so tests his people's patience that, with the help of a god, they distract him from his predations upon his people by seducing him into friendship with a wild man of the forest, named Enkidu.

Enkidu is a semi-magical being still able to talk with the ani-mals and live completely at home in the wild sanctuary of the still untouched forest as part of its seamless web of life. Gilgamesh grows quickly obsessed with his friend, seducing him into aban-doning life in the forest. The two become inseparable and go off on a series of Boy's Own rampages. Enkidu receives and Gilgamesh duly ignores a series of great warning dreams, that are dreamed on their way to slaying the massive demon guardian of the ancient forest, just for fun. That cleared the way to hacking apart its sacred groves to make furniture and temple doorways for a luxury-loving city goddess.

But when they kill the Bull of Heaven, which the goddess Ishtar has sent against them to punish Gilgamesh for spurning her sexual favours, they go too far, and the gods decide that one of them must die. It is the wild man Enkidu who succumbs to a mysterious mortal illness, dreaming dread dreams of the grey shades who dwell in the desolate lands of death. After twelve days he dies and Gilgamesh is left inconsolable. He misses his wild brother as if it were his own soul that has been ripped from him. But then a terrible fear of his own mortality overtakes him, gradually possessing him far more deeply than his grief for his friend.

Driven by terror, he makes an all but impossible journey alone to the land beyond the world, where Utnapishtim—the sage said to be one of the very few who survived the Great Flood and so gained the gift of immortality—is rumoured to live, together with his wife. After crossing the mighty rivers that divide life from death he does reach that far land and is set a simple task by the sage: stay awake for seven days and nights and the secret of immortality shall be his. But Gilgamesh soon snores his way into oblivious sleep. Utnapishtim and his wife bake a loaf of bread each of the seven nights he sleeps with which to shame him when he wakes.

Gilgamesh wakes, admits defeat and leaves, devastated. But the wife pities him and urges Utnapishtim to tell him how to fetch the boxthorn plant growing at the bottom of the sea that holds this most radical of secrets. Although Gilgamesh manages the great feat of getting hold of the magical herb, he grows distracted long enough for a serpent to slip under his guard and steal it. He returns, bereft, to Uruk, full of the scared, itchy, unsatisfactoriness of 'What will become of me?' and 'Never enough, never ever enough'.

The urban human being

Gilgamesh can create and rule a great walled city in the face of wild natural forces, and shape his people and the city to his will. He can harness all the energies that are required for the massive, irrigated production of an agricultural surplus, and the complex marketplace that organises its distribution, which brings into being the city, this place of civility or semi-tamed impulses, and the fount of that surpassing drug, which is centralised power. Great achievements. But the story of *Gilgamesh* is also the story of a self-indulgent perpetual adolescent, unable to find contentment, unable to live awake.

When he is drawn (through the wisdom of those he is oppressing) into tempering his misuse of power, by profoundly recognising and falling into fraternal love with Enkidu—who is that missing dimension of soul that we intuitively always protect from naming, taming or manipulating—*still* this does not trigger a growing-up in our hero. Instead, connecting with this fertile energy lures his soulmate into joining him in a delinquent rampage of slaughter and wholesale environmental destruction. Monsters—whose ferociousness in story can be a way of understanding a wise guardian of our worst impulses—are slain; forests fall forever, transforming the land. Into the first human-made deserts, in fact.

Real magic—for what is more magical than the powers of creativity, productivity and sustainability expressed in the wondrous complexity of a mature forest, a coral reef, indeed any ecology in its harmony and fullness?—is the natural capital of the earth that is ignorantly trampled to dust in the rush of the city-state to create a heap of momentarily magical short-term 'goods'.

The city-based Gilgamesh seduces Enkidu's indigenous or natural human soul—and by extension, his own (and yours and mine) as well—away from the natural world and into a testosterone-fuelled project of tearing down the forest. For a while, it's all a lot of fun, but when they go too far and awaken the anger of the goddess of earthly fertility, it is the wild man—Gilgamesh's sense of his own soul, you could say—who begins to die.

Here's where the story links human destructiveness of the natural world with the rise of the walled-off city and with an intense refusal of mortality. Gilgamesh grieves deeply for his beloved friend but his horror of his own death overtakes the submerged longing for wholeness that was always implicit in his powerful attraction to Enkidu. An heroic quest for personal immortality now possesses him far more thoroughly than grief for his lost soul. But although he has the fortitude to battle through great difficulty and finally lay his hands on the secret of immortality, holding on to it turns out to require a more disciplined awareness. This eludes him, and the immortal secret is lost through his easily distractible mind.

Childhood perpetual

A serpent was the ancient way of saying 'unnatural monster', 'powerful spirit', one that appears silently and mysteriously from the earth, the very source of life. The Genesis serpent has since been pronounced to be the Devil, but it shares a direct line of descent from the one that also proves to Gilgamesh the limited nature of his (our) self-control and self-awareness, and fear of his own mortality.

Gilgamesh, even as hero of a story that can endure for 4000 years, is actually (like numberless celluloid action heroes after him) more child than man. He has no capacity to put another ahead of himself or place any value on humble impulse control. Most of all he is childish in his abject refusal of his own mortality, never allowing it to spark in him a more adult curiosity that can dare turn back towards that great existential mystery, which is inseparable from the mystery of being, and look it in the eye.

The city—that striking creation of human beings that is most costly to natural systems—is simultaneously enriching and expensive to the spirit of human beings. Urban life has generally been the seedbed of education, philosophy, libraries, advances in medicine, art, literature, architecture, music—all of them powerful nourishments for the human spirit. But while the city's technologies and synergies furnish a degree of leisure time by cushioning us from some of the toil for life's needs, it also historically locks whole lives into class-bound, cog-like servo-mechanisms within a kind of perpetual-motion machine.

The meaning of a city-bound life can be understood less as a self-sufficient whole than as a part, dependent for its meaning and sustenance on its place in many networks, each of which ultimately regard it as replaceable. The city, the domain of Gilgamesh, is in a way composed of dependent part-lives, kept in place by mortgages, debts and wages, caught in the intense competition for adequate money-based wealth and material status.

The twentieth century has been dubbed 'the century of the self'. And yet Gilgamesh already anticipates the aggressive individualism that arose exactly at the same time as an individual's risk of vanishing into the anonymous, lonely mass of industrial city life. A keen ego is needed to overcome the sheer indifference of the marketplace to your existence, let alone your fate. If your number comes up unlucky in the draw, there's no point in protesting; in the words of *The Godfather*, 'It's not personal. It's business.' Gilgamesh foreshadows this harsh edge to the citified ego all too well. And four thousand years later we are seeing the resilience of the natural world finally begin to falter before its ferocity.

The large-scale irrigated agriculture needed to feed a city like Uruk fed far more people than slash-and-burn garden agriculture could ever do, and the large-scale concentration of people in one place yielded prodigious energy to harness to the projects of the city. But it also drained far more time and labour from greater numbers of people, as well. Uruk marks the first step towards agriculture on a massive scale, which has now morphed into highly industrialised coal-, oil- and chemical-based agribusiness, feeding infinitely more numbers of people again but further weakening the ancient ties between people and the land, the knowledge and skills involved in growing food, and the instinctive relationship between human beings and food grown right where they live.

The first city-states like Uruk, and warrior kings like Gilgamesh, appear on the world stage with the first armies, raids and wars to defend or plunder stored surpluses of grain, oil, food, treasure, and to seize the prize of cities, slaves and the rich cultivated hinterlands that support a city. Meanwhile, in the driven character and incivility of Gilgamesh we find the seeds of the self-dedicated, self-entitled individual, formed by the explosive rise in huge urban-centred economies based on ever denser forms of energy. This may prove to be the most expensive idea ever conceived on earth. *Gilgamesh* is our earliest discovered shards and fragments of a mirror in which to clearly glimpse its fleeting face, as in an ancient dream.

And *Gilgamesh's* dream—our shared trance—of hoping never to die is utterly expressed in the rise of the city, which is a kind of boast against death; its buildings and monuments, that nevertheless will end in ruin and dust, defy gravity and decay for as long as they can by freezing time in stone. In a way, the city is a rigid expression of our reluctance to accept death and the fact of one thing continually becoming another in an ever-moving world. The obsession of Gilgamesh with pleasing himself and eluding death drives his life, while in fact he is losing his battle with mortality at every point in the story, dissipating his mind and losing his life to the power of fear inside his obsession with mortality.

Erisychthon: 'Ours for the taking'

Ovid's long first-century BCE poem *Metamorphoses* recounts in Latin for Roman consumption a series of much older Greek myths and stories of humans transformed by the gods into something other—and usually less—than human. Among them lies the story of Erisychthon, which, like *Gilgamesh*, holds portent for our times.

It is another story that begins in the vulnerability of the untouched green world to human predation. But this time unrestrained greed is the focus.

Erisychthon, yet another king of highly impulsive appetite and temper, ignores the restraints advised by the gods and observes no taboos. His very name means 'Earth Tearer'. He takes it in mind to harvest the timber of an ancient forest grove of oaks sacred to Ceres, goddess of the harvest and the earth's fruitfulness. While others see a natural temple in the most venerable oak, which is fifteen yards around and hallowed by the streamers, garlands and prayers tied to its branches, Erisychthon just shrewdly sizes up the lineal yards of fine timber it offers for his personal use.

As he approaches, axe in hand, the tree shudders. He orders his servant to fell the oak, but when the man wavers and falls back, sensing that he stands on holy ground, the king seizes the axe from him and lands a mighty blow upon the trunk. The tree blanches grey-white even before the axe lands, then gushes a fountain of blood from the wound as the nymph spirit of the tree screams in agony. Horrified, all step back, bar one brave soul who leaps into the path of the axe to stop it. But Erisychthon roars, 'Here's the reward for all your piety!' and decapitates the protestor with one swing of his axe. He hacks the great trunk apart, bringing the sacred oak down with a terrible roar, crushing the grove to smithereens. The nymph of that holy tree curses him with her dying breath.

When Ceres hears of the offence from her dazed dryads, she orders one of them to fly to the remotest part of the Caucasian mountains where terrifying Famine—the colour of dead moonlight, skin stretched so thin you can see her vitals clinging to her bones—dwells in stony wasteland. The nymph comes as close as she can bear to the bottomless hunger of Famine, gives Ceres's orders, then flees. Famine, by nature, cannot meet with the goddess of fruitfulness herself, but she willingly carries out her orders to punish such desecration. She flies through the air to where the king sleeps in his palace, hovers over his insensible body and kisses his dreaming lips, breathing into his pores insatiable hunger.

Erisychthon wakes to an all-consuming rage for food that nothing can satisfy. Halfway through one vast feast he anxiously bellows for the next, but the more he eats, the more ravening his hunger. Into his belly he pours all the wealth and resources of his kingdom until everything of value has been devoured. What is left? His eyes fall upon his daughter. He pimps her immediately to the first stranger he meets, but she is aided by her desperate prayer to the shape-changing god Neptune, who promptly transforms her from a lovely maiden to an old sea-dog sailor the moment the money changes hand.

Her gift, of changing form and slipping from grasp immediately a deal is sealed, is the perfect way to keep a bottomless greed alive. She is like an avatar of modern advertising, arousing an appetite and promising so much, yet never quite providing what was dreamed of. And it works a treat for Erisychthon.

At least for a time. For at last the famine in him exhausts even his daughter's resourcefulness, and as food only ever increased his ravenous addiction, he finally tears at his own wasted limbs and, in utter despair, devours himself alive.

Eating ourselves alive

Is there anything that needs explaining here? How eloquently Ovid's knife finds its way to the canker of soulless, deathly greed that can turn a sacred *source*—forest, animals, water, air, minerals, seed variety, the human genome, life itself—into mere *re*source, passively awaiting our use and exploitation. And how quickly that relegation of the world to mere matter becomes a bottomless appetite for material consumption, an addiction that will take an axe to the tree of life and strip bare the world around us, until we have eaten ourselves alive.

The story shows how even our own children are fair game for such predatory appetite. The strange fate of Erisychthon's beautiful child, sucked into her father's madness, is like a foreshadowing of the power of spin in advertising, which so readily substitutes appearance for reality, story for truth. All those who buy her from her willing father hunger for what she really is—for the *real* that is constantly distanced from us by the spin—but all end up with only a disappointing counterfeit reality.

Meanwhile, that deep human appetite for the true or the real decays into a self-consuming, insatiable greed for more and more stuff, which can never even *touch* that true longing.

Faustian bargains

Although the world is still exquisitely beautiful, the economic fundamentalist mind can look on what's left untouched and, like Erisychthon, see only massive resources, ours for the taking but stupidly not yet seized. Downstream in time from the three foundation-level stories I have touched on here, Western culture is full of stories of human overreaching, often figured as a pact with the Devil, the archetypal overreacher. Our soul in exchange for unlimited wealth, knowledge, power, pleasure is always a bargain that looks impossible to refuse at the start of the term of the contract (after all, what do souls contribute to the bottom line?), but grows profoundly melancholy as the payment date falls due.

Living now in the time that our debts are being called in by the earth, it's time to check the fine print on the contract.

The Faust legend, in all of its incarnations in chapbook, play, poem, opera and film, involves Doctor Faust, a theology scholar who drifts towards magic, alchemy and proto-science, frustrated by the limits of theology to get him all that he dreams of having. The Devil, in the form of Mephistopheles, is drawn by the power of his longing and offers Faust everything he dreams of up to the very zenith of human happiness. When he truly exhausts all desires, only then will Mephistopheles collect his due—a small thing, nothing to be too fussed about: Faust's soul. Faust leaps at the promise of boundless self-gratification and the obvious bargain he is being offered, perfectly confident such a moment will never arrive, that the debt is infinitely deferrable, that no pleasure could ever satiate him completely. Besides, what *is* a soul? Where is it—can anyone point to it? You can search a skeleton and find nowhere for it to lodge.

But what if our immortal soul were not a thing but an unending negotiation with the true nature of ourselves; not a noun but a most subtle verb? Certainly, *loss* of soul is a constant, subtle process. Long before the debt is called in, the ever-mounting and more complicated appetites of Faust, and ever more devilish ruses

Mephistopheles creates to fulfil them, is an *action*, twisting reality, exploiting others, ransacking goodwill.

To seek the Devil's powers is to be careless with the core of self that is beyond price, yet so subtle and mysterious that it is not sufficiently noticed, let alone prized, until it has been ceded—for what always looks suddenly like a bill of cheap goods. The emptiness that follows is the purest of terrors. Suddenly the appalling hollowness of the bargain—the hollowness of Faust himself that drove him to scramble for sensations, gee-gaws, flatteries and the intoxication of power over others—shows its true face. We seem to find it too hideous to contemplate. Easier, simpler, to turn away to other things.

Aliens on earth

Just as economic rationalism was taking hold of the political landscape of the Western democracies, the *Alien* cycle of films (especially the first two, in 1979 and 1986) began to explore the Faustian bargain we had long been making with the natural world. They offer a space-based, science-fiction mirror to the corporate-military-industrial-complex that has long been forging a monstrous bargain with the worst part of ourselves.

The Alien is a species of parasite or even virus whose entire 'personality' is one unstoppable appetite to colonise and destroy other bodies and species without mercy, in order to proliferate with appalling energy and populate any planet beyond all bounds. Does this sound a little familiar so far? Virulent defence of its young is the sole shred of what we might call love or tenderness in the Alien. Its fierce, utterly simple and ruthless intent to invade and destroy its host species makes it to military eyes the perfect weapon. Of course, that is also what makes it impossible to be controlled, and what will inevitably destroy all warm-blooded life on any planet to which it is introduced. A small consideration for such a military prize. So nothing can match the equal ferocity and ruthlessness of the corporate-military-complex in its determination to acquire it.

For both entities—alien parasite and corporate/military

enterprise—feelings don't come into it. They understand each other. The sole agenda, for both, is self-reproduction and cease-less proliferation. Hatched, the alien blends a strangely humanoid feel with compelling reptilian details and several sets of complexly retractable jaws, dripping with slime. But perhaps the most inti-mately awful feature is its pupal 'face-hugger' stage, a kind of octopus-come-placenta with unbreakable grip that welds itself to the face of its human host, erasing all trace of personality and silently gestating its next stage of hatching through a tentacle into the vitals of its host, who is destined to become its mere disposable cocoon. At term, it bursts full bore from the belly of its victim, leaving a shattered corpse behind.

The analogy with both unfettered corporate consumer capi-talism and unrestrained superpower militarism needs little explanation. Likewise, we are left to catch sight of our own species' alienation from itself into something monstrous and barely rec-ognisable as residually human, when limitless, oil-fuelled material growth acquires the ferocity of addiction.

Thus *Alien* hatched into the late twentieth century one of the most telling images for our time, capturing the plight in human consciousness I am exploring: that octopus-placenta suckered so tightly to the victim's face, blinding them and masking all personal features, its umbilicus rooting deep into the vitals through a mouth forced open, protest utterly silenced. The *personhood* of a human being reduced to mere host body for the gestation of an unstoppa-ble parasite that will destroy it in the process of its metamorphosis into a planet-destroying alien.

Rolling Stone took up the image in its moment of ferocious anger at the vast harm done by Goldman Sachs in bringing on the financial crash of 2008, which ruined hundreds of millions of suckered victims of its publicly licensed greed. The world's most powerful investment bank at that time was pictured as 'a great vampire squid wrapped around the face of humanity, relentlessly jamming its blood funnel into anything that smells like money'.

A more comprehensive image of the 'octopus' on our faces, as we grapple to see, think and speak the crisis we are in, is difficult to imagine.

That sense of becoming the aliens on earth was foreshadowed in the earlier stories I've examined, stories that have helped us grow parasitic on the rest of the natural world, depleting our vitality of mind and will to be otherwise. It reproduces itself by extinguishing species at an unprecedented rate and threatens to destroy a human future.

Avatar (2009) tilts the mirror at a slightly different angle. Bottomless corporate-military greed is abroad again, this time targeting the rarest of rare metals, 'unobtainium', available only on a planet ominously named Pandora, which is every child's dream of an untouched, infinitely lush adventure world. That is, before applications on gadgets replaced childhood adventures with a fully 'imagineered' childhood. It is an ironic footnote that to 'imagineer' the live-motion capture that brought this three-dimensional dream of a lost world to vivid life, the computer firepower needed was immense.

The story follows Jake, a burnt-out ex-marine amputee bound for the military scrapheap, whose mind is downloaded into an avatar body, making him a blend of cyborg and 'second world' internet avatar. To infiltrate Na'avi society in order to persuade them to accept the mining operation that will ruin their ecosystem, he takes the form of a member of the tall blue Na'avi 'people' of Pandora with their long magical tails that not only swish like a cat's but end in tendrils that can join with others in lovemaking, and plug into the sacred planetary energy that sustains the vast web of life.

This humanoid form inspires no horror. Instead, we enter that enchanted, luscious world, with and *as* the avatar, leaping with joy, falling in love with its amazing beauty that could only be born in the imagination of a child of earth. Time spent in an avatar body on Pandora ironically lets us back onto our own planet deeply touched by memories of how it was before its profligate living diversity was swept away by a great dead, post-industrial sameness.

Of *course,* like Jake, we readily go over to the 'alien' Na'avi side, wanting their disciplined delicacy and intelligence to prevail against the crass material overkill of our own rapacious species. Who wouldn't? Through the eyes and body of Jake, we have half become Pandorans already. Or rather, retrieved our lost earth souls in the company of tall blue aliens who are, ironically, far less alien and unacceptable to us than we have grown to ourselves.

Our overkill as an all-consuming species; the pact with the devil involved in commandeering and engineering the life of a planet to satisfy the bottomless greed of a single species; the dream of limitless growth appropriate only to an infant or parasite; and our shamefully overbearing posture as a species—all are vivid to different degrees not just in the foundation stories I have visited here, but in dozens of hyper-budget blockbusters of our time, as the media industry searches out our deepest fears and oldest stories to mine for drama. *Avatar* was first to eclipse *Titanic* at the box office. *Titanic* may have had a syrupy love story pinned prominently to its breast, but nothing could disguise the fact that at heart its mythic roots lay in our fascination with the vast catastrophe of this overly huge and engineered civilisation of ours heading straight towards an implacable limit point.

Our civilisation, perhaps even our species, is a doomed dinosaur, still rampaging as apparent ruler of the earth—but we all know the abrupt fate of the other dinosaurs. In *Jurassic Park*, and other blockbusters about dinosaurs, we catch sight of how we try out in advance our own spectacular rise and possible fall as a species. Do we suspect we might appear to the other species right now a bit the way we self-admiringly view rapacious *Tyrannosaurus Rex*?

For examining ourselves in the light of these stories, *we* are the tyrant kings, smashing through the land, shredding the trees, flattening the earth with our devastatingly heavy carbon footprint, who may yet return the world to the torrid climate of the

Carboniferous era, in which the dinosaurs rose. A climate that suited cold-blooded creatures so well is rather unlikely to suit us warm-blooded ones.

Apocalypse now (or very soon)

The sense of an ending is as intrinsic to a story as it is to a life. Any story continually implies an ending, even if it is a cliffhanger that invites its sequel. So the very nature of story can encourage an eschatology, or sense of everything approaching 'last things' (usually death, judgment, heaven, hell).

However, it is one thing to see this sense of an ending as an aspect of sojourning here on earth together with night and day, birth and death; it is quite another to see the entire unfolding of the world through the lens of a narrative heading insistently for a highly anticipated doomsday. This is the self-fulfilling prophetic mood of apocalyptic thought. The very word means an unveiling or revelation of what must transpire. The deep longing in human beings to know what will happen next finds in apocalypse a very strange form of release from fear and personal responsibility: Don't worry, there's nothing we can do, the worst must and will happen, but it's for the best.

Anyone taking up the great questions of climate change has to guard against falling prey to apocalyptic doomsday thinking that can inspire a dangerous fatalism and undermine our humanity. Computer modelling of climate change might attempt to anticipate the direction of change and set benchmarks by which to measure its rate, but we don't know what will happen, we never have. History evolves, like life itself, in chaotic fits and starts and unexpected 'tipping points' that slide change in a rapid new direction. As Stephen Jay Gould has said, history can never be predicted with any precision. It includes far too much chaos and depends on too many minute and unmeasurable differences in conditions, which can trigger massively divergent outcomes that stem from tiny and virtually untraceable differences in starting points.

Apocalypse and the end of the world has been a leading story of Western culture since its Judaic-Christian inception, reaching back to earlier Persian Zoroastrian underpinnings that see the world as a vast struggle between good and evil that must come to a final showdown. Playing out in thousands of forms, from Revelations to *Lord of the Rings*, this eschatology proposes that the end of the world will burst forth at some moment in time, bringing to a final head a great ongoing battle between the forces of light and dark, and ending time itself. Even older pagan myth cycles imagined an end time. The Old Norse myths, for example, have the image of a mouse perpetually nibbling at the roots of Yggdrasil, the World Tree, finally cutting right through and bringing it down forever.

Apocalypse anticipates the end of history and the world in catastrophe for the wicked and the flawed, while often holding open a dream of a thousand-year aftermath of history-less, time-less, peaceful righteousness.

Perhaps the Cold War threat of nuclear apocalypse was so passively tolerated because of a deep grain of apocalyptic expectation already well established in Western culture. The development of nuclear weapons and the dropping of the bombs on Hiroshima and Nagasaki were a crime against humanity and against nature, but remain entirely unacknowledged as such. On the contrary, blatant pride is taken in the prestige of having nuclear 'capability'. Nuclear weapons development fed seamlessly into the massive enterprise of the nuclear power industry which, especially since Three Mile Island, Chernobyl and Fukushima, itself offers rich doomsday possibilities.

The difference between the doomsdays that hang over our heads from climate change and nuclear energy is that the former steadily approaches as the ongoing consequence of our polluting the atmosphere, while the latter hovers threateningly as a perpetual *possibility* of human error, systems failure or mishandling of waste. Still, it is chilling to recall how thoroughly and calmly our culture swallowed its possible fate of abrupt nuclear annihilation for almost four decades of Cold War, managing to live with a sense of existential absurdity and numbness in the face of an uncontrollable threat of apocalypse.

Regardless of how much long-running apocalyptic narratives in our culture may have normalised it in advance, did this obscenity of threatened nuclear annihilation also help prepare the way for our decades of passivity towards the steadily building threat of global warming?

Scientists observing the world's first test explosion of a nuclear bomb at Alamogordo in 1945 did not know for certain whether or not the explosion would set off an unstoppable chain reaction that would consume and unmake the entire world. They actually gave themselves leave to find out. It seemed at the time that the chain reaction from that event did *not* take place. Perhaps they sighed in relief too soon. Not only does the spectre of nuclear warfare and meltdown continue to stalk the world despite the fact that our eyes have been drawn away to other threats; it is fair to say the apocalyptic thinking that could quieten their scruples enough even to contemplate conducting such an experiment rolls on in a continuing chain reaction of uncanny acceptance of the unthinkable.

'End times' are also peeking at us from around the corner of 'peak oil', unmistakable signs of 'limits to growth', a planet shrinking under sheer weight of human numbers—all of them signs of the end point of the fantasy of limitless exploitation of a finite, one-off planetary endowment. The story of global economic growth itself carries at its core a darkly knowing, apocalyptic image of its own inevitable and catastrophic ending. However, while the fantasy of an end time with raptures that will transport the chosen few to a heavenly place engages the imagination of millions, the reality of the profound rupture we are creating in the fabric of our living world struggles for recognition.

Our foundational cultural narratives, including *'Apocalypse now, or very soon'*, secrete warnings about what dangers the world is drifting towards. But, while the warnings may excite our imaginations and even longings, they do not have the energy to rouse us to imagine and create a world that can survive and heal from our excesses. In fact, they may have primed our minds so subtly but thoroughly for a feared and longed-for end that we're left resigned and even expectant when we need to be alert and appalled, and more likely to concede ground to creeping disaster when we need to resist and fight for a future.

Thinking seven generations deep

The North American Hopi way of approaching any big communal decision is one that will seem strange, and strangely beautiful, to ears tuned to the urgent din of 'growth at all costs'. It is, 'What will this mean for the next seven generations?' To fully ponder this question, the Hopi would close their eyes and reach deep inside to visualise the faces of the generations downstream from themselves—those unknown stewards of the earth yet to be born.

There is a roundedness in such a sense of time. It goes far beyond the logic of 'what comes around goes around', a far deeper sense of 'karma' than that. This is not about karma as a burden from the past, or a supernatural system of reward and punishment meted out through forms of rebirth (or life after death). Instead, it evokes a reminder of how creatively and imaginatively human generosity and awareness can feel out and meet with that of the earth; how that opens the way; how it seeds a thousand possibilities that may yield a liveable future and green the earth.

Inside it is a willingness to sacrifice something you would like to have for yourself—momentary ease and comfort, say, or a quick personal advantage—for something that belongs to the much bigger, more unknown and imaginative sense of who you are, best described as 'we only have each other'. That 'we' is boundless, extending to all living beings.

This is the sense of consequence that evolves from 'paying it forward' rather than from the exacting of past debt. In an industrialised democracy, an analogy would be conceding rather than refusing the taxes that will maintain and develop the infrastructure that supports the obvious common good of any sane, functioning society—schools, hospitals, public transport, affordable housing, roads, emergency services, environmental protection, etc. To this extent, a society that opts for extended tax 'holidays' for some or for all of its citizens is one that has lost a shared interest in its own future, and grown stone cold towards the next seven generations.

In contrast with this rounded sense of time, the linear future implied by apocalyptic thought flows from a sense of an originally blighted creation that is insistently heading towards an apocalyptic end time that will be a relief from the anxious waiting. This sense of a future is curiously flat and depthless in time. Everything could be over tomorrow. And why act upon concern for the world and for each other if this is the case?

End time is, admittedly, a more easily riveting story than the far more subtle drama that the earth presents to quiet contemplation. Ecologies move from simple to complex, but they don't progress from first thing to last thing. They occupy time quite differently: a constant play of interdependent co-arising energies finding their best balance moment by moment in mutual and evolving relationships. Ecologies, you might say, are empty of purpose and judgment; in fact, in a real sense they are empty of 'things'; they are instead better described as an evolving communion of subjects, or forms of sentience, in mutual relationship and co-existence.

The Buddhist understanding of 'anatta', 'no-self', is very at home in this ecological mind. It holds that, while there is a *sense* of self that to some degree necessarily pervades every sentient being (at least we can say with authority, human beings!), in fact there is no *fixed* self to be found, when you really look. In the place where that vanishes, something far more astonishing emerges: a profound experience of the infinite interpenetration of all beings, at the core of your own sentience. This is not at all just a metaphysical thing of wonder. It informs the choices we make and the actions that follow, and it allows that the self is not just richly permeable but always ethically transformable, malleable in the light of whatever wisdom comes its way.

The infinitely intricate ecological 'intelligence' of the earth that shaped the circumstances that ushered or drew each of us into being offers a very different sense of how every action shapes the whole, and opens a very different sense of the ethics and creativity of each moment.

And this changes the sense of how we inhabit past and future into one that is less confined to self-interest and far more ecological in spirit, closer to the Hopi stance of listening deeply to the unfolding story the earth is always telling us. Human freedom becomes visible and momentous in a new light, here, but that will be visible only to someone who has understood the far-reaching and irreversible impact on oneself and others of all the choices we make. In other words, always open to the subtle work of mending that the ever-evolving earth is always teaching.

Earth has her stories too

So may the earth herself, and her long and continuing emergence as the most highly creative and generative speck of the vast universe that we know thus far, be permitted to offer the final comment here? In this time of increasingly sharp responses from the earth to our headlong rush towards disaster, it is important to recover the skill of holding a sensitive conversation with the earth, which has never stopped speaking to us, in a universe that never stops transmitting its magnificent nature clearly. And that begins in listening, as with any great story.

For the earth herself has stories—all of them fragments of a masterpiece.

Perhaps there is just one ultimate masterpiece, and that is the way things really are, moment by moment, here on our magical planet. Look at the leaves on any nearby tree. Watch the waves, their power and unending variety. Listen to the music of the earth when human noise subsides. Consider a feather, a mountain, a river or an ocean, or perhaps just a cloud, and the fact that there is something called 'a cloud'. Contemplate an epoch. Remember the impossibility of what the rocks really are, the soil, the earthworm. And the fact that we are, each of us, virtual planets for a multitudinous variety of microscopic life forms.

The time of the dinosaurs was an epic of the earth. Here's another, a tiny and yet vast story that shows how nature meets our aggression with an ingenuity that is masterly and will always finally prevail over our excesses, even if it means prevailing over us. Be warned that there's always pain in such stories. And the mercy they disclose is one that appears only when we shift the frame and take a longer view. To hear the earth's stories we will have to look past our small sense of self towards the larger self, the perspective of the whole.

The now abandoned Berkeley Pit open-cut copper mine in Butte, Montana, is an open scar on the land. It was 540 metres deep and had yielded over a trillion tonnes of ore when the Anaconda Mining Co stopped digging in 1982 and turned off the water pumps that had been keeping out groundwater. Now the scar is slowly filling with that water, blood-red and metallic, the water level rising each year as a truly lethal brew, containing a wide array of heavy metals, and an acidity level that will burn flesh. Tourists flock to the site to marvel at the spectacle, perversely beautiful in its toxicity. The pit has become a popular tourist attraction, with paid entry to a viewing platform, and of course, adjacent gift shop.

In 1995, a flock of migrating snow geese caught in a fog bank were forced to land on the lake. They drank the water and quickly died from internal and external burns. Necropsies showed their insides were lined with burns and festering sores from exposure to high concentrations of copper, cadmium and arsenic. If the pit water level eventually reaches the natural water table, which is estimated to occur around 2020, the extremely toxic pit water will reverse flow back into surrounding groundwater, polluting Silver Bow Creek in the headwaters of Clark Fork River. There is no guarantee that the efforts to stop this from occurring will succeed.

Against all odds, organic matter has now been discovered living in the deadly soup. New fungal and bacterial species located nowhere else on earth have been found to have adapted to the extreme conditions in the pit lake. Intense competition for the limited resources caused these species to evolve the production of highly toxic compounds to improve survivability. Some natural products such as *Berkeleydione*, *Berkeleytrione* and *Berkelic* acid, which have been isolated from these compounds, show potential in the treatment of cancer, which may be good news for humans facing the old foe. But there is good news for the natural world, as well. It has been found that one of the 'slimes' that now live in the lake is a yeast that has the ability to extract heavy metals from the water at a rate nearly seven times more efficiently than the average yeast. This yeast has until now only been isolated once before, when someone discovered it in the rectums of geese. The dying snow geese, floating on the red, misbegotten waters of the lake, left a legacy. Life lost becomes life found.

The complexity of this unfolding may elude the usual calculus of human 'mercy', 'kindness' or 'love', but it can reach us with the speed of light if we're looking at the earth as our marvellous home and not with the eyes of a giant corporation. We need to understand the creation of the universe not as a singular past event but one that both arrives complete at every moment and never stops unfolding. We need to realise it is a pattern too rich and charged with unceasing change to ever swallow into some final form of comprehension but one that our minds can deeply apprehend, given sufficient prompting from love, imagination and wonder. Such an act of apprehension can turn us back into people who belong here, no longer riddled by some worm of perpetual doubt about that fact. Such a great narrative as the story of the universe lets us back into understanding that five billion years ago the molten rocks of the uncooled earth already implied our own hand and eyes, along with the minds of Shakespeare, Mozart, da Vinci, Galileo, as well as the sheer unlikelihood of birdsong, roses, dragonflies, thistledown, sticks, dung, and even unicorns. And knowing our place in this large, inclusive story, and knowing that we are not only all part of it but taking our own part in creating how it unfolds, may help to rouse the energy we need right now to mend the earth.

PART III

BREAKING THE FRAME

Chapter Five

Natural mind

The indigenous peoples of the world live in a universe, in a cosmological order, whereas we, the peoples of the industrial world, no longer live in a universe. We live in a political world, a nation, a business world, an economic order, a cultural tradition . . . in cities, in a world of concrete and steel, a world of business, of work, of highways, parking lots, shopping centres. We no longer see the stars at night or the planets or the moon . . . Summer and winter are the same inside the mall. We read books written with a strangely contrived alphabet. We no longer read the book of the universe.

Thomas Berry

In Herman Melville's great novel *Moby Dick*, Captain Ahab, gazing spellbound on the great white whale for the first time, was asked by his terrified seamen what on earth he could possibly do with so large and terrifying a beast. After a long pause he replied, 'I think that I shall praise it.'

Children don't have to try to lift the earth into their hearts. It just arrives. Praise, or wonder by its other name, is continual in a child safe to wander freely in the natural world. When my sister and I ventured out in the early North Queensland morning—the sun already lying warm as a cat on our shoulders, puddles brown with last night's rain, and the latest hatch of baby cane toads hopping vigorously all over the road—we had no doubt of our naming rights to the world, so fully did it know us. No doubt of how to place our bare toughened feet on the ground, trustingly avoiding prickles while secretly loving the squelch of cool mud between our toes. Even a momentarily painful pressure of stone on nimble soles had its sharp informative value.

All this satisfaction was a seamless play of mind in constant frog and bird music, dizzy variety of leaf shapes, bush and tree presence, scuttle-rustle of lizard—or snake!—threading through the fantasy game we were always weaving in collusion with this unlocked natural treasury, to which our very bodies were the key.

There was no creature that missed out on our tender regard. Some became incorporated into our games in ways they may have preferred to avoid. Baby cane toads, for example, abundant after every heavy downpour. We'd line them up at one edge of a huge half-clam someone had brought back from the Great Barrier Reef, now incorporated into our backyard rockery as a little pond, and force them to swim the length of it. The very unwilling, prodded on by our fingers, occasionally sank to the bottom and died, something we were worried about doing ourselves under the command of our ruthless swimming instructor in the children's section of the local public swimming pool. We were sorry for the toadlets, but we had to be tough: they must learn to swim—for their own good, we told them.

I had a book I loved above all others. *The Golden Treasury of Natural History* by Bertha Morris Parker, published in 1952 by the Chicago Natural History Museum, was a big book, its cover shiny yellow, cool to the touch, teeming with life forms. Its wondrous subtitle was as follows: *The birds and reptiles, fishes and insects, mammals, amphibians, plants and trees, flowers and fruit that have inhabited the world, as well as the minerals, fluids and gases of the earth itself and the suns, stars and planets that surround it.* I was very fortunate; all that was mine.

My sister, two years older than me, had taught me to read the moment she went to school and learned the surpassing magic of allowing the world to flow through marks on paper and into your mind from the mind of someone else. She passed the contraband goods on to me in rather strict school games that I awaited every afternoon, vigilant for the sounds of her return. What a gift!

So from the age of three I sank into reading and disappeared into other worlds, minds, and amazing facts whenever I liked, usually perched out on our breezy back steps with their good view of the yard, chickens, kelpie dog, family comings and goings. My father worked from home at that time, so he was there to help out whenever I came to some odd or indecipherable word. I'd take my book down into the darker coolness under our Queenslander house where he had his workshop, hand-tooling covers for the books in our home library, and point to the problem word.

'I' for example. What was a single capital letter doing there, out at large in the middle of a sentence? I can remember the ice of shock when I took in the understanding that this was the assertive public face of me, the universal sovereignty I shared with all others while being also, from my point of view, blazingly unique and intimate, never to be seen before nor afterwards again on earth. And a more slow-dawning and sobering intuition, that this grand 'I' somehow carved the more humble 'me' out of the seamless universe, creating by proclamation in the same breath a powerful idea and tremendous solitude, leaving an exile in its place. Perhaps I was dimly aware that this 'I' would die, and have a tombstone with dates on it, while the 'me' of the universe clearly went on as good as forever in all directions. Exciting and disturbing news, at once.

But this 'I' occurred nowhere in the Golden Natural Treasury.

In its place was something so extraordinary that decades later, I am still not 'over it', nor even remotely left out of it: Namely, the entire prehistory of the planet and all her fantastic creatures who have ever blossomed into life—and those who still struggle to keep a foothold today. The vast slug of human-centred greed and need was fatly advancing even then, but not yet enough to bruise our minds. DDT was being poured out onto the wetlands of Cairns to suppress mosquitoes and dengue fever, and beginning its slow leach into all human breast milk and the intricate bones and eggs of birds as Rachel Carson's 'silent spring' got underway.

But we didn't know anything of this yet. The sky full of signs, the humans all with their heads down, hard at it.

Children are hard at it too but purely in play. So instead, we knew wonder. Bertha Morris Parker's introduction to my wondrous book way back then ended with these prescient words:

> In science, 'truth changes', because better scientific instruments and methods are constantly revealing more of nature's secrets. But one can foresee little or no change during the coming years in the basic ideas presented in this book—that the story of the earth is indeed one of great changes; animals and plants are fitted in wondrous different ways for living as they do; and our little earth is part of a universe so vast that it passes our understanding.

Much later I would catch the echo of the words from the *Vedanta* that she brings to bear on the sense of earth in endless change: *Shanti, shanti*—'the peace that passes understanding'. Words that my father would wonder over softly in his dying days, several decades later.

This placed me securely within an orderly scale that was so huge, and yet so immediate and in perfect proportion, as well as staggeringly tiny and microscopic. The perfect fit was wonder, and our trust in that. The entire cosmos beckoned our imagination.

And seemed to ask some great question of us, which curiously did not daunt us but seemed to draw us to itself.

The form the question took for now was the adventures we created every day, wandering out from home by foot or on bicycle while keeping it *just* in safe distance, naming the animals, the plants, the paths we made, the places we discovered, eating the dusty little bush tomatoes sweet and warm from the bushes, every day the First Day, creating the world with our wonder and imagination and anything that came to hand.

One thing always becoming another

As children we have no great problem with the impossible, and are at home in that which passes our understanding. Change is our element; though we thrive only if we have sufficient security of food and touch and love, in childhood we confidently know ourselves to be change itself. A crawling baby is undefeated by the impossibility of standing on two feet and wobbling forward, and can meanwhile safely ignore walking while crawling extends its great pleasures. Every child lives uncrushed by the vast horizon of the unknown; we knew it then as the not-yet-known instead, and just got on with whatever alluring game we were playing at the time. While every game, in some unplanned way, tested us and drew us safely enough to the edge of the not-yet-known.

And perhaps the other side of the uncrushable nature of children is that mysteries are close all the time, intensely infused with imagination, with easy border crossings going on all the time between play world and real world. Consider the moment when my father invited me down to his workshop to witness the miracle of magnetism. He had to interrupt my reading this time. I looked on as two heavy nails leapt from the workbench to cling to a magnet held above them. He watched intently for my amazement, but I was disappointingly phlegmatic. 'Ah, magic,' I said, being very familiar with it already, and went back to my book on the stairs.

'Impossible' has long been our stimulant to ingenuity,

creativity and imagination. This reaches far beyond necessity being the mother of invention; it points to the vivid sense of wonder that may be intrinsic to our peculiar situation: of possessing a consciousness that has no beginning or end (when we look into it), and which blooms in a body that is limited in time and capacity. This places us in a fascinating spot of bother that is vulnerable, painful, ridiculous, astonishing and delightful and—when we notice the strangeness of being here at all—energised by that very strangeness.

Our potential to become a catastrophic disruption to the sequence of life unfolding on this planet stems from our peculiar situation; but so also does our potential to rise magnificently to the occasion, reinventing our humanity to the shape and size of the challenge that it presents. That challenge falls to the moment-by-moment decision of every one of us—that's the core determinant of our fate. But adults forget the playfulness and plasticity of the world they knew as children; we fall into silence about it, and isolation from each other, and conform our lives to the prevailing story as best we can.

Which of course helps makes clear what we need to do to turn things around: break the silence, end the isolation and change the story.

What children know

We must do everything we possibly can to recover our natural exuberance and entrancement with the living world, towards which our million-year-old minds are receptively shaped, as most young children so clearly display. Even a little path half-choked with weeds, an earth bank or sandpit carved into a play world, or a mud-luscious puddle reflecting the whole sky, can be more than enough! But best of all is for a child to be free to wander and play, led by the imagination, in a place in which every rock and twig has been shaped almost entirely by natural circumstances, some small corner of the world not overwhelmed by human interference and human static.

Without access to a world not too bent or damaged by human purpose, where each thing has been free to grow according to its place in a schema that can teach us how to catch infinite subtlety and surprise, human beings cease to hear the harmonic or the natural world, and its benevolent aspect begins to escape us too. We simply don't know how to lend ourselves to it anymore.

The earth's magnetic field has shifted several times in its history, completely reversing north-south polarity. It is as if the magnetic field of our relationship with the earth has shifted in an equally extreme way, in the shift from Paleolithic hunter and forager to pastoral, agricultural, historic, literate, urbanised, industrialised, and then digitalised, carbon-addicted, twenty-first-century human being. What has been lost, what has been gained, and what damage or imbalance must be repaired in this gradual polar shift from culturally embedded in the natural world to culturally and technologically insulated from it? The earth has always provided all that is needed for life and for loving and falling into entrancement with the mystery of earth and universe. You could say that we and the earth are by nature inclined to sing each other up. That mutuality has been broken.

Yet the song continues. Thomas Berry speaks of a random childhood memory of the natural world that fired his entire life as a priest and theologian turned 'geologian', or passionate defender of the holy fact of the earth. For him, it was a simple glimpse of a spring meadow across a creek as a twelve-year-old boy. It was 'just' a meadow in early afternoon May light, covered with white lilies that rose above the thick grass. It was more than lilies, it was cricket song too, and clouds in the bright sky. Nothing conscious happened. Just a boy glancing across to a nearby field.

> Yet, as the years pass I seem to come back to this moment and the impact it has had on my feeling for what is real and worthwhile in life. *Whatever preserves and enhances this meadow in the natural cycles of its transformation is good; what is opposed to this meadow or negates it is not good.* My life orientation is that simple. It is also that pervasive. [My italics.]

That glimpse, deep into what is, is not just a consoling memory from childhood. It is a motivating force for a whole rich life, which indelibly entered a child because imaginative children exist in open rapport towards the conversation of the earth, conducted in such immediate and complete form as an open meadow blowing with white flowers.

Young children seem more easily to know how to see and be seen by the natural world. They still intuit their role in the unending creation story quite forthrightly. They *rely* on fluid change rather than fear and resist it—how else could they expect to grow? I have been moved to see how children seriously ill in hospital seem to find the courage to give themselves over to what is happening with serious trust, rather than 'childish' demand for another fate. The ability of young children to lend themselves unreservedly to the reality of what is happening both creates and springs from an essentially imaginative rapport with everything around them. They are not positioned there simply as an insular victim of unkind forces; they are more simply the whole of what they are in.

But in our culture this ease of knowing yourself to be the whole grows hard to sustain past early to mid childhood. This is in part the result of an education that requires us to distinguish objects one from another and identify them primarily by name. This takes us away from the thinking that perceives relationship between subjects rather than analyses the features of the object called by this name, relative to the object called by that name.

When you go walking in country with the Aboriginal elder, Uncle Max Harrison, he obliges you to begin to see as he was taught, not through learning the *names* of things but by perceiving their web of enlivening interdependencies—between 'this fella' (a tree, perhaps) and 'that fella' (a bird that appears this time of year and sips the nectar from its flowers), which indicates that 'that fella' (migrating humpback whales, say) will now be showing up off the coast on the way from Antarctica to the breeding waters up north. It grows agreeably hard to separate one fella from another. Each organism is a clear signal to every other of a wholeness plain in everything, but it's hard to see that if you are looking with an eye that sees objects and you don't allow the time it takes for the 'mind' of the whole ecology to slowly resolve in your own mind—a hologram revealed in every part, your mind included.

This way of seeing and being with the world lies much closer to the endless metaphoric learning that is the brilliance of childhood play. Metaphor is that place of most rapid-fire learning where names are infused with time and change, leaving us happily slipping between one entity, one role, one form of sentience and another, with the ease of dream. In time our culture expects this constant creation of a whole world that children engage in to give way to the more analytic routines of learning. Although we are likely to stay easily hooked by ready stories all our lives, the experience of deep immersion in a mysterious story can start to fade from the sky of our minds.

Once I sat in a bar in Calabar, the old slave port of Nigeria, watching Chelsea play Manchester United, with a ten-year-old boy who leapt about, beside himself with joy. Television was available only on the rare occasion when the bar's thunderous generator was working. The rest of the time the boy was at school or at play, in circumstances poor in material comforts but rich with people, chickens, a scraggly cow, a sandy sidewalk crammed with itinerant traders, where anything could happen next. 'We must keep our eyes *busy*!' he urged me repeatedly, as we shouted together at the television set and drank our sweet malt drinks.

Our eyes turn cool towards the world because we are drawn in to studying or manipulating it from a slight remove, such as encountering it through written words or on a screen rather than entering it wholesale. Twenty-first century urban children have been largely robbed of a childhood that ensures a good measure of free play with the natural world. When they encounter wild nature, it will likely be an image on a screen. Not much of a conversation to be had there. Snappy digital animation that intimates the natural world draws the eyes much faster than the real thing and glues them to a brightly coloured simulation. Even a coral reef teeming with jewelled life can seem drained of its potency by a trillion created images that have preceded its arrival on the retina of a child. A child who is in one sense being drawn into a life trapped on a screen as much as the fast-disappearing animals.

Can we know our world is in dire straits if we have forgotten how to have the conversation with it? Children are of course still born with that propensity perfectly intact, richly sensitive and ready to respond to the presence of another creature, but often little or nothing engages it.

Animals make us human

Of course, there are still our pets, those household gods that offer an uncomplicated enough place for our unconditional love to lodge. Everyone loves their cat or dog, but while we fuss over them with food and veterinary bills that exceed what many people could ever scrape together for their own children's health needs, we hardly glance at what is being lost from our world as the species one by one exit the planet. The animals, insects, fish, trees and plants in their myriad exacting forms of sentience and character, who have held up a mirror from ten thousand different angles to catch sight of who we are; have fired our imaginations with their strangeness, excellence and beauty; and have tipped our minds into metaphor by the sheer fascination they induce, that draws us halfway into themselves.

Metaphor is the intrinsically human use of the marvellous way the universe has of constantly inducing one thing to become another, leaving nothing fixed, but rather fluid and composed of time itself. Metaphor is the quicksilver energy of imagination flowing between things saying 'I am also you'. It is that shape-shifting capacity in every human, born of our fascinated encounters with other sentient beings and the whole world they each portend.

So the animals shape-shift us, they relieve us of ourselves for a time. Once, they carried a numinous force of their own, a holy presence. Our oldest stories knew this intimately, and our children's books carry on the knowing, peopled with animal characters who help us to divine who we may be: tigerish, piggish, doggy, catty, beetling, crabby, slippery as an eel, busy as a bee, a snake in the grass, wormy, weaselly, bullish . . . Human nature needs every single animal attribute to be complete. The movement of an animal draws the human eye like nothing else can. To mimic an animal in ritual dance is to draw up a god. For a wild animal to return our gaze, unforced, or to advance a trusting contact, unbidden, can be a defining moment in a life. Are gadgets and playstations fair substitute for this ravishingly prolific life and the grace it bestows?

That rich, million-year-old responsiveness of the child's brain to just where they find themselves in a natural environment, in company with significant humans and other animals, tame, semi-tame and wild, is now barely addressed in a purely urban world. It lies dormant or else is rapidly diverted to the moving images on a screen. A little further on, the child become a young adult and will barely even sense that they have been deprived of something profound. The 'time-pollution' of incoming signals, rendering our time ever more casually interruptible, will not even leave them time enough for that.

The conversation the earth is holding with us takes some time and quiet. We have allowed ourselves to become fractured and made small by technology's voracious intent to talk at us incessantly, beam ever-changing images into our minds, have us talk more to more and more people but fewer and fewer face to face, and to strain to do everything in less time. We are subject to incoming messages, opinions, tweets, sound bites and spin, a ceaseless bombardment from proliferating varieties of electronic platforms. Only a fraction of these interruptions are important enough to deserve the unhesitating priority they are given. Many undermine rather than add to knowledge. And truth—a word rendered relative to the point where it attracts scare quotes, irony or lofty postmodern dismissal—is rarely a concern.

What if we can no longer even gauge how much has gone missing from what it is to be human?

And what happens if we forget we are animal too, and that in the ecology of the earth, every species is an unrepeatable idea of the earth, one that is needed and implied by the presence of all the others?

Where do we draw the line?

One of the most important twentieth-century philosophers of ethics, Emanuel Levinas, wrote an essay entitled 'Name of a Dog' about his time as a prisoner in a Nazi concentration camp. By some unlikely means, into that benighted place wandered a small dog who adopted Levinas's work team. They named him 'Bobby', and he became a most important part of their lives. He wished them goodbye in his fashion when they left for their long hours of labour, and smiled and wagged his tail fulsomely when they came back. In other words, he was the only being who treated these prisoners like human beings.

And yet thirty years later, when Levinas came to write about our capacity to respond to the ethical call of the other, he concludes that only other human beings can make an ethical claim on us. He erects a boundary: On one side, humans; on the other, Bobby and all the rest of the life of the living world.

As anthropologist Deborah Bird Rose put it, 'Bobby doesn't make the cut.' She went on to speak of one of her senior Aboriginal teachers (the word she prefers to 'informant') Old Tim, a senior Aboriginal law man and clever man in Yarralin country, in the Roper River area of northern Australia. Dingoes—Australian native dogs—were a big part of Old Tim's Dreaming. His relationship with them was a very inside one. He could talk with dogs and report on things dogs said, and they said things like, 'We are the father and mother of you people' . . . 'We made you, in important ways, and now you chuck us on the rubbish tip.' He's right. Our close connection with the non-human life that helped grow us human has been severed; we live in a time of massive rate of extinctions beyond anything humans have ever known, beginning to look like one of the five or six great calamities on earth.

In the face of this trashing of the living world, what does Levinas's position offers us but a loneliness and emptiness as a species in a faltering biosphere. He's saying 'We're humans, we live and die as humans, and the rest of the world can't make a strong ethical call on us.' Which feeds the cycle of violence against the living world while shielding us within a human-only world for a time from the reality of what's happening all around us. The unprotected but ultimately only secure alternative is to know how much we overlap with the other animals and share their fate. Until then as the extinctions continue and all the animal partners to our lives are dying, as Bird Rose says, like a dingo or any other animal caught up in the cogs of human exploitation of the world, we too are being poisoned and flayed right back to the bone and bleeding out onto the ground. We have to ask ourselves is this how we want to live, is it bearable to allow all this carnage which is our own carnage as well?

If we can throw any species onto the scrap-heap, we're effectively conceding that life itself is a scrap-heap and that we are fit for the same fate, that our own lives and deaths are without intrinsic value. That we, too, may be considered essentially inappropriate and beside the point.

And yet the moment we really take in another creature, being to being, the magisterial creativity of the universe is sharply clear and complete in their presence. That can't be brushed aside any more. We can get by without moving to acknowledge this fact or to live by its light. In other words, we can choose to junk the offer life makes in every moment we are here. Its mysterious force will compose and animate us in any case, in every detail of our lives. But so will the choice to be dull towards it. That too will decide the world that chooses us.

Tuning in to the conversation and warning calls of the birds, reading the signs of animal scats and tracks, of rubbed areas on tree trunks, of geological eras in roadside cuttings, knowing that the blossoming of those trees means black cockatoo sightings on the coast and whales passing further out, becoming lucky in the finding of bird nests, snake skins . . . The earth treasury opens of its own accord, but our indifference to its mystery lays it waste.

When we are lucky enough to glimpse it clearly with no choice but to return its gaze, the critically important practical questions finally have a chance to arrive in us: What threatens to damage this holy fact? How do I act upon recognising it? How can I best serve in taking care of it? What kind of awareness can inform and even transform me here?

The matrix of mind

In 1898 a meeting of cattlemen in West Texas recorded the following declaration: '*Resolved: that none of know, or care to know, anything about grasses, native or otherwise, outside the fact that for the present there are lots of them, the best on record, and we are after getting the most out of them while they last.*' The spirit of Gilgamesh and Erisychthon was evident at that meeting. The declaration to know nothing and proceed 'after getting the most out of it' received unanimous support. It took less than sixty years after that for the quality and carrying capacity of the rich West Texan range to be thoroughly destroyed.

Annie Dillard tells of a moment in her childhood when someone brought a large chrysalis to school in a glass jar in winter for show and tell, and left it, forgotten overnight, in the premature spring of the heated classroom where its hatching unnaturally accelerated. The creature emerged, but the sequenced lamination of its large wings as they tried to open in the cramped jar hardened them into crumpled deformities that could never fly. Later, Annie watched the teacher tap out the jar onto the drive, and saw the misbegotten insect hunch its way over lumps of dirty snow towards its sorry fate.

Paul Shepard remarks, 'A history of ideas is not enough to explain human behaviour—the behaviour that places us so far outside stable and coherent harmony with the natural world and our fast disappearing fellow species.' For Shepard, the harsh state of things is not finally traceable back to the fault of the idea of Descartes that the universe is mechanical and animals feel no pain, or of Francis Bacon that nature should serve man and be ransacked without mercy; it is the outcome of something that has gone far more fundamentally astray.

He looks to our whole process of coming into being in the world and how far that has drifted from its original state, of being, as a child, fully embedded in the natural world. He argues that this is an unnatural set of circumstances for the developing mind itself, estranging us from the wisdom of our senses, and paralysing the will and imagination to repair and heal the world.

To the extent that it is no longer fully established and integrated as children, we must create every possible opportunity to recuperate the fullness of our natural mind as adults.

Shepard traces our acquiescence to the ongoing ransacking of the natural world back to the increasing replacement of a living world by a world of things and landscapes that are entirely human-made. The result is our loneliness and gradual autism as a species, cut off from the conversation that is the living world.

The million years our species has been on the earth has formed the 'matrix' of our minds, meaning the sequence of states of readiness towards mimicry, language, athletic skill, symbol-forming, and so on. These are states of high receptivity to particular stimuli, and they correspond to what was repeatedly encountered for the longest time we've been here. Only relatively recently—during the last several thousand years—has that opportunity for childhood immersion in the natural world begun to taper off and be gradually replaced.

From earliest mobility up to the age of ten or twelve, we are programmed to move in graduated stages out from our mothers into increasing immersion in the greater matrix of the natural world. Of course, that happens still, but we no longer encounter what shaped

and triggered our mind's proclivity: a world that was itself graduated in a navigable way from the domesticated hearth to the wild
fringe of camp. The first move was from inside to outside the shelter, then from the periphery of shelter to the fringes of camp and
edge of bush or forest. To foragers and hunters, that entire world
was utterly *alive*. Camp dogs, toads, beetles, dragonflies, lizards,
sudden birds, puddles, mud, sticks, a dangerous crackling in the
undergrowth that sent you fleeing excitedly . . . the world was made
of fascinating presences. And each one lent itself to the magic of
observation, mimicry, myth, metaphoric learning.

Despite the physical fact of moving outwards into the world,
the natural world was actually an ever-expanding and deepening
inner life.

This living continuum of play, leading freely out into the *natural*
from the ground of the *human*, fostered an entire 'calendar of mental growth, cooperation, leadership, and the study of a beautiful and
mysterious world where the clues to the meaning of life were embodied in natural things, where everyday life was inextricable from
spiritual experience and encounter'. Other forms of sentience were
ritually encountered and creatively absorbed into the human—first
by simple mimicry of the movements and sounds of birds, animals,
fish that drew the attention and woke the imagination. Later that
became danced in human ritual that reincorporated you bodily back
into that sacred *flow* shared by everything.

As you grew through childhood into puberty and beyond,
human complexity and meaning began to richly layer itself upon
this matrix but did not replace it. Instead, the individual stages and
passages of life, formalised through ritual, marked a continuing
reiteration, into body, mind and imagination, of the ongoing creation of world and cosmos.

In the post-agricultural, post-industrial world, such a fundamental childhood experience of immersion in the natural world
has been an ever-receding possibility. Two hundred thousand
years of *homo sapiens* experience of life on earth prepared the

mind of a human child to unfold in progressive stages ready to be triggered in response to stimuli which are decreasingly commonplace in the world of the child. In much of the developed world, childhood has now been literally screened from most real contact with the earth, and increasingly channelled into so-called interactive devices, leaving whole latencies of mind to wither, never coaxed to bloom. And so what was once an entirely natural fellow-feeling for the earth becomes remote or obscure to us. That leaves us stranded perilously short of sensitivity towards the natural world, unable to respond either to its beauty or to its urgent demand to notice how we are impacting the natural systems that support all life.

The Spanish philosopher Ortega y Gasset described the sensibility and sensitivity of that ancient hunter-gatherer way of seeing like this:

> The hunter does not look tranquilly in one determined direction sure beforehand that the game will pass in front of him. The hunter *knows that he does not know* what is going to happen . . . Thus he needs to prepare an attention which does not consist in riveting itself on the presumed, but consists precisely in not presuming anything and in avoiding inattentiveness. It is a 'universal' attention, which does not inscribe itself at any point, and tries to be on all points (my italics).

This is the kind of wide-bodied 'field' awareness familiar to meditators, bushwalkers, artists and of course young children—anyone with the capacity to be deeply immersed in focused attention that extends an intuitive openness towards whatever subtle possibilities may be glimpsed. Clearly, it involves resting in a state of alert curiosity shaped by no preconceived ideas. Despite its quiet openness, it is a most dynamic state of attention, continually providing a finely shaped willingness to place trust in 'knowing that we do not know'.

To stop disfiguring ourselves and being the wreckers among the species, it is urgent that we find the story that can re-establish us psychically within the reality of the unfolding cosmos, and help us shed our stance of bored spectatorship. We need to recover the mind that can receive the true significance of 'ordinary' things, and be knocked back into our senses by them, back into full engagement with reality.

For all that comes into being without our agency—wind, clouds, moss, rocks, water dragons, fern fronds, petals, you name it (until names run out and there is just the pleasure of each thing itself)—all such things are beautiful and impartial, doing exactly what they do. Luckily, this astounding fact of each thing-in-itself cannot be owned, nor taken with us when we go. Eternity is to be found right there in that fact.

Their eternity is not the same as 'everlasting'; it lies in us to see the difference. William Blake's 'Auguries of Innocence' saw heaven in a wild flower, a world in a grain of sand. Everything but us embodies time with no hold barred, freely burning with it, not suffering it. No other creature lives the moments of their lives forward in expectation, or holds back from them in disappointment.

The earth swims among the stars and galaxies, green-blue, swirling with water vapour. There we are. This is us. But how deeply can that now reach into us, if the developing mind, so finely geared to cues from the natural world, receives no input? Fertile for cues that now no longer arrive, the earth concreted-over, the magnetic power of animals, birds and other creatures now replaced by human-made moving images and 'animations', the ancient matrix of mind and its earliest stages of unfolding left misshapen, cut off from the world, riddled with gaps, unable to fly.

One time, around the age of four, I spent a deeply memorable day as a small mother bird of some unknown species. 'That fella', probably. There were four or five nondescript bushes along our front fence, and one of them was selected to be my nest. I hollowed out a secret haven and assumed the demanding business of being mother bird to my nestlings for six or seven hours. I flew about our yard collecting twigs for my nest and food for my babies, but much of the time I simply sat on my nest for long spells looking out, thinking very little at all. I broke for lunch when called, but silently slipped back to my bird life the moment I could get away again.

Luckily, my parents were entirely undisturbed by this behaviour. I have never forgotten the intense happiness of that timeless day of swift intent and calm non-thought.

In our pantry we have the occasional antechinus visitation. These endearing little marsupial mice are not wholly unwelcome. Their urine leaves no acrid mousy smell, and they are fearless and curious towards humans, whisking themselves with impossible speed around the room and up and down the walls. They will even come and sit silently on your shoulder, if you grow absorbed enough in a book, late enough at night. Even given the droppings they deposit in small mounds on their favoured pantry shelves, it is impossible to encounter them without becoming somewhat affiliated by way of delight with their very interesting clan. Once initiated, *antechinus* joins your metaphoric bloodstream; *antechinus* begins to dream your mind a little way on from its old boundaries.

It is always a mournful moment when you find them looking so utterly shocked in the harmless antechinus trap, and carry them up the road, apologising softly all the while, to release them at sufficient distance to ensure they won't be right back inside the salted cracker packet one week later.

Secretly, you hope they will. They are your kinsmen. You are for them, too.

If we are to survive and grow beyond our relative infancy as a species we must regain the ability to give human voice and mythic shape to the great unceasing flow of metaphoric truth: that this living planet is not just for us, but equally *we are for it*.

We are for it

It begins with tuning back in to what's always subtly here and at hand when human mental noise is not so busy drowning it out. Where I sit writing is in an intimate valley three hundred metres up and seventeen kilometres inland from the sea. Around me, across the creek flats, creeper-hooded layers of rainforest climb through shreds of mist to the ridges where eucalypts succeed in forming a final crown among the sandstone cliffs. There's a clear creek running through—one long song of audible praise. I am aware that this perfection that surrounds me rests entirely on change and chance; nothing is guaranteed.

Onto one twig of this utterly contingent perfection, a Splendid Blue Wren alights, then skims over grass tips to perch on an upright star picket. His five tiny brown wives congregate busily in a branch over by the longer grass, then suddenly they're *here*, slipping in and out of the chicken wire of the vegetable garden as if it barely exists. An exacting insectivorous world creates the exquisite quickness of the wrens. Now upright and alert on this wire, then instantly over to that one—immaculate and effortless in a way so beguiling and instructive you cannot but stare, and drink in wrenness. Their swift visitation leaves me swimming in their particular style of sentience. It arrives wholesale in their very shape, movement, timing, twittering, brilliance of eye. I can't say quite how this happens, nor whether they absorb me as keenly as I do them, learning them by heart without even trying.

The wafting cloud of cabbage moth butterflies floats through. Their numbers have exploded in warm days, that favour a lazy flit and flow. They are airy with drift, casual with indecision. A pell-mell fluttering before settling on grass stem here, bare patch there, with softly shrugging wings that suggest all the time in the world, just for the moment.

Now the red kelpie pup sends them flying. Hyper alert, ears tilted, a grin from ear to ear, and quick as a flash, but with a stumble at the end that sends him rolling twice then back onto his feet. Effortless being. That done, he slumps in the shade.

Each thing that swims into our awareness can be its own gift when allowed to be exactly what it is—which in turn lets us more deeply into what *we* are. Brief gifts, enduring gifts—they weigh the same.

When I was around six years of age, my sister and I had the job of entertaining a visiting child while the adults were talking and clinking teacups upstairs. We talked to the stranger while idling on rope swings in the cool under our Queensland house where she informed us importantly that God saw and knew everything we did. In self-defence we told her that *our family* believed in Mother Nature. I recall my heart beating hard as I suddenly took this interesting stand. After all, despite the formal agnosticism of our parents, my sister and I visited God whenever we liked, usually after lights out when we rode Midnight and Lightning, our swift horses that could fly through the sky. For some reason, though, it felt important to press the case for nature, which we felt was being too lightly brushed aside in favour of God. Suddenly the conversation lost all cautiousness.

Each picking up seamlessly where the other left off, my sister and I let rip. To our own surprise, we found ourselves taking the other girl on a fantastic journey into Mother Nature. It unrolled with such assurance it was as if we'd travelled many times before down *inside* a green blade of grass, deep into the earth's dark through roots and root hairs and the lairs of worms and beetles, deeper in again into the rocks and then down even into the magma, remaining unscathed by anything except our own growing amazement, until we finally had to return for a bit of ordinary light and air. It was as if some force ran through us and took charge.

Our visitor was as astonished as we were by our casual but total authority on the matter. We all fell silent for some time afterwards, hearts beating, a strange feeling in the air. Even God seemed pressed into that silence.

The imagination that can conceive a universe and a whole planet lives in us as deep as where our childhoods lie, which is in almost no time at all and pretty much all time at once (except when a birthday, or the end of a school afternoon, is taking too long to arrive). To bring it back to light, we need to be able to remember how it is that a child sees. To remember how to respond naturally to what lives and breathes in us, and to let that trigger the natural artistry of the adult imagination.

Fortunately there are ways to stir and recover a receptive mind that can bind us back into reality. One way is through the imaginative power of story. Another is the ritual practice of paying sustained attention while not wanting anything—sometimes known as meditation. One more is through the tiny-looking questions known as koans, which open as the night sky does, stripping us of our habits of mind and leaving mind awake, ready and creative.

What's the *story* here?

What stories do we have available to us that can open the world—and the universe—to the human spirit and imagination? The stories we have depended on up to now, which stem from the time of the earliest city-states, are inherently cautious, even dubious, in their attitude towards the natural world. It is seen to offer opportunity but invites no deep trust. If all myth is a working out of the relationship between the human world and the force of nature, it is plain that our given stories tend strongly towards the longing for safety and redemption *from* this force and cannot picture seeking redemption *within* it.

The gods and heroes of the Greek and Roman myths that flesh out the imagination of the ancient world of our civilisation provided us with a prototype psychology, a way to grasp the emotions that this struggle sets up within us. They gather the deep-lying patterns of human mentality into the heightened forms of the gods, who are then depicted as influencing our human fates in capricious ways. Such myth addresses, and by addressing creates, a very human-shaped world with nature at its edges, one riven by powerfully contending human impulses.

But the body of myth that lies outside the domesticating impulse that has shaped our most fundamental post-Neolithic stories are quite different. The hero figures that survive in the oral cultures of the world seldom even think of slaying monsters, in fact they are not much drawn to slaying in general, and are wise enough to let their foolishness be as clearly seen as their cleverness. They are often rather hard to tell apart from an animal. In fact they may be quite plainly called Raven, Coyote, Brown Mouse, and so on, and folklorists speak of them as Tricksters.

This kind of myth is often called 'wild myth', and its logic is a kind of *ecology*—a whole pattern of earth intelligence and emotion, disclosed in story that is seen to have been dreamed up by the land itself, together with human beings. Human sentience is not seen as carved out from and in opposition to the ways of the earth and universe. It's seen as co-creative. People are needed to sing up into consciousness a whole set of ecological relations between all the discernible 'powers' of the earth—humans, animals, mountains, waters, stones, trees, sky, earth itself. It is the whole ecology that has ultimate significance, and the separable powers within it cannot take precedence over that.

Sean Kane describes the interweave of interlocking patterns almost as intelligences: 'Ecological complexities behave as if they have intelligences or minds guiding them, responsible for them, protecting them.' You *could* name this as the resilience and integrity that ecological patterns create and maintain through their multitude of mutual partnerships, but that takes nothing away from how clearly we can feel the intelligence of these 'minds', or sentient systems, when we stop in our tracks long enough to sense our way back into them.

We have to drop into a more embodied, imaginative mode of consciousness, entirely natural to our minds when we relax from that narrow beam of consciousness that misses subtle relationships, and drop into wider field awareness.

It's a little like what we do in dream. Nothing and no one in a dream can really be other than inside our own consciousness and open to us; we can shift from one subjectivity to another, even transit into the 'mind' of an object or animal. Somewhat similarly, keeping up our end of the conversation with the earth at times requires moving beyond what we usually think of as ourselves and shifting into the thinking of an animal, a stone, a river.

There is a subtle fit between the creative dreaming imagination of human beings—so able to absorb other styles of sentience, and to shift between modes of awareness—and the dreaming imagination that is expressed in the natural ecology of the earth. If the likeness between mind and earth seems hard to grasp, consider for a moment the mind of a seed. A seed has a full complement of DNA information, a bundle of potential, and an irrepressible urge to express that. In that sense, a seed has a *mind*, full of ideas of becoming a tree. 'The tree flourishes as the dream of the seed,' says Sean Kane, 'and then takes up that seed Dreaming itself.'

And so it goes on, on and on as roundly as the turning earth itself. We may have forgotten about it for a while, but we human beings have always been able to attune our minds to this dimension of reality. It's our thing.

This apprehension of our connectedness with the presence of the living world does not come cheap. It will always require a protocol of paying attention. The Matole Indians of California, for example, saw water itself as a live presence demanding great respect. The protocol around water was tricky and full of humble fellow feeling.

Here is a Mattole elder's advice for engaging with the acute sentience of the presence called 'water':

The water watches you, and has a definite attitude towards you, favourable or unfavourable. Do not speak, just before a wave breaks. Do not speak to passing rough water in a stream, do not look at water very long for any one time, unless you have been to this spot ten times or more before, for then the water there is used to you and does not mind if you're looking at it. Older men can talk in the presence of water because they have been around so long that the water knows them. Until the water does know you, however, it can become very rough if you talk in its presence, or look at it for too long.

Notice how far from any impulse of manipulation or exploitation this sensibility stands. Pre-domesticated stories offer a human world that is open and responsive to sensing the ideas and emotions of the earth, while withholding all impulse to manipulate them. Connectedness cannot go along with manipulation. When the impulse to grab asserts itself, fine-grained attunement dies.

Aunty Beryl Carmichael of the Nyanntpia people out by Broken Hill once said, very simply, 'Connectedness *is* reality. If you're not in connectedness, you're not *in* reality.'

Awareness of the web of connectedness was once second nature to human beings, carefully guarded by ritual observances of remembering. It is still there in practices like the saying of grace before a meal, or the prayer of gratitude before taking the life of an animal or plant for food. But over time—many centuries of city time, clock time, empire time, electronic time—we have lost our thread of the intricate relationships, embedded in patterns that recur with beautiful insistence within the continuing drama of change. We have shed this awareness as a 'natural' concomitant of the brave project we call 'modernity'.

Modernity—that most energetic and enthusiastic antithesis of a sense of eternity. The dream of the machine, the engineering of ourselves to a level we dream of being 'above' nature. The ever more highly geared engine of innovation, of one 'product' giving way to the next as fast as possible, in pursuit of some ever-elusive escape clause from the fact of personal impermanence.

Once we had rituals of awareness that could sense the eternity *inside* the fact of one thing always becoming another. If we are to make it through this crisis, we are going to have to establish new ones that can help us find our way back to deep accord with the earth. There's nothing primitive about such awareness. It still survives in places where literacy—and its many consequences, including rapid industrial development—has not yet taken great hold. Literacy extends the world we can imagine and equips us with tools that give us greater agency in our lives. Giving women the gift of literacy is the most effective way to 'famine-proof' a society and turn the tide of persecution of women and girls. But literacy can also disengage some of our most valuable and highly evolved faculties. It can undo our skills of direct awareness of the natural world and subtly distance us from the evidence of our senses. We can be quite blind to the loss of these faculties, unaware that in some critically important way our ability to see and preparedness to respond has been reduced to a primitive state.

The Mau Forest in Kenya, on the rim of the great Rift Valley from which our species first emerged, is the source of much of the water that feeds Lake Victoria and the River Nile. The forest has been subject to ruthless illegal logging, a plunder that has been hard to stop when corruption is so rife. The Ogiek people are traditional Mau Forest dwellers and are known as the beekeepers, the honey gatherers, entirely dependent on blossom-bearing trees of the ever-shrinking forest. They have fought hard to stop the predation that is stripping not just their home and livelihood, but drying out the source of the chief tributary streams feeding the Nile, that great artery of Africa. An Ogiek elder spoke some haunting words:

We are people from yesterday. The forest has been our home since immortal times. Now we are chased out. We look like fools because we know nothing of the world. But tell me, who is primitive—we the illiterate, or the others, the literate, who are organised into groups so they can destroy nature?

We are needed here too

Evolution has drawn our particular bodily form and style of sentience into being out of several billion years of life on earth; our minds in turn have drawn language and then writing into being, which has strongly shaped our minds further, both expanding what mind can be, while also distancing us from sensuous immersion in the continuum of the natural world. Digital technology is currently reshaping us again, further sharpening our sense of exile from the earth by substituting virtual forms of reality for direct contact with the living world.

However far away we may have got from where we started, we will surely fail to survive if we cannot recover our sense of being wanted here, and needed. Our minds and awareness are needed to *mind* this astonishing planet in its multitudinous life. Such a strong sense of belonging is critical. It gives us a humble, grounded and creative ingenuity in defending it and mending it.

The mysterious awareness we bear was implicit in the primordial event that gave birth to the stars and the elements they forged, beginning with hydrogen. Exploding supernovae generated stars that spun off planets that on at least one occasion spawned complex organisms, an informed sequence of genes, and the explosive variations that followed on a theme of limbs, organs, scales and feathers, as well as the linguistic forms and symbols that transmit minds, thoughts and feelings across space and through time.

Our lives are finite but our minds are close to unlimited. This ignites the meaning and urgency of human life. It opens up each moment to a potential infinitude of depth and timelessness, from the moment we grow fascinated by being the intersection of the natural and human worlds and are drawn in deeper. That fascination cannot end because the world itself is endless change, and infinite variety of styles of existence. Our imaginative minds seem to be the planet's way of collecting and refracting this immense array of sentience and ways of being. Our minds are where metaphor enters the world, and multiplies its expressive and interactive possibilities ten trillion-fold.

The plenitude we swim in is completely granted, from our birth to our growing up to our eventual disappearing, and everything we experience along the way. But nothing about it can be taken *for* granted, unless we are prepared to waste and lay waste the gift. Our earth is the jewel of the universe, as far as our perceptions can yet reach. Jupiter will never bring forth a mountain from its gases; no other ocean has yet been found in this galaxy, no lake, no river, no seeds, no genes. The green, wet, moist, erotic tenacity of life-and-death appears to be the peculiar specialty of Planet Earth. Remember how that extended childhood address went, on and on until all naming ran out? 'Planet Earth, Solar System, Milky Way . . .' and when that could go no further, in the words of Thornton Wilder's *Our Town*, this unfixed, ever-moving address of ours ends at last in 'Mind of God'.

And in its ending finds its beginning.

Chapter Six

Stories we need to hear now

*Everything is held together with stories . . . That is all that is
holding us together, stories and compassion.*

Barry Lopez

When I was seven years old I was snatched from what most
call reality and seized by what some call a vision.

It took place in the course of the most ordinary and practical
of moments. I was on my way to the girls' toilet in the playground
of my small school in Cairns, barefoot as always then, picking my
way down the short cut worn by other children's feet through the
grass and prickles at the back of the toilet block. I watched the
prickly 'sensitive weeds' droop their fronds where I touched them.
The sound of children chanting their multiplication tables floated
from some classroom. I may have been humming as you do in that
swim of childhood thoughts and dreamy observation. Suddenly I
was stopped dead in my tracks by an experience that overwhelmed
and replaced all that was around me.

Abruptly, suspended in vast dark space, I was *blazing*, a pure body of inexhaustible radiance. Later I would call this 'a star' since nothing else comes close, but 'star' sounds magnificent and remote and too defined, for this was both boundless and utterly intimate. This was *me*.

The surprise was enormous and arrived in successive waves. First, electrifying astonishment—so *this* is what we are! Then pure joy of coming home to find everything in place and completely at rest—of *course* we are this! And then came the realisation that there was star upon star upon star as far as I could see, each being unique and yet entirely of the same 'stuff', each alone in vast space and yet entirely *held* in undoubted relationship which was the velvety dark of space itself. Remembering the unshakeable clarity and reassurance of being flung entirely from my seven-year-old self into this extraordinary confiding of what we really are can still bring me to tears.

I cannot say how long I stood suspended there, spellbound, streaming with the revelation. There was no time happening. It feels wrong to call it a vision since it was not so much looking at light but letting it pour endlessly through me into all that could possibly ever be. I knew myself to be completely safe in whatever happened to me. And somehow I knew that I did not have to wallow in this experience. It would never abandon me.

And children are immensely practical. So in good time, I released myself to go attend the call of nature, and then went on back to my classroom, just as if I were a small girl passing through an ordinary school day, which of course I was as well. I bicycled home that afternoon with my heart still almost too big to fit into my chest, everything lit and glorious, yet managed as well. I felt a kind of duty to try to tell my parents about it, though I sensed in advance that putting it into words would never succeed.

I found my mother in the kitchen, chopping carrots. I stood beside her and said something tentative and exploratory like, 'Mum, isn't it amazing what we are?' She considered this lovingly but a little distractedly, continuing to chop the carrots, and I could feel the great business already failing to make its way across to her intact. Finally she said something like, 'Yes, darling, it's wonderful, we're all so lucky that we have each other, our family is healthy, we all love each other . . .'

All of this was true, and good indeed, but did not touch it, not at all. I knew a little sorrowfully that I needed to put it away safely inside, where nothing could possibly harm it, that silence would look after it best. So I just ran out to swing on the roman rings in the backyard with my sister while it was still light.

In our right minds

Throughout the human ages, reality has reached through to rearrange the mind of people in this way. That's why it is called 'realisation': it returns us to reality. The goodness or rightness of that moment is so strong you cannot find a single thing you want to change.

Realisation can come as a fortunate blow to the mind. Sometimes, though, it comes with a blow to the body, a sudden agonising event that throws you not into panic but into the great wonder of your right mind. Neuroanatomist Jill Bolte Taylor has vividly described what she called her 'stroke of insight', the oddly powerful, clear and seamlessly connected state she was left in while also being progressively shut down in language and mobility by a massive stroke affecting the left hemisphere of her brain, from which it took her eight years to fully recover. 'I felt like a genie liberated from its bottle. The energy of my spirit seemed to flow like a great whale gliding through a sea of silent euphoria,' she says. And it also comes, less spectacularly, the way day dawns or night falls—a thousand tiny realisations in a gradual shift of consciousness, one that is equally irreversible once it has restored you to the fullness of reality.

Realisation is the great and tiny mental shift of rejoining what Thomas Berry, the late geologian, has called 'the dream of the earth'. The one that dreamed our lives into being, out of the inchoate vast event that gave birth to the universe. Waking up is the return to greater conscious agreement with and participation in that astonishing, ongoing dreaming. It is realising how deeply 'I am the whole dream of these things'. And from that awareness compassion naturally flows.

Story is the way we hold the world in mind, how we grasp the amazing story of this universe, this earth, this life. This is not a cold, implacable story of an inhumanly hostile universe, one that could snatch our lives away at any moment. That's the small story of a small, frightened, vulnerable mammal, clinging to its crevice of safety, big-eyed with fear rather than wonder. The great discovery is that the loss of that small self, in the true amazement of letting reality all the way in, is the discovery of a greater self, one that is not cramped by birth and death but at ease with the fact that we extend in every direction that the senses, mind and imagination can now embrace. This self is composed like the universe itself of sheer becoming; it is not fixed in time, is never born and cannot ever die. The small sense of self dies into this larger one, which is often called 'no-self', as it belongs to everything, including (of course), the one called 'you'.

The astonishment comes from discovering that 'I' am empty of all that I thought I was. And that this discovery is instant access to the fullness of being. That *nothing* is left out of what 'I' am and can be.

This story of the universe belongs to everyone too. It is a profoundly human story, in fact, as it is born directly from the human capacity for astonishment and vast curiosity. It is created by the sense of immensity that, if it does not swamp us into a sorry tale of personal insignificance, can fire wonderful powers of human creativity. We take up the dreaming of the universe *in person*. We already embody it most personally (for this human body cannot possibly be left out of the entirety of the universe), and now our minds have a chance to begin to embody what the body quietly and soberly understands from the moment it is born onto the earth.

It belongs to everyone in another very important sense. Our sense of the story of our species and its coming into being has shifted profoundly, and is now, for the first time in human history, one that can be held in common by everyone on earth. We can all effectively look through the lens of the Hubble telescope to the earliest moments of the universe and peer back into the fossil record and prehistory of the world. Instead of a shallow linear time of human history thought to be around six thousand years long in Biblical terms and soon to end, we now can know ourselves to be twelve billion to thirteen billion years old.

How blinkered that old story of a brief and irremediably damaged creation begins to feel when we are free to embrace the seamless story of our universe and planetary unfolding, all the way back to the places where time itself gives out. The evidence of an unfinished, ever-unfolding universe also becomes coherently available to us for the first time ever. It is as though we are offered a glimpse into the mind of God. What an extraordinary and timely gift to lift the imaginative powers of human beings past the banality of taking the entire mysterious world for granted and finding it a curse to be endured.

Truly knowing ourselves to be inseparable from the ceaseless creation of an unfinished cosmos can be a powerful realisation. Skilfully handled, it can help provoke a profound shift of heart and mind *back* into a more awake and earthed kind of sanity.

As Thomas Berry has said, our sense of the earth has to be sound enough to support the dangerous future that is calling us awake. We need stories that can dream us back into proper stewardship of the earth, that can reawaken a 'mythic commitment' to the grandeur and functioning of the natural world. He finds in the great story of the universe and our planet that necessary archetypal story with the essential ecological imagination at its heart. It is a literally universal story that can mend the dangerous disconnect between the micro- and macro-phase dimensions of human awareness. One that can provide a functional mythology with the power to form a more mutual and integral human/earth relationship at this critical juncture.

The uses of astonishment

For too long, such 'universal' matters were seen as the province of poets, mystics, theologians, romantics and moral idealists. The micro-phase view of unfolding events—what's happening right now under our noses and how can we take the most profitable advantage of it—was thought to be the proper preoccupation of realists. If we thought about the macro-phase at all, we probably thought it more properly God's business.

Macro-phase change has trouble registering on the mental horizon of micro-phase awareness, leaving us vulnerable to massive incremental change that we never saw coming. When it finally does begin to register as palpable shocks, as with global warming, the micro-phase response is to a quick technological fix and for ways to turn a nice little profit from it. But as Berry says, 'Now we begin to recognise that what is good in its micro-phase reality can be deadly in its macro-phase development.'

To tap back into the forces that have guided life from the beginning we need imaginations that can move freely between the micro-phase reality of infinitely subtle relationships that compose and condition a given ecology, and the macro-phase reality of epochal shifts in earth's unfolding. This is the imaginative reach of the word 'geologian'. It may take a geologian to be able to catch sight of the massive crime of geocide, which would otherwise slide right past our eyes as if we were asleep. To become a geologian is to respond, as an earth-born creature, to the psychic and indeed spiritual energies deep in the structure of reality itself.

To understand how this planetary crisis sits in the geological record, and to end our autism as a species—and thereby also soften the lonely fear of personal extinction—we need a frame of mind wider than just our one life. We need a framework of life itself and the planet that has birthed it and every creature that ever walked, flew or swam, all the way through to our species with its marvellous and difficult self-reflective awareness, its ability to hold the entire Universe Story in mind. This story invites us to appreciate our own direct participation in the immensity that surrounds us, not just *with* our minds but—when we really look—*as* our mind.

If we really look, the immensity and nature of the universe is revealed in every detail that our senses can take in, and in our own miraculous mortal bodies, as well as our minds and imaginations, our dreams and our emotions. It is astonishing. Even more astonishing is that the means of becoming imaginatively aware that this depth of seeing is not given any priority in the stories we value and that we allow to shape the education of children. Our culture remains largely asleep to the full, mind-expanding context of our own humanity. It's not just the earth and our fellow creatures that made us human and continue to tell us who we are, it is also the all but unthinkable universe.

What a thought!

Cosmogenesis: The Universe Story

'Cosmogenesis' is the name that has been given to the revelations of physics, geophysics and palaeontology concerning the origination and continuing unfolding of the universe and life on earth. Since the mid twentieth-century we have been able to look with increasing coherence all the way back to the original flaring forth of the universe, as well as looking billions of years back into the fossil record of life on earth, and ever deeper into the subatomic universe of energy and matter. This offers a continuous and coherent narrative of our genesis that is for the first time open to all of humanity on the same basis, of both testable physical evidence and contestable hypotheses. At the same moment, it is a narrative with great natural mythic presence. It offers a chance to see ourselves not imperilled by but actually *made* of this great force of nature, born into this wild and mysterious reality, participating in it, a conscious spark of its huge fire.

Entering the imaginative reach of this story can help frail human beings like you and me take the leap *not* into a nihilistic smallness in the face of a crushing immensity, but into a larger, more robust and audacious sense of identity that is yet properly humble, and earthy. From this can come the confidence and mental eloquence to initiate a renewed conversation with the earth. It lets us meet the universe and our existence as a singular sacramental event—and to discover in nature itself our most intimate and sustaining 'other'. That the nature of the universe is also our nature, that the earth's physical expression in a multitude of forms is fundamentally inseparable from the expressive fact of this actual body and mind, opens the space for ritual, emotional, artistic and philosophical rapport with the earth.

As Thomas Berry puts it, 'Everything tells the story of the universe. The winds tell the story, literally, not just imaginatively. The story has its imprint everywhere, and that is why it is so important to know the story. If you do not know the story, in a sense you do not know yourself; you do not know anything.' And when your eyes and ears are open it is impossible to miss it, for there is nothing that is not making it clear, singing it up, speaking it plainly. To be deaf to it is to miss your life, functionally blind and illiterate to what Psalm 19 calls 'the glory of God':

> The heavens declare the glory of God; the skies proclaim the work of his hands. Day after day they pour forth speech; night after night they reveal knowledge. They have no speech, they use no words; no sound is heard from them. Yet their voice goes out into all the earth, their words to the ends of the earth.

Earth is estimated to be around 4.6 billion years old. Life came forth as early as 3.8 billion years ago when the first single-celled organisms, called prokaryotes, appeared. The first atmospheric oxygen was evident by 3.4 billion years ago, indicating the presence of photosynthesising cells. Complex cells called eukaryotes were present

2 billion years ago. Sexual reproduction began 1.2 billion years back, triggering an explosive acceleration in the rate of evolution. Multicellular life was present by 1 billion years ago, the first simple animals. Colonisation of the land began, and ancestors of most modern animals appear in the fossil record in the 80 million years leading up to the dawn of the Palaeocene, 55–60 million years ago.

The Palaeozoic era of life opened with the first extruded hardened shells of trilobites, clams and snails; it saw life form skeletons, grow lungs and leave the sea, develop the wood cell and begin forests, and reptiles appear, and ended in the Permian extinctions that eliminated between 75% and 95% of all species, around 245 million years ago. The Mesozoic era that followed came forth with dinosaurs, flowers, seeds, warm-blooded birds, marsupials, the first placental mammals and earliest primates, and ended in the abrupt Cretaceous extinctions, probably caused by the nuclear winter that followed a major meteor impact 67 million years ago.

The Cenozoic era—our time—is the period of supremely rich biological development of the past 65 million years up to our time, with the earliest hominids appearing around 2.6 million years ago, using fire, flints and stone axes by half a million years ago, and with earliest signs of Homo sapiens appearing 300,000 years ago. Finally, modern language-bearing Homo sapiens sapiens appears a mere 40,000 years ago.

And yet across just the last seven or eight thousand years of this amazing life history, greatly accelerating across in the last three hundred, we have come to our present moment of single-handedly, as a species, precipitating the greatest mass extinction for 65 million years on land and in the oceans. This too is part of the Universe Story, the chapter scientists are now formally recognising and naming 'the Anthropocene', epoch of man-made geological change.

A communion of subjects

Thomas Berry frames this wipe-out as optimistically as possible by seeing it as the terminal phase of the Cenozoic and the convulsive birth of what he calls the 'Ecozoic Era'. This is an era in which humans will be obliged to form an integral earth community founded on the principle established by the Universe Story: that 'the universe is primarily *a communion of subjects,* not a collection of objects'.

The alternative, a massive engineering of the earth and atmosphere now on the drawing board, that hopes to hold the reality of climatic and ecological collapse at bay for a time, and provide a temporary bubble for human existence while the life-world falls apart around it, is a puerile dream, a human-cooked Disneyland that Berry dubs 'the Technozoic Era'. The world reduced to a collection of objects and gadgets—including us. It is difficult to imagine the fragile bubble of this dream withstanding for long the pressures from reality: of coastal inundation, extreme weather events, water wars, acute global food shortage with the loss of arable land as population billows even further before a natural decline is possible, increasing scourges of insect-borne disease, dead oceans, collapsing ecologies . . . And it is simply impossible to imagine *loving* a monotonously human-referenced, human-choked world labouring under its brown 'engineered' skies. Was the loss of Eden never something that happened in the past but always our dread dream, of a future in which the gift of human consciousness finally succumbed to a failure of wonder—wonder at the extravagant gift of simply existing in a world like the one in which we came into being!

The Universe Story, like any story of mythic proportion, offers ever-deepening levels of initiation and engagement. From early childhood education through to full adult maturity and old age, it never bottoms out but goes on opening minds to the style and shape of the universe, establishing ritual rapport with the earth along the way. It opens as much into poetry, art, music, film, dance, play, religion and dream, as it does into science and scholarship. It opens into how we think about each other: political and economic arrangements with a stronger grain of sanity and commonality. And it draws us away from 'the thinking that created the problem' to thinking that recognises all life as kin, and the earth's web of ingenious ecologies as sacred. On this ground, any knowing or intentional act of harm against what constitutes the source of life is to be recognised not just theologically as a sin, but ethically and legally as a *crime*.

Berry, a Catholic priest, considers redemption-oriented theology in its traditional forms to have now served the main part of its historical mission. It must, he says, consciously expand to include a cosmological religious awareness as the only viable way into the future: 'We need to recognise the story of the universe as we know it through our empirical sciences as *our sacred story*.' We can no longer afford the high cost of a religious stance that sets human beings apart from others and from the earth, but must establish a psychic and spiritual stance of mutual confidence in the ongoing revelation of the nature of the universe, especially as it expresses itself on this life-filled, sentience-bearing earth. We urgently need the story that renders that back into commonsense and makes it again entirely natural to defend the needs shared by all life: clean air, clean water, fertile soil.

Knowing and revering where and what and who we really are, within the seamless story of *becoming* in an emergent universe, is a way of recovering the grace of trusting the earth. This is redemption in a new light—the light of the unprecedented impasse we now find ourselves in, which the old stories could not conceive and cannot adequately address. The spiritual force of this the Universe Story redeems our fears and can lead us back home to where we are.

In the light of this story death becomes the mysterious boundary shift or transformation within ongoing life—not just a tragic loss of personal access to that life. When the experience of the self is infused into all that it encounters, 'I' don't disappear but it becomes hard to carve myself and my life out of all that I am experiencing. I can no longer draw such a clear and certain divide between the animate and inanimate, or the psycho-spiritual and material.

In the Universe Story, the nature of the universe is neither simply an accidental, inexplicable, random fluke of matter and energy; nor is it merely a physical and ultimately dispensable means to a transcendent human end, or End Time. Rather, it is revealed as an evolving, self-organising cosmogenesis, a perpetually creative and participatory cosmos that tends to express itself in a sequence of remarkable, irreversible transformations.

This leaves us, as participants in a communion event, in a very interesting and roomy place. As Berry says, 'We bear the universe in our being as the universe bears us in its being. The two have total presence to each other—and to that deeper mystery out of which both the universe and ourselves have emerged.'

This experience of the universe has sympathy with the ancient ways in which humans have loved and communed with the earth and cosmos, at the same time as it is informed and stirred by the work of the empirical sciences. We can enter the intelligence of where we are and what we are encountering, rather than mentally standing outside it while analytically probing an earth we have stripped of any pulse, sentience, agency and mystery.

An Ecozoic Era is one in which the earth, that formerly controlled itself directly, now begins also to control itself through us. Consciously taking on such great weight of collaboration requires that we respond to the creative urgencies of the emerging planet just as it responds to ours. A strong ritual rapport with the earth implies a sense of mutual presence within a web of relationships that shape the biosphere which has evolved within a universe that is coherent throughout the space of its being and its sequence of unfolding in time. Until we understand such coherence and mutuality we're left with the gnawing fear that the earth may not be fundamentally congenial to our kind. Why would it, as long as we exercise only our capacity for 'conquering', engineering and holding nature and other creatures at bay by whatever ingenious and destructive means we can fashion?

A finely balanced turbulence

Can such a story induce trust once more in the creative urgencies that shaped the galaxies, ignited the sun and formed the earth; that brought forth the seas, continents and atmosphere; that awakened life into numberless forms and eventually brought us into being and got us through the million years to an awakening of our present understanding of ourselves in relation to this stupendous process? We will have to find out. Berry bravely hazards the view that, 'Sensitised to such guidance from the very structure and functioning of the universe, we can have confidence in the future that awaits the human venture.'

But that can't remain a hope. Rather, what was once a human commonplace (we belong here, completely) is now an instruction, beckoning us back to sanity. We urgently need some immersion in this story to help shape our minds and imaginations back into the image of the universe—to inspire, educate, heal, guide and discipline us.

The Universe Story can create exquisite appreciation for the delicacy of the 'choices' evidenced in the sequence of its unfolding. Take, for example, the curvature of space and time recognised by Einstein when he attempted to peer into the mysterious energy that has sculpted the universe from the moment of the Big Bang: gravity. Physicist Brian Swimme explains that a fractionally larger curvature would collapse the universe down into a massive black hole; fractionally smaller, the universe would explode into a scattering of lifeless particles.' He sees the universe as *shaped* in its largest dimensions from its earliest instant of emergence by this state of poise between collapsing, due to gravitational attraction, and flying apart by the force of its original expansive energy. This curvature of the universe is, miraculously, sufficiently closed to maintain a coherence and sufficiently open to allow for a continued blossoming of an extraordinary creativity.

It is this same gravitational attraction that sculpts earth as a life-bearing planet, holding the planet together, maintaining the physical integrity of life forms, and stabilising its circling of the sun, while exerting inner forces that, together with earth's inner, molten state of nuclear energy, 'keep the earth in a state of *balanced turbulence* whence its continued transformation takes place' (Swimme's words, my italics). Other planets in the solar system failed to achieve or maintain the exquisitely balanced dynamism that brought forth earth's cornucopia of living forms.

How starkly it then emerges that we'd have to be insane to put at risk the finely tuned climate harmonic that emerged from such turbulence to bless our arrival as a species.

So this Universe Story celebrates, above all, the marvel of precarious existence itself. Every detail of the emergent universe and our tiny and yet vast home, Planet Earth, confirms that we are all equal participants in a singular sacramental communion event. A great continual exchange of consciousness and energy is going on. We're completely in its loop: in drinking in the presence of the other, in living and dying, eating and being eaten, all taking place within this exquisitely shapely and finely balanced turbulence, this complexity of call and response or, if you prefer, cause and effect. We see it in the mysterious perfection of the life cycle, water cycle, seasons of abundance and scarcity, in every corner of the highly unlikely fact of *being here*.

We can draw heart and energy from this poised turbulence that appears to be the natural setting to which earth and universe return continually. The imagination and intelligence of that tendency is inside us, when we can recognise it in everything that is. We find it in the mythic power of this great story to which we all belong.

And we find in that the birth of real fellow feeling. For we are all in this together, not only in the wonder that expands us beyond ourselves, but also in the suffering that comes with ordinary pain, loss and mortality.

Stories, and compassion

All of the natural, unavoidable afflictions that come with existence only deepen the realisation that being here, as a conscious, self-reflective part of this emergent universe, requires a kind of necessary peacemaking with mortality, difficulty and loss. There is a sacrificial dimension to the natural world revealed in every premature death, seed that never matures, wildfire, flood, drought, earthquake, tsunami—and indeed, in every birth as well. Autumn makes it clear each year in drifts of leaves. Supernovae express it in explosion. Prey falling to the predator reveal it plainly. Age-spots on a human hand, wrinkles on the face speak of it too: 'Ripeness is all.'

Making life safe and easy—for *us*—has brought its own suffocating misery on top of the bill now arriving for damage to the living world. Accepting a measure of personal hardship is not an easy sell, despite the selflessness and resilience that can come to light in people in the face of a dire emergency. Yet the hardship intrinsic to living on a planet of unceasing tides of birth and death is a problem only when we value comfort and a fragile dream of security more highly than the amazing possibilities of living at full stretch. Then we turn our immense reserves of human ingenuity and willpower over to the service of what are finally puerile and ignoble ends. When we baby ourselves this way, human magnificence disappears. To learn our way back to a grasp of how to be whole within that balanced turbulence, or as the old Chinese Zen masters would put it, 'riding the clouds' or 'walking in the red sky'—that's the possibility offered by deep imaginative access to the Universe Story.

Brian Swimme considers the example of the hawk as a way to value the difficulty of existence in a universe of perpetual change. It is difficult not to admire the acute, poised and deadly beauty of the hawk as it swoops upon a mouse streaking for cover. The magnificence of a predator is shaped into being and honed by the evasive skills of its prey. The beauty and acuity of the hawk depends upon the alertness and the swiftness of mice. If mice were just a little slower off the mark, or if they took to walking casually right past the hawk, hawks would gradually become a little roly-poly;

their extraordinary speed and eyesight, no longer needed for survival, would slowly diminish and dim, and a terrible beauty—let's call it 'hawkness'—would slowly leach from the world.

It is difficulty, and the urgency of life enlivened by awareness of death, that shapes the arresting qualities of every species. This beauty and intricacy of the living world is strong enough, once we recover our wonder, to call us into acceptance of our likely share of hardship and difficulty. Strangely enough, it can become a kind of ease if we trust the direction of the earth, trust ourselves to the universe—knowing it's our direction too. And it is suffering, as much as wonder, that opens us to the mystery of other creatures and human beings. Empathy with the whole of creation is an important maturing waiting to happen to our species.

If we fail to ask the questions of the earth that come from empathy, we may not avoid rendering the earth a wasteland. For all our ingenious intelligence and manipulative powers as a species, we have not yet learned to ask the earth: 'What ails you?' and 'How can I help?' And yet buried like a recessive gene in the DNA of our cultural inheritance, that has done so much to make a wasteland of the living world, is a persisting human legend of the West concerning the secret of compassion.

The Grail legend

Ambiguous in meaning and mysterious in origin, the Christian- and Celtic-inflected Grail legend centres on an unconscious quest for a mysterious object. It is represented in this story by the chalice said to have contained Christ's blood. Some accounts see the Grail borne on to ancient Britain, where it forms part of the cycle of stories of King Arthur.

A very young, green, would-be knight, Parsifal, or Percival, rides out into the dangerous world in quest of knightly glory, despite his mother's best attempts to stop him. His name means 'heart-torn'. He has many comic misadventures before blundering into a strange kingdom where everything is wilting and dying. He learns that the strange king of this place, known as the Fisher King, is lying ill, close to death but unable to die, with a thigh wound that cannot be staunched. The king is stranded at death's door and his kingdom reflects this deathly state. The Grail castle stands in the middle of a place that is called the Waste Land. Percival is painfully unaware that the king and his entire kingdom awaits with bated breath the one thing that will free him—a turning word or gesture from Percival.

It is very rare to stumble on the castle that houses the Grail, but Percival reaches the drawbridge, finds it open and clatters across. On entering, he finds a vast banquet hall. A feast is laid out, and people are silently serving the food in a grave and beautiful ceremony. The Fisher King sits at the head of the table, and Percival is invited to sit beside him as guest of honour.

At some invisible signal, into the room comes a procession of lovely women bearing an array of beautiful objects. The room falls silent as, one by one, they are ceremonially paraded through the hall, past Percival. All eyes are upon him. What will he do in response? Finally, the most solemn and beautiful object—a chalice of gold—is borne aloft by a young woman, the Grail maiden, whose name is Rebounding Joy. She seems to pause before the young knight.

There is plenty of time for Percival to ask, 'What's this strange chalice, what's happening here, what's this got to do with the sick king beside me, and why does he suffer so deeply?' But he is silent, struck dumb. Finally, the young woman moves on with the chalice, the procession ends, and everyone looks at him in silent grief. If he was supposed to do something, he doesn't know what it could possibly be. He's a stumblebum who has blundered into a vital initiation and missed it entirely. Not unlike the rest of us. Open-mouthed in the presence of both suffering and the miraculous, he did not know what to say or do.

The banquet tables are cleared away and Percival is shown to a luxurious bed, where he falls fast asleep with a head full of dreams and mysteries. When he wakes in the morning, the castle is empty and bare, the only sign of life his tethered horse. Greatly shaken, he leaves, painfully aware that he has missed the most important thing in the whole world but without the slightest clue what it might be. Now, too late, he burns for it, heart-torn indeed.

Luckily, because we're human beings and it often works this way, after some time and many hazardous loops of life, the impossible does come by again. (After all, it does so every day we wake to the sun rising, heart beating, mind stirring, in the midst of an inconceivable cosmos . . .) Percival is given a second chance to find and enter the Grail castle. The same extraordinary event happens all over again—the old king with the wound that cannot heal, the solemn procession, the strange cup, the maiden of rebounding joy. But this time Percival is a little more mature and seasoned by life. He is roused by such suffering and he spontaneously finds himself *sharing* it.

He asks the questions that come to him the moment he looks upon the Grail. 'Dear Uncle,' he asks the king, 'what ails you?' And then he turns and asks the Grail maiden, 'How can I be of help?' He offers all he has, which is of course simply himself. Two life-giving questions, entirely to the point, and they are enough. They set the world in motion once again towards wholeness. The first question mysteriously sets the grey Waste Land rippling back into colour, ripeness and life, soon after granting the Fisher King his longed for release into easeful death. The second saves even Percival, releasing him from being the imitation of a human being and knight, and initiating him finally into the start of his real life as a man.

The Grail legend implies that each of us must find the essential question in our own word. But in every case it will be the heartfelt opening of a conversation that changes everything and begins to bring the kingdom of earth back to rights. All beings are released from a frozen spell of the self, when we come back to life. And coming back to life begins in this story with the awakening of natural curiosity about the other, and the empathy that comes with that.

The spirit of curiosity is pivotal. Percival's empathic curiosity does not try to control events, engineer the world or impede the flow of one thing becoming another. It has no interest in an attempt to have things 'just right for me', for that creates the Waste Land.

Percival's compassion is a state of openness towards the unknown. Even death is not a problem to be solved here. The Fisher King has been unnaturally held back from death—a frozen state that is like any life lived holding death at bay. So tightly gripped by mind, life becomes a wound that can neither be staunched nor healed. In this condition we neither live nor die but blur the two into each other. Percival's first question embraces suffering: 'What ails you?' In recognising the other as himself, feeling the suffering of the other as his own, compassion flows as naturally as a blessing. The question that follows straight on is the simple offer to do whatever he can to serve an ailing world. 'How can I be of help?'

'Heart-torn' is exactly the kind of opening in consciousness that restores a Waste Land back to the cyclic productivity of life. The Grail legend seems to say that Percival's immaturity of heart, which could not embrace mortality, kept the Fisher King—and by extension, the living world—laid waste, able neither to live nor die. The Fisher King's restoration to health and wholeness is not 'and they all lived happily ever after', but a willing release from death-in-life. Our civilisation fights off death—as monstrous, tragic, cursed, the wages of sin, a technical or technological problem to be solved. We need to see into the relationship between this fear and a limitless global growth economy based on the fast-as-possible conversion of this planet into The Waste Land.

Love and lament

When my sister died of breast cancer in the thick of her life, just days before her forty-ninth birthday, a great chunk of my own life was ripped from me. Had I been able, I would willingly and joyfully have split my remaining years with her. My dearest joy would have been her companionship as long as I live. 'Darling' was her final word to me, over and over. 'Darling, darling, darling.' My mother's death came more in season, at the age of eighty-seven, but still the vehemence of her loss tore my heart as if I were a child once more. 'You know you are the best mother in the world,' I told her in our final conversation in this life. 'Yes, I know,' she told me calmly.

Every loss of a beloved human being brings with it the arrival of a much greater appreciation of the human being at exactly the moment they pass from reach. Is it like this for us, the generations who are witness to the passing of the Holocene era, which had been the gift of earth at her most full tide of vivid and diverse life? The gift, squandered.

Even lament for all that is torn away from us is its own strange form of praise for the whole, which is large, terrifying and magnificent. A wild cry flung to the hills, to which the hills and rocks reply with the unstinting fact of themselves. The Yugoslavian poet, Charles Simic, speaks of flinging himself into a ditch along with his parents and other refugees as a small child, when warplanes strafed the roadway they'd been walking down. It is hard to recall the faces of those lost people now, he says, but the faces of those humble pebbles in the ditch are completely clear to him still, and still continuing to save his life.

Jonathan Franzen goes so far as to call this acceptance of vulnerable love 'Going for what hurts'. He tells how, in his childhood and youth, he *liked* nature well enough as something pretty, but then as a young man grew furious with our whole exploitable 'gravel pit' approach to the numinous world, until, overwhelmed, he consciously decided to stop thinking about it as there was nothing he could personally do to stop the madness. Better to get on with loving what you could love in this world, he thought.

Then the world—or at least its birds—took him in hand. Franzen fell hopelessly and unexpectedly in love with birds and became a devoted birdwatcher, going to any length to see a new bird but equally finding it impossible to look upon even a common pigeon or robin without overflowing with love. He discovered that he felt even more anger and pain than before, because he now felt such love and despair for the fate of birds; but paradoxically he also found it easier, not harder, to live with these strong feelings.

He describes how loving birds forced him to confront a self that is alive for a while but will die before long, which he sees as the real root cause of all our anger and pain and despair. You can either run from this fact, he says, or, by way of love, you can embrace it. 'And who knows what might happen to you *then*?' he wonders.

So rather than a cold infinity that makes us curl up in fear, we can discover in the Universe Story a humanity capable of both astonishment and compassion. From here, we can begin to sense and engage the unique intelligence and creativity of the earth as our own.

CHAPTER SEVEN

Earthed

We are the only protectors, and we are the thing that needs to be protected, and we are what it needs to be protected from.

Robert Hass

One time I was driving home with Aboriginal elder Uncle Max Harrison through his tribal Yuin country—forested, mountainous far south coast New South Wales—when he suddenly decided we should veer off the highway and up a track to the top of an escarpment to check some country that had been badly burned in a recent bushfire. He wanted to see how the mossy hanging swamps up there, the ones that filter the headwaters of all the little feeder creeks to the big rivers below, were recovering from the burn.

What we found was fascinating. Where the fire had blackened the heath and trees, the moss beneath was either barely moist to the touch or crumbly dry. Yet immediately uphill from there, above the fire line, we found the mosses verdant and bulging with water. How was it possible for all the water up there not to be draining freely down a slope to wet the scorched and desiccated area below?

Uncle Max explained: 'Well you wouldn't give great big gulps of water to some poor person suffering serious burns, would you? Those fellas up there, they're holding it back, just giving little sips to these burnt fellas down here.'

It was an extraordinary moment of seeing right through the illusion of separable parts to the plain realisation of an inseparable forest community working—in fact, thinking—as a whole. Suddenly the *mind* of the forest was evident, visible in the way it impinged on every part of what we were seeing. Each one of these fellas—trees, mosses, birds, lizards, beetles, ants, waters, and also us humans—was suddenly clearly saying to the other: 'I am also you.'

Forestry ecology is now beginning to catch up with indigenous understanding of the way plants interact to help each other survive. Darwinism has been crudely interpreted by an aggressively competitive era as individuals competing for resources at the expense of other individuals. The sharing of resources is invisible to the eye that sees only the workings of individual advantage. The 'fitness' in 'the survival of the fittest' referred as much to 'good fit' as it did to 'most fit and healthy'.

'Good fit' is a fine way to understand elaborated community, or ecological niche. The most successful plant communities have a high diversity of species that coexist in intricate relationships of beneficial mutuality. Looking only at what can be detected above ground, we miss the vast, subtle benevolence of the below-ground neural network of the forest community. Subsoil fungi contribute massively to the subtle network by which forest members share carbon dioxide and nitrogen, by providing a maze of threadlike underground channels that connect the root systems of individual trees—particularly radiating out from the vast roots of the grand old 'mother trees' that are beginning the slow process of dying, allowing them to transfer their immense legacy of nutrients through the fungal network to young saplings coming up. Suzanne Simard, a forestry professor in British Columbia, comments that the way all these individual parts work together is a lot like the neural networks in our brains, with physically distinct neurons and axons working together so intimately and mutually that they are at once physically and almost metaphysically related.

This connectedness of the forest community, which of course includes pollinating birds and insects, as well as seed dispersal in bird and animal droppings, enhances and builds the structural biodiversity that a forest community needs to ensure it can survive fire, flood, disease and plagues of pests. The 'ones left standing' set about nurturing the re-creation of the network of sharing that will rebuild the damaged community. This is the deep meaning of the traditional Chinese saying, 'Heaven is ruthless'. Benevolence, Heaven on earth, is the complete sharing of life by life, in life and death. What gives life also takes it back completely; or more subtly, what gives life never stops sharing it out and out. Perhaps we simply haven't been on earth long enough, as a species so very capable of discerning one thing from another and manipulating that value of *difference*, that we haven't become quite 'earthed' enough yet to discern how deeply one thing is also another, and could not otherwise be at all.

The official final statement issued in 1972 by the Stockholm Conference (precursor of the 1997 Kyoto Accord) described this richly frugal connectedness in the following statement, which is quite startling in its context:

Life holds to one central truth: that all matter and energy needed for life moves in great closed circles from which nothing escapes and to which only the driving fire of the sun is added. Life devours itself: everything that eats is itself eaten; every chemical that is made by life can be broken down by life; all the sunlight that can be used is used. Of all that there is on earth, nothing is taken away by life, and nothing is added by life—but nearly everything is used by life, used and reused in thousands of complex ways, moved through vast chains of plants and animals and back again to the beginning.

Ecologically intelligent design

The advent of the industrial era has produced an exaggerated sense of split between the human domain of industry and technology, and that of nature. We have not yet really discovered at what level of development the human and the natural can be present to one another in a mutually enhancing manner. Technologies have only just begun to function in an evocative manner towards nature, as bio-mimicry begins evoking its structures, energies and spirit in inventing materials, and solving design problems. For the main part, we've gradually made ourselves an increasingly irregular part of the world's ecosystems with every 'progressive' increase in our interruptive powers.

Sustainable development must be sustainable for the whole earth community or it is not sustainable at all but an unacceptable waste of natural capital and a burden on the earth. Abuse of soil, air, water, forests and arable land that closes down the basic life-system of the earth is the ultimate non-negotiable form of any deficit, and an unaddressed failure in these terms is a failure of last resort. A fact that has not penetrated the thinking of growth economics, so remote have we become from the reality of the earth.

Examples of technology designed to benefit and integrate with the earth community—such as the fact that the agricultural soils of Northern Europe are now more fertile than they were in their original state—are painfully rare. But we are now beginning to see the start of design thinking that heals the rupture, in examples of integral design that learns from nature and extends through to the entire life cycle of a product *and* its waste products. Ecological design takes the pulse of *place* and aims to accord intimately with the terms of the earth, its natural flows, fractal patterns, and linking of scale. 'Scale linking' refers to the large hidden in the small, and vice versa. The water cycle, for example, links a single dew drop with an expelled breath, an urban puddle, a great river, ancient fjords, Antarctic ice. Natural processes are constant recycling systems that depend upon the flow of energy and materials across diverse scales, ranging from nanometres to the size of the earth itself. Water in a creek flows in microscopic whirlpools, escapes into large eddies, recedes again into the microscopic. The vast and the minute are in a constant dervish dance, a dynamic interpenetration of subtle harmonies in which everything is influencing or being influenced by everything else.

The principles of ecological design, derived by Sim Van der Ryn and Stuart Cowan, are: first, that solutions grow from place. Place is all of the subtle harmonies that make up exactly where you are in space and time; it is not 'somewhere in general', as digital connectivity insists. Centralisation and standardisation, economies of scale and ignorance or disregard towards what must be learned from place tend to produce design solutions with poor fit, low uptake and high levels of wastage. Knowing (and loving) the peculiarities of an individual place, tuning in to the local conversation of winds, rivers, birds, animals, insects, can lead to original and uniquely beautiful buildings and local design technologies.

Second, that ecological accounting informs good design. For example, a composting toilet that recycles human waste without depending on diluting and transporting sewage eliminates wastage of water, nutrients and energy and avoids damage to freshwater and ocean habitats, while costing far less. Life-cycle accounting is part of this process, developed to reveal the impact of the various stages of a commodity's production, from resource extraction to consumption and discard. Recent German legislation requires car manufacturers to take back each car they make and completely recycle its component parts, and the next step under consideration is to make all manufacturers responsible for the entire life cycle of their products.

The intelligence and value of ecological accounting is revealed in the 'clothesline paradox' identified by architect Steve Baer. Oil drilled in Alaska is sent thousands of miles through pipelines to be refined, then shipped to an oil-fired electricity generator, which sends energy out through the grid for hundreds of miles with transmission losses all the way, to a clothes dryer which then converts electrical to mechanical and thermal energy to dry your clothes. When you could have simply walked out and hung them on your clothesline.

The third principle of ecological design is design following the flows of nature. For example, composting reveals an essential structure within nature that materials are continuously broken into their basic components to be rebuilt into new living forms. Ecological design incorporates natural processes and 'thinking' wherever possible, and mimics all the best billion-year-old, thoroughly road-tested design ideas of feathers, scales, vortices, fractals . . . Everyone from designers to users seem to grow unusually enriched and enlivened by moving in this direction of a covenant with nature. To observe and follow natural systems is to compost and recycle with sensitivity, and realise the principle that 'Waste, by design, equals food', or other forms of valuable, finite resources.

Fourthly, everyone is potentially a designer. People with a local design problem to be solved are invaluable to good design, which depends on the intelligence of shared needs, values and circumstances. The best design experiences occur in situations where no one can claim personal credit for the solution, when the solution instead grows organically out of a particular problem, process and style of communication about it. Consider a hillside of terraced rice paddies and silage ponds, a beautiful dry-stone wall curving over a hill, a vernacular building with innate sense of proportion and grace, like a large Australian corrugated-iron shearing shed, or an old French barn-house . . .

In a similar way, good land stewardship needs a sufficiently high ratio of local 'eyes to acres'—meaning the number of knowledgeable and experienced land-husbandry 'eyes' that can detect subtle differences in soil types, changes in plant communities and wildlife habitats, and variations of microclimate and topography. It takes a good while of looking and living in a place to begin to *see* a plant community, or to really learn the local song of the frogs. Steward-ship is not 'management' that can be organised from a far office. It needs to pay careful and respectful attention to detail and to be able to compare the natural flow patterns of complex local systems with subtle changes in that pattern, so as to work in consonance with the land, rather than impose upon it unwieldy schemes that brutalise such systems. This implies that humble, local acts, each respecting the whole earth and web of life, are what add up to valu-able and sophisticated stewardship, scaled both to the actual limits of ecosystems *and* to the present limits of human understanding.

Philosopher Bryan Norton has said, 'The value of biodiversity is the value of everything there is. It is the summed value of all the gross national products of all countries from now until the end of the world. We know that because our very lives and our economies are dependent upon biodiversity.' Biodiversity, 'the most exquisite form of complexity in the world', is revealed as the irreplace-able 'true harvest of four billion years of evolutionary design', the pattern of connections that maintains life on earth as a great shim-mering web of life-becoming-food, waste-becoming-regeneration.

There is solace in the discovery that the chain of being, includ-ing the food chain, while it may be sculpted by intermittent acts or events of violence, is founded in a continuous flow of practical empathy. It quickens the imagination of what human beings, too, may really *be*, more fully earthed.

A single life in this world—yours, or mine—is a fragile, momen-tary marvel with a lineage deep in time. The web of connectedness passes back through trillions of other earlier lives to the rocks and waters and elements liberated by a supernova explosion that gave birth to our sun and solar system, and extends forward in virtually infinite sweeping curves through unknown lives to follow. And at this very moment of being, it renders our lives possible. Or to put it another way, our very existence actualises the entire web of life. The one is found inside the other.

And at the same time every particle of matter and filament of energy in the universe (including the particular momentary and unrepeatable arrangement that composes you and I) manifests the no-time, no-space, no-inside, no-outside that was the state of reality at the moment of the birth of the universe. This no-thing that gives birth to all things continues endlessly bringing forth you, me, the frogs and trees and stars, as well as this moment and then this one, so that you and me and all things in all our particularity share one undivided nature of *no-thing*—no separate 'thingness'—that is the very font of our connectedness.

(Before I could complete the word 'connectedness', I was waylaid for minutes by a tiny flying creature—I guess we can safely call it 'that fella'—landing pointedly on my thumb tip. I've never seen one before. Its wings, shapely silver and black with tiny transparent panes, its torso luminous blue-green, its business unknown. It seemed happy to move from one fingertip to another, but to prefer to contemplate the world from the vantage of my thumbnail, for a time. Then it was off.)

This metaphysical grasp of an ecology is implicit and made inhabitable in the stories of the first people. It has always nudged mystics, and begins to nudge science; and to see it restores a sense of continuum between human culture and the forces of life, nature and universe. Heaven remains ruthless from the viewpoint of *bios*, an individual life (that will come to an end); but from the point of view of *zoe*, the larger life form of a whole species and whole ecology (that continues ceaselessly), the kindness and mutuality of all beings makes good sense of the word 'heaven'.

Two-sister Dreaming

There is an Australian Dreaming story from East Arnhem Land that lets us catch a glimpse of the long human process of learning to establish and embody ritual rapport with the earth. Shifting consciousness into stone or animal is one thing, but this story shows the high price that can be exacted for merging consciousness with the source of the creative force of the earth itself. I have found this a deeply arresting story from the moment I heard it, as one who was dreamed into being in such closely merged consciousness with a sister as to know myself to be a two-sister human being. It follows the journey of the Wagilag Sisters, two young women who dare to take a walk into the unknown. The younger sister has not yet come of age but the older sister has slept with a man of the wrong moiety and is pregnant with his child, so together they flee the anger of their clan.

These two seem to share the world the way I knew with my own sister, in which it is never entirely clear where one ends and the other begins. As they head north towards the sea, it is the first days of the world. It is they who confidently name animals, trees, bushes, mountains, waters—all the significant features of country. They create culture, too, finding the right grasses and emu feathers to weave the first ever dillybags.

Their journey creates a songline in country whose fertility depends upon the annual monsoon. But these are first times, so the entire sense of country—the network of kinship relations that extends over every animal, tree and landform, and reaches all the way back to the old ones of the ancestral past, who remain present in country—is still being formed, brought into being by what happens to the sisters.

They find a fertile waterhole and prepare to camp for the night, unaware that its water is the resting place of the giant olive python who created this country. The older sister builds a gunyah, for she is ready to give birth. Meanwhile, the younger sister builds a fire to cook their food. When the baby is born, the new mother goes down to collect water in her coolamon. Immediately, over at the fire where the younger sister is cooking, the killed animals begin jumping up alive from the ashes and running away. A bad sign! A drop or two of birthing blood has mingled with water of the serpent's pool, which rouses him in anger. The serpent rises up and lowers over the sisters with thunder roaring and lightning crackling, spitting out the ceaseless deluge of water that becomes the first great wet season of the world.

The sisters keep him mesmerised and at bay by dancing and singing, but the moment they begin to tire, he draws nearer. The older sister grows too weak from childbirth to go on dancing. The younger sister dances even more energetically, so hard it brings on her first menses. She is helpless to stop her blood from flowing with the rain into the sacred waterhole. Now nothing can hold back the great python. He swallows the two sisters and baby just as the party of men who have been pursuing the sisters arrive at the pool. They angrily demand the women and child back. The python regurgitates them—straight onto a thick bed of wet season furry caterpillars that sting them back to painful life.

But not for long. He swallows them a second time, and then speaks directly to the amazed men in the voices of the sisters. The sisters teach all the important songs and ceremonies for cyclical continuance of rain, monsoon and menstruation, as well as the laws of kinship to be followed from now on. And in the place where the sisters last stood on earth, two large stones, and one small one for the baby, are left by the side of the pool, forever marking the site of this tremendous event.

At this, the rain eases and a glorious rainbow arches over the waterhole called Mirarrmina, a sign of a covenant between human beings and the earth. The sisters' fate of twice dying and being twice resurrected, the second time by becoming one with the creativity of the earth itself, speaks of the way an intensely practical spiritual relationship of mutuality manages to be successfully translated, from the raw creative energies of the earth into human speech and customary law. All myths attempt this primal conversation in some form, but this one *enacts* it, offers it as an embodied event. The Wagilag Sisters Dreaming has been carried forward through thousands of generations and remains prominent in song and art throughout that region today. It is a mystery story harmonising creation, monsoon, menstruation, birth and law, for all who can be initiated into its hidden depths, which do not lie on the relatively simple surface of the story but must be worked for.

Clearly it's not easy or comfortable learning to hear and impart the speech of the earth in human terms. As the story of the sisters shows, in some sense, it is the end or else transfiguration of you, a form of becoming incorporated back into the mind of creation itself. Those who plumb such places of mind—mystics, shamans, contemplatives—sacrifice comfort and risk the sense of self. To merge with nature itself and yet return intact to the human world, you need a rock-solid sense of self. To successfully bring across an understanding of that creative force of nature in a form the human world can use, you have to risk and be able to sacrifice much. The story lets this be seen. While it will by nature have many more highly particular initiatory levels within it, this great Arnhem Land creation story maps the depths of self-sacrifice involved in the adventure of becoming fully human *and* fully earthed. Equally it shows how a fundamental transgression can have vitally instructive consequences for a community, illuminating a path for surviving and prospering.

That fact that blunders are our usual way of growing wise may be our saving human grace. In a way, every human break-through—in science, art, medicine, religion, technology, enlightenment—requires a kind of holy fool, a person prepared to step beyond the established safe bounds of tradition and run the risk of seeming foolish and ending in failure. In this regard, this Australian story, tens of thousands of years old, is an interesting comparison to the primal scene of transgression—also involving a first woman and a snake—in Genesis. One ushers humans into accord with nature and the sacred, a way of being in good standing with both; the other condemns human beings to a sense of being permanently and historically cast out of accord with nature and the sacred, into an endless fight with ourselves. The natural world becomes lost to us in its original balanced form, a mere backdrop to a primary struggle to live with our metaphysical 'wrongness'.

An integral human-natural world community

In turn that supposition can distract us from seeing how thoroughly we are capable of laying waste to the gift of Eden—not in some distant Biblical time, but right now. Thomas Berry outlines six foundation principles for establishing an 'integral' human-earth community, rather than one in which human beings stand outside or against the natural world. His hope is that these can usher us beyond the crisis of the end of the Cenozoic era into the potential of the Ecozoic era.

The first is to understand the need for new religious sensitivities. To put it bluntly, if a religious body of thought and understanding cannot address the fact that we are in danger of destroying the life systems of our planet and the earth community of species, then it has reached its use-by date and cannot offer salvation in any meaningful terms. Berry's terms are equally blunt: 'There is no effective spiritual or religious mode of being for the human in isolation from this community. The visible world about us is our primary scripture, the primary manifestation of the divine, and this for human communities throughout the entire planet.'

Berry's second principle is a call for a new ethics, one that can look beyond suicide, homicide and genocide, to even more violent crimes now on the horizon of human agency—biocide and geocide. Biocide is the wanton killing of the life systems of the planet; geocide, the killing of the planet itself in its major forms of expression. Berry holds that while humans cannot extinguish life on the planet, we have it in us to severely damage the planet beyond recovery to anything resembling its former grandeur within any human scale of time. An interruption to the earth's capacity for life on such a geological scale warrants the chilling and arresting term 'geocide'.

The third principle for an 'earthed humanity' is to simply note the fact that 'the human is derivative, the earth is primary'. The consequence of this profound reversal of order is the beginning of the ethics called for in the second principle. 'The primary concern of every profession, institute, and activity of the human betrays itself unless it makes this larger earth community its primary referent,' says Berry. Economics, admitting that it is only within the ever-renewing cycle of earth productivity that human productivity can be sustained, must proceed to place the economic integrity of the planet first, not last.

The fourth is taking deeply to heart the fact that: 'In the emerging Ecozoic period almost nothing will happen that will not in some manner be related to the human.' We will never control the inner workings of the planet. As Berry notes, we cannot make a blade of grass. 'But there is liable not to be a blade of grass if it is not accepted, protected and fostered by the human. We have completely new and comprehensive responsibilities now that we never had before.' This means not just accepting but fostering the wild fertile forces of the planet. Granting to the other members of the earth community their rights to habitat, meaning a viable share of the earth's benefits, will actually be restoration of full *human* rights of relationship to the earth.

The fifth principle redefines 'progress' as progress of not just the human community but the entire life community. 'To designate human plundering of the planet as Progress is an absurdity beyond description,' says Berry.

And the sixth holds that the Universe Story is not a mere account of how we got to be here, but a *celebration*, basis even for a liturgy of communion with the earth. As Berry sees it, the universe throughout its vast extent and sequence of transformations in time can be seen as 'a single multiform celebratory event'. Within it, to his eyes, the earth emerges as a privileged planet that exhibits 'a culminating celebratory mode of expression'—enough to justify the supernova explosions that forged the elements, the galaxies that emerged, the forces that shaped our solar system. To bring this mystery down to earth, he asserts, 'When we ask what is the meaning of the flight of the birds, their song; what is the meaning of the quiet gliding of fish through the sea; what is the meaning of the evening song of the cicada: we can indeed assign some pragmatic answer, but that would not go to the deeper meaning of the phenomena.'

He contends that if we cannot understand all these expressions of existence as celebration, we have missed the meaning of our own existence. Berry's namesake, St Thomas Aquinas, observed that 'every human person is *capax universi*'—capable of the universe. That universe-capable mind needs awakening and practising, but it is latent in every human being.

It will take courage, this immensely demanding transition from a dying Cenozoic era to a slowly recovering and flourishing Ecozoic era. But unrestrained population growth and globalised predatory capitalism set on a course to devour a limited, one-off planetary endowment is an obscene fantasy that is also devouring our entire human future and setting the scenario for hell on earth. A crime against life and against the earth—wilful geocide.

It's admittedly not easy to withdraw our personal lifetime subscription to geocide. I write these words on a computer made of oil products and rare metals sourced in eastern Congo that are so critical to the vast market for 'smart' communication technology that the world is willingly blind to the interminable civil wars and hideous war crimes, especially against women and children, triggered by competition for this trade in such highly demanded rare metals. Although this book is my own struggle to push beyond the thinking that has created the overwhelming problem, the technology I am using rests upon damage I am not being made to face directly.

There is no road map to safe arrival in the Ark of the Ecozoic. But it is clear that it is the only safe and sane ground we have to get to. A passionate understanding of the Universe Story can help initiate consciousness towards that ground that lies beyond a narrow frame, where surviving forms of indigenous wisdom can meet the story and help it break old habits of 'knowing it all', show it how to tune in through scientific revelation to poetic and mythic levels of the dream of the earth. This can open the way to a more intelligent, practical and artistic partnership of humans with the earth,

of consciously assuming self-control over our heightened technological and industrial capacity to profoundly affect the biosphere.

An ecological economics

'Climate change doesn't conflict with demands for a new kind of
economy,' says Naomi Klein. 'Rather, it adds to them an existential
imperative.' Economic redesign in accord with ecological sanity is
critically important if we are to rapidly grow an alternative to a
global system that currently locates all power in global financial
institutions capable of recognising *only* financial values and seeking *only* individual financial gain. Klein sees a managed transition
this way as one in which growth would be reserved for parts of the
world still pulling themselves out of poverty. In the industrialised
world, steady state forms of economic activity, such as the public
sector, co-ops, small local businesses and non-profits, would be
encouraged to expand while the corporate sector seeking constant
growth would be obliged to contract.

Such a proposition rests on a series of planks of change. Defined
in the light of climate change as a collective problem requiring a
collective response of shared interest, the first plank is reversing
privatisation to revive and reinvent the public sphere—the sense
of the public commons; the common good expressed in affordable
housing, public hospitals, schools and transport; collective responsibility for society.

Another plank of change is a turn away from goals geared to
three- and four-year election cycles to long-term participatory
democracy planning at both national and local levels so as to manage a transition from fossil fuels. Corporate profitability would
have to retreat from the forefront of economic life and take a more
minor and regulated role in economies based instead on collective public priorities. That means offering incentives for renewable
energy use and good environmental citizenship, but also barring
behaviour that endangers life on earth—the Canadian tar sands
project, for example. Klein again: 'We are not talking about a return

to authoritarian socialism . . . but a turn toward real democracy. The thirty-odd-year experiment in deregulated, Wild West economics is failing the vast majority of people around the world.' She sees this failure as the reason for growing open revolt against elites of wealth and corporate power, a revolt being led outside of the established and perhaps complacent democracies.

A steady gradual return to localised production and the abandonment of globalised production and shipping of goods is also inevitable in a decarbonised economy. The National Academy of Sciences recently found that emissions from industrialised countries that signed the Kyoto Protocol had stabilised, largely by moving their 'dirty' production to China. It reported that the rise in emissions from goods produced in developing countries but consumed in industrialised signatories to the protocol was six times greater than their emissions savings achieved by the developed countries. Klein foreshadows that an economy organised to respect natural limits would localise economies, rationing long-haul movement of goods to those cases where goods cannot be produced locally or where local production is more carbon-intensive. Climate change demands an end not to trade, but to the reckless form of free trade enshrined in every bilateral trade agreement and pushed ruthlessly by the World Trade Organisation. She admits that 'the challenge this poses to the capitalist project should not be underestimated: it represents the reversal of the thirty-year trend of removing every possible limit on corporate power'.

And it means ending 'the cult of shopping'. In Klein's words, 'an ecological crisis that has its roots in the overconsumption of natural resources must be addressed not just by improving the efficiency of our economies but by reducing the amount of material stuff we produce and consume'. Frantic production of goods to satisfy the most short-term of briefly excited 'wants', in the factory economies of China, India, Indonesia, cannot be endlessly sustained if we are to have a viable Planet Earth.

David Korten argues that as we restructure our economies into *living economies* based strongly in local place and posited on a profoundly different set of values—economies that balance aggregate human consumption with the regenerative capacities of earth, and sharply reduce wasteful consumption while investing strongly in the restoration of healthy ecosystems—they will increasingly mimic and integrate with the biosphere's natural structures and processes. A living economy, like a functioning ecology, proceeds from recognition that no individual or group is born with a natural right to a greater share of the common heritage than any other.

'Like the biosphere, the living economies we seek will self-organise within a framework of market rules,' he proposes. Locally rooted, and primarily dependent on their own resource base, they will need built-in incentives to encourage producers to optimise creative adaptation to local microenvironments. He sees the decision-making powers of ownership distributed more evenly across the community; with everyone taking roles as producers as well as citizens there would be sufficient natural incentive to internalise costs and manage resources responsibly.

The ecological matrix that generates the culture of a living economy emphasises at every point the mutual responsibility of individuals to meet their own needs in ways that contribute to the wellbeing of the whole and thereby optimise their own wellbeing. Businesses likewise. Making a profit would remain essential to the health of any enterprise; but contributing tangibly to the health and flourishing of the 'economic bioregion' and all its constituents, human and non-human, would be an equal, tempering demand.

The whole earth implies an ethics

An ethical re-evaluation of how well human law and governance manages to protect and serve the commons on which the entire community of life depends—reliable climate, clean air, clean water, living space, fertile soil and resilient ecologies—needs no comprehensive philosophical defence. For it is a given at the very basis of human ethics not to destroy the foundation of life. Corporate mission statements, which are virtually interchangeable, and quickly whipped off the table in order to allow business as usual to proceed, bear no genuine relationship to ethics. The stock-in-trade phrases of public relations and spin have debased the currency of moral discourse. The very idea that ethics are essential to human survival and the flourishing of community needs to be rehabilitated from its long neglect.

'Living by damage' is all too easy at one level. There is no cause for serious moral discomfort at all, as long as our sole motivating principle is our exclusive survival as an individual and species. But deeper down, a heavy price is paid in fear—fear of death, fear of nature and her justifiable reprisal, fear of the downtrodden and their understandable rage, fear of how hard we strain to avoid knowing we are not quite inside reality. All this feeds back into insane levels of consumption and 'helpless' debt. To have no morality, choice or question in the universe apart from our own survival and self-interest makes us the deadliest and most ruthless creature on the earth—the very image of the Alien that obliterates the face of its host to gestate deep in its vitals. As long as our political and economic behaviour can see no alternative to living by damage, and growth at all costs, we have to actively suppress a genuine ethics from ever stirring back into life in our hearts.

This feat is accomplished by making pious gestures towards the 'neutral' yet benevolent hand of that blessedly guilt-free god, the marketplace that will take care of everything. Of course that is when it is not seesawing, crashing or conning a docile public with economically toxic 'financial products'. Such religious faith in what Ronald Reagan called 'the magic of the market' is obliged to painstakingly overlook the fact that the real economic bottom line is a one-time endowment of a functioning atmosphere, clean oceans, rivers and lakes, fertile forests and soils, a managed use of minerals, and the intelligent flourishing of human beings alongside many millions of fellow species.

The alien this makes of human beings must be tricked out in

brand gadgets, clothes, accessories, fetishised food, houses stuffed with—well, stuff—in order to distract us from the ugliness each shiny thing is masking. Which is a virulent form of self-interest that will devour the earth, as helplessly hooked as Erisychthon. In going along with it, we are the mad king eating ourselves and the lives of our descendants. At least Alien fought vehemently to ensure the survival of its offspring. Do we even bother trying to justify the harm done in our name and the pressures placed on other lives by our patterns of consumption? The full measure of our self-alienation may be that, as a culture, we don't bother much with trying to justify it but prefer to ignore ethical questions altogether. According to Levinas, it is the *justification* of harm to another sentient being that always reveals the root of what must be called immorality. By not even moving to justify the harm we do, we keep ourselves abstemiously clear of the ground of morality altogether.

He argues that simply to possess and be aware of possessing sentience is to be 'called into ethics'; the call comes with that very recognition of sentience in oneself and in the other. Before parents, moral codes, laws, social traditions, religious commandments or precepts, and the prevailing social order can call us into ethical awareness and greater consideration of others, the primary existential *fact* of our sentience has done so already.

So once we turn our hearts towards an earth life system and a universe regarded not as a collection of objects but a communion of subjects, what call does *that* make upon us? And is the ethical framework we have available strong enough to overcome the flood of doubt and hopelessness in view of the enormity of what lies before us as a species? Can we come to an ethic that understands not just a value in conserving nature, but a sacred force to the proposition that in fact nature conserves *us*?

Chapter Eight

Reinventing the human

The tiger fears the human heart. The human fears the tiger's kindness.

Korean Zen koan

A genuine ethics cannot be retrofitted to our circumstances. In the words of Levinas, 'One is commanded to goodness even if it is futile', simply by empathic awareness of the other who may be harmed or helped. This is a salutary pointer to how much an ethics of the earth may ask of us, what stretch of our imagination and other faculties that extend consciousness beyond our own small perimeter of wishes and needs. The Universe Story may stretch us to the point where we can dare to embrace the aliveness of the earth and universe as our own great life, and draw us into acting to avert a catastrophic collapse of the earth's life systems, and to heal the damage already done. But what Levinas is saying is that even if we fail in this, acting for the earth remains beyond question a necessity, regardless of outcomes that we might judge as failure or success. The earth makes its own call on us, once an ethical sensibility is aroused (sometimes painfully) from its sleep. But to be awake is to be alive and empathically connected, which is a joyful state even when it hurts. Just to be hopeful is not enough. Hope can open the door to ethical action, but to repair and restore a damaged world we must walk through that door.

Empathy is born from the fact that we can imagine our way into and feel the situation of another—their plight, their joy—and lights up the same neurones in our brain as if we were experiencing what they are suffering or enjoying. Such 'mirror neurones' have been observed not only in human beings but in elephants too, as well as other complexly social animals such as chimpanzees. A resounding absence of empathy is what marks all acts of intentional or disinterested harm to other beings, or to the environment and life system that sustains them. In this respect, a great communal narrative like the Universe Story is a prime empathic civilising medium with the power to reawaken some of the energy of neuronal mirroring needed to draw us into caring about the experience of all the beings with whom we share the planet, reaching out through time and space far beyond merely what is immediately in front of us.

Our only final failure would be to allow futility and despair to overwhelm us just as if we were alone in the cosmos and simply guilty as charged.

But such despair, while understandable, submits too much to the thinking that created the problem. In the case of defending the earth from harm, despair shares the assumptions of human, not *earth,* jurisprudence. The history of waves of successive life upon the earth discloses periods of great setback, but nothing like despair. No life can *be* without the entire field of other lives, including the life expressed by water, the mineral realm, the wind that blows as it pleases ... Despair has trouble surviving the wholeness and connectedness of this beautiful world, even in its suffering. Our human laws are centred purely on individual rights and responsibilities, and while we are indeed individually responsible for our actions, who we are and what we do makes sense only in a vast network of relationships. It is actually impossible for any sentient life form to be 'on its own'. This is the understanding of the earth, towards which all life must bend, but to which human law is functionally blind.

A Korean Zen koan holds up a beautifully sharp mirror to how deeply we thus endanger ourselves and the whole world—and where to look for relief from such danger. It goes like this: 'The tiger fears the human heart. The human fears the tiger's kindness.' Reasons for the endangered tiger to fear the scared human heart need no more elaboration; but why do we fear the tiger's kindness, and what could such a thing possibly be?

As with any koan, you meet the tiger in your own heart and mind. But meanwhile of course it will include the 'kindness' of the great food web, the gift cycle that will in time see every body that has eaten others to stay alive in turn become food for bacteria, worms and moulds. It will surely include the eventual mortality that initiates and continually ignites all of the possibility, joy and splendour of being alive.

But I want to suggest that the tiger's kindness also includes the *ethos*—the entire ethical and compassionate teaching and understanding—discoverable in the terms of the earth when we look without self-pity. As long as we are ignoring it, we have plenty to fear from the acuity and power of that kindness. Plenty to fear about ourselves, plenty of basis there for the crippling shame that makes us even more dangerous to the life of the world. Plenty of reason for sorrow, caught up in the very moment of such self-recognition. It's quite some tiger.

As Joanna Macy says, being with our world and giving full attention to the perils confronting it can invite an excruciating tension:

> It is the tension between seeing the enormity of the peril—such as climate chaos, mass extinctions, nuclear warfare—and seeing the inadequacy of our response to it. It takes courage

to endure these tensions, yet endure them we must; for to be conscious enough to act responsibly requires being awake to the possibility of failure.

She sees a strong spiritual grounding as essential for finding the moral strength to keep us from shutting down or succumbing to wishful thinking. She values any practice that steadies the mind, opens the heart and lets the world be more present and no longer separate from 'me'. In those moments we experience our existence as an equal expression of all that is, and fear dies away. It disappears into what is.

It disappears into this cool morning. Into magpie carolling coming through the valley fog a little muted, pitch-bent. The quiet occasional remark of other birds, liquid and twittering. The fog lightening to silk, then shrugging a thicker shroud back around the shoulders of the hills. The rooster finding none of this an impediment, lets his cries evenly acclaim the world, the day, his clutch of hens, and possibly the trickle of damp finding a way through his feathers.

Earth law, wild law

Fundamental to the emergency of our time and the profound change of heart it demands is an earth jurisprudence based on survival, healing and restoration. Many years ago Aldo Leopold spoke of this charter for a more harmonious human-earth relationship as a 'land ethic', proposing that we might place willing and agreed constraints on ourselves in recognition of the essential whole that is at stake. 'An ethic, ecologically, is a limitation on freedom of action in the struggle for existence. An ethic, philosophically, is a differentiation of social from antisocial conduct.' He goes on to say that these two do not yet quite coincide with the one thing that is of supreme importance; he wisely does not name that but locates its origin in the fundamental ethic of mutual accommodation that all ecology displays.

You could call this singular matter the intrinsic kindliness of all beings, by nature, towards the web of life that sustains us all, a kindliness that has gradually grown lost to us from the time we first forgot to extend it. It is the tendency of interdependent individuals or groups to evolve modes of cooperation—symbiosis—in which competition for the resources of life are replaced in part by what Leopold called 'cooperative mechanisms with an ethical content'.

Human politics and economics express this ethic most commonly only in the breach by fighting for power, material gain or self-interest. Natural ecologies more simply and straightforwardly live or die by it. But what if we were to break back through to seeing the whole earth as vivid expression of the fact that we are all in this together, turning any sensitive human heart towards the survival of the living world, instead of seeing only the main advantage that can be wrested from it for the short term of a small human life? *Love* of the earth may be a reasonable name for this mainspring of a relationship of mutual care.

That vivid, mind-expanding awareness of the living planetary whole quite naturally begins to forge an earth ethics. The vital brake to a runaway world system must be provided not only in the rules of engagement in our economic and land management behaviour, but enshrined in ethics and actualised at law. 'Wild law' or 'earth jurisprudence' have become names for the project of evolving a body of law that recognises the earth—both ethically and in legal practice—as the subject, claimant or 'client' whose claim to rights that must be protected *pre-exists* the rights of individuals. In other words, it seeks to regulate human behaviour towards the biosphere by balancing the rights of human beings with the rights of non-human agencies—species, plants, rivers, oceans, ecosystems. And then actively protecting those rights by advocating for them and restraining human beings from infringing them, in a process of seeking a just balance between contending rights.

Wild law does not accept the fundamental understanding of property law, which sees the earth as a passive body of resources

that human beings are naturally entitled to claim in material ownership and exploit for an exclusive form of benefit. Wild law sees
in this prevailing attitude a profoundly unacceptable risk to the
long-term survival of ecosystems and species, including our own.
Wild law eludes the traditional legal paradigms of substantive,
procedural, private or public law. Without a paradigm shift in our
thinking, the two kinds of law appear to be on different planets.

It is perhaps useful meanwhile to see earth law as an essential
earth *etiquette*, a prudent, respectful and frugal brake on human
compulsiveness, more an ethos of human self-governance than a
collection of laws, though these must evolve as the idea begins to
penetrate the way we think more soberly about our entitlements as
a species.

We are completely entitled to meet our own basic needs (as
distinct from bottomless wants). Are we not also entitled to the
companionship of other species? To live on a planet alongside the
tiniest and also the most monumental life forms it has ever brought
forth, such as the imperilled blue whale? To know that tigers still
roam their traditional forests? To be able to rely on the preservation
of the great rainforests that have long been the lungs of the planet?
To know that a legal principle of fairness prevails over ruthless
competition directed against both other species and other human
beings?

Property rights evolved in a different universe to one that understands the supreme importance of biodiversity to the survival of *all*
life on earth. Wild law sees the rights of the earth as 'primordial'—
that is, as the foundational rights from which all other rights flow
and find their definition. As Mike Bell points out, they are 'primordial' in the sense of being shaped by the very nature of the earth.
Because shaped by the earth, these rights are normative, which is to
say they let us understand what a genuine 'right' might actually be.

So, rather than searching human law to find wild law, we have
to turn that upside down and relearn human rights by finally
coming to understand the rights of the earth. Thomas Berry has

eloquently described a bill of rights derived for and from the earth, and they begin with the proposition that 'Rights originate where existence originates. That which determines existence determines rights.' What a radical revision of 'I exist therefore I have rights.' It requires that we look deeply into the nature of existence of universe, earth and ourselves in order to apprehend the primary referent of *being* itself. It requires that we have a reliable means of doing so—a practice of awareness that can return to us what Aquinas called our quality of being capable of meeting, knowing, being fully realised by the universe.

When we look with eyes awake to the Universe Story, we can readily perceive that the primary referent of being is not the human individual in relationship with other human individuals and a collection of objects, but to Berry's *communion of subjects*. In this understanding is a profound recognition of the sentience of all beings. And of the intelligence or even *mind* of mutuality embodied in all ecologies. This recognition renders human property rights provisional rather than absolute. It concedes the existence of species- and ecology-specific rights that have thus far been oddly invisible to 'civilised', urbanised, industrialised human beings. Wild law recognises such rights as river rights, bird rights, insect rights, tree rights, as well as vital human rights!

These rights *in every case* include the right to be, the right to habitat, and 'the right to fulfil its role in the ever-renewing process of the earth community', as Berry puts it. Wild law includes rights of mutual nourishment, for it recognises eating and being eaten, including the predator-prey relationship, as integral to the comprehensive community of existence.

Berry adds to his bill of rights for the earth a final one that acknowledges that we have a right as human beings to satisfy our hunger for wonder, beauty, imagination and connectedness. 'Not only a need but a right of access to the natural world, not only to supply their special needs but also to provide the wonder needed by human intelligence, the beauty needed by human imagination, and the intimacy needed by human emotions.' I would add to this the right of close encounter with other forms or styles of sentience—to be found not only in creatures but in trees, forests, rivers, oceans, mountains, rocks—for without these we cannot fully plumb human sentience itself, in its fullness and completeness.

Even as I write this, a clutch of hens and two rather grand and foolish roosters strut and roam and bob and sometimes rush about on the grass in front of me, foraging, gossiping, creating short-lived scandals to liven up long intervals of peaceful musing. It is a constant pleasure to glance up and watch them. It's not just the pleasure of seeing into their social lives, or idly loving the glossiness and intricate patterning of feathers, the curious shapes of combs, the pert shapes of chooks against the green. It is the fact of their creaturely existence that is so satisfying when I drink them in.

They drink me in too, not simply responding to the slightest movement that might suggest food, but looking over and wandering close with what feels like an equally idle and satisfying curiosity. The wild birds darting freely in and out of this half-domesticated world are like quicksilver by comparison, with the vivid intelligence of survival that has grown a little more negligent in chooks, so long removed from their Asian guinea fowl ancestry. But still the pull of their company is steady and undeniable, the pleasure of half-dissolving into chook-mind, chook-world, chook-rhythm, walking about on unlikely scaly feet, fluffing and tilting my under-feathers towards the sun in a warm dirt bath . . . Ah!

Restorative justice under earth law

Indigenous ways of understanding wrongdoing may provide some clues to how to get from a present ethically impoverished starting point, to flesh out the principles of wild law into a jurisprudence based on survival, healing and restorative justice. The traditional observances of aboriginal peoples, says Mike Bell, generally offer 'the concepts of the sacredness of the land, the seasons, the kinship relationships between animals and humans, the dependence of the human on the munificence of the earth, the spirituality of living in harmony with the land and its species, and an ethic of appropriate use of resources'. Any act of sharing or frugality reiterates the expansive whole of life and of the social group, rather than ever narrowing the world down to fit a frame of 'my life', 'my property', 'my rights'.

Bell draws lessons in particular from what he has discovered of traditional Inuit jurisprudence, which like many indigenous forms of social regulation is based on the concept of restorative rather than punitive justice. He sees it as offering a rich prototype for a framework of earth jurisprudence. When we look, such a framework can be found to inhere and already exist in natural systems, and a jurisprudence that develops according to the terms of the earth can extend the laws of nature in a human direction through our careful self-reflection.

Inuit restorative justice systems evolved in arguably the most severe conditions on earth for human life. Survival in a frozen world requires a great measure of willing self-discipline on behalf of a communion of subjects that of course includes the powerful arctic realm of earth herself. Such an extreme environment creates exceptional understanding of the fact that 'we're all in this together'. The traditional model of Inuit self and community fully included the non-human world on which it depended, and extended respectful forms of equity to the animals that shared the human environment. To become *inummarik*—a genuine person— required an active, lifelong study of and engagement with the needs and nature of both the human group and non-human life forms, thinking, dreaming and meditating your way ever more deeply into comprehending the mysterious fruitfulness of where they meet in mutual respect, and how they actualise each other.

The Inuit saw limited value in punishment, which was invoked only when the life or survival of the group was seriously threatened by someone's actions. Resentment and alienation of members was itself seen as a threat to group coherence and survival, so punishment was avoided in favour of creating a change of behaviour and restoration of relationships. The power of this approach rests on trust and good faith. Take those away, dismiss or fail to recognise them under law, and there is nothing to fall back on but coercion by whatever means it takes—shaming, fining, confining, corporal or capital punishment. The steady climb in the rate of incarceration in the countries that regard themselves as bastions of freedom and enlightened values speaks eloquently about the erosion of communal trust and good faith under regimes of unrestrained material exploitation.

Survival of the earth community can be taken as the foundational motivating force behind a restorative earth justice. As Bell remarks, our current human law assumes our survival as a given, and so cannot be expected to come to grips with the present fundamental threat to our survival, which simply lies outside its frame of reference and understanding. The law itself needs a revolution in consciousness to begin to grasp that our survival as a species depends upon attentively recognising under law our relationship with that vast community of species scientists call the biome, without which human life cannot even begin to be possible.

Punishment of national, corporate and individual offenders against the environment has rarely achieved 'justice'—in fact, most commonly it has failed to achieve even the payment of penalties awarded. Wealthy corporations can frequently wriggle their way out of legal responsibility on some slight technicality of law, and punishment is largely ineffective in a world that is both globalised and profoundly unequal, allowing losers of an environmental legal action simply to move to a location impoverished, politically corrupt or desperate enough to be more 'friendly' to environmental abuse. Witness, for example, the obscene and wilful desecration and ruin of the Niger delta—once one of the most fertile and biodiverse regions to be found anywhere on the surface of the earth—by the world's biggest oil companies.

'Get what you can take' rapidly becomes 'and get away with

every cost to the environment and everyone who lives there'. Now Nigeria, then the Gulf of Mexico, next the Arctic Ocean, and the tar sands of Alberta that alone promise to yield enough oil to finally cook the planet. Anyone would have trouble getting their mind around this magnitude of criminality; little wonder that the people of earth have trouble finding the full magnitude of fury that it deserves.

Traditional restorative justice seeks to create the ground for a change of heart in offenders—seeing this as what is vital for the survival of the group. For the survival of the planet, this would be a fundamental change of heart in corporations, nations, educational systems and religious orthodoxies, allowing as many as possible of seven billion individual human beings finally to recognise and come to terms with our despair at the devastation of our unprecedented Planet Earth. There is no getting around how remote that presently looks from here, with capitalism on coal- and oil-fuelled hyper-drive prevailing as the orthodoxy in almost every corner of the planet. But there is also no getting around its inevitability. The question is how to get humanity to come to meet inevitability— and in time.

Unlike legal systems that create adversaries, the Inuit restorative justice approach sees the creation of winners and losers as far too costly to the chances of the group to survive and flourish. So mediation—with its wise and creative energy to search for the common ground and common good, which has winners only—is what is prized. But Bell stresses that the common ground cannot simply be established as a midpoint between, say, pro-development and pro-conservation forces. That can too often be a painful lose-lose compromise. The truly creative move must always be to find the vital *new* common ground between the rights of the human world and the rights of the other-than-human world, always giving priority recognition to the limited carrying-capacity and resilience of this one-time gift that is the earth.

However, in a profit-driven commercial world, sensitive

awareness of community survival rarely reaches such a high order, and commercial incentives routinely put the world's ecosystems at grave risk. Establishing the rights of the other-than-human world may take some time; until then, making destructive practices unprofitable, and finding an even stronger *dis*incentive, is too urgent to wait.

Truly egregious acts of harm to the environment that destroy an ecosystem on a massive scale have begun to be identified in legal argument as 'ecocide'. For example, British Petroleum's 2010 Gulf oil spill; or the decades of oil spills in the Niger delta, including the pipeline rupture in 2008 for which Shell was finally forced to admit liability and pay hefty compensation to the 68,000 people whose delta homes and livelihoods it has laid waste for decades to come. If ecocide were criminalised on a basis of strict liability, heads of corporations would face prison terms if they approved activities that led to such 'murder' of the natural environment and destruction of communities. Some are proposing that ecocide be recognised as the fifth Crime Against Peace by the United Nations. This would place ecocide alongside genocide, war crimes, crimes against humanity and crimes of aggression, and therefore punishable in the International Criminal Court.

This widened frame sees economic development as fundamentally inseparable from and guided by the principles that support the natural world in its most robust, resilient form, and vigorously refuse all forms of economic behaviour that threaten the planet with geocide. This actually repositions economic development as a version of natural ecological development and sustainment rather than as adversary or rival to its needs, thereby making it subject to the principles constantly revealed in nature. The wonderful thing is that knowledge of those fundamental patterns of earth intelligence and self-maintenance is already knowledge of a powerful ethic; internalised, it is actually identical with the ethic of 'how to be a real human being'.

Heaven is ruthless

None of my urging to resume a mind and way of life more informed by the earth's terms, one that can more safely hold the earth in trust, should be taken to imply a sugary notion of nature as gentle or maternal. The Universe Story does not reflect nature in this way at all. Its power lies in its very invitation to meet the precariousness of existence and unlikeliness of this extraordinary universe while embracing the exquisitely unlikely threshold moments that have continually emerged in the unfolding from simplicity to complexity, bringing forth life and consciousness, and the benevolence of earth's systems towards life itself. When we see the endlessly refining principle of mutuality inside those systems, we catch a glimpse of the originating impulse of empathy that becomes human compassion. Of seeing ourselves in the other, feeling and knowing ourselves also in the light of the experience of the other, and so quite naturally suffering *with* the other, free of pity or fear or any self-referential motive of 'doing good'.

And shared suffering is both healing and enlightening. Everyone comes away wiser. Paradoxically, compassion arises from the ground of suffering yet is often experienced expansively, as joy and gratitude. Compassion shifts us from closed to open, fearful to trusting. Shared suffering leaves everyone with a wider frame of identity.

If heaven is ruthless, it spares nothing in bringing us to this more open and expansive form of awareness. To meet the earth and the universe in such a mind is to meet our *selves* more fully—which will be the subject of the next chapters of this book.

Together with the wonder and depth of the Universe Story, an earth jurisprudence is a call to bring to bear the weight of all of our scientific and technological acumen, guided by the developmental principles of the earth as well as what can be drawn from traditional indigenous wisdom. Together these consciously evoke the imaginative power latent within the fact of our *being here*, and the breakthrough to reality this can inspire. That is what is needed to consecrate the massive transition we have to make as a human species.

Which is no less than turning the ending of the Cenozoic from a catastrophic collapse of the planetary systems that support life as we know it into a new octave of human awareness, transforming the unconscious Anthropocene (human-shaped) era of the last few thousand years of human history into the dawning of a conscious and more awake and intentional Ecozoic era.

Coda: Reality check

It has to be admitted, however, that our record in making radical change as a civilisation in order to save our souls, or even to save our skins, is not an encouraging one.

For a few days in late October 1962, during the Cuban Missile Crisis, the world sat knowingly on the brink of nuclear war between the USA and USSR, the two superpowers of the Cold War. Schoolchildren of the day remember discussing in the playground whether or not they would still be there the next morning. I was only very young but shared the icy, unreal sweat of waiting to see whether or not a hydrogen bomb would explode over Sydney, which was widely considered to be targeted by the USSR as a major population centre. A violent electrical storm on one of those waiting nights woke our family bolt upright in our beds. Was that great crack of light the explosion of a bomb? The gigantic drum roll of earthly thunder that followed a split second later was one of the most beautiful sounds I have ever heard. They were amazing days: humanity collectively contemplating its cataclysmic end, awaiting a fate that was being decided by two vastly militarised states with opposing ideologies and enough weaponry at their disposal to exterminate all of humanity several times over. And there was nothing we could do.

Even more astonishing was the way that ordinary life resumed within a few days of the two nations finding ways to pull back from the brink without losing too much face, just as if nothing had happened that might suggest a fruitful change of ways! Instead, over the next twenty years this visit to the brink triggered a dramatic acceleration of the arms race, and the world apparently adjusted to the idea that intercontinental ballistic nuclear missiles could be released at any time; moreover, that ceaselessly *expanding* the means of doing so was the only logical and safe way of making this less likely.

How did people respond when Western civilisation actually did experience a cataclysmic decimation of its population centres almost on the scale of a nuclear 'exchange'? The great disease pandemics of the past perhaps come closest to a moment when the threat of human extinction became a sudden reality that could no longer be denied. Waves of bubonic plague first appeared in Europe in the sixth and seventh centuries, then largely disappeared until the fourteenth century, when many population centres of Europe and the Mediterranean experienced several waves of the Black Death, with catastrophic mortality rates. Larger towns and cities lost—in dramatically rapid fashion—anywhere from 20% to 80% of their population. Europe's population fell by more than half in that century, and further plague outbreaks continued to occur sporadically until the eighteenth century.

According to Berry, the devastation this pandemic wrought on medieval society dislodged human confidence from what had been a relatively hopeful sense of God and benign sense of nature, setting a sharply different course that ran in two paths. One was the tilting of the religious worldview much more towards pessimism and a search for supernatural redemption from what now looked like a dangerous and disaster-prone world. Accordingly, the religious response of gratitude for life and praise for a marvellous creation suffered a serious decline. The other was a drive to master the natural world and make it 'safe' for human beings. This was a very different kind of search for salvation, powered by 'godless' scientific enquiry into the most intimate secrets of nature, which gradually brought forth industrial, technological and medical advances that did indeed afford a measure of insulation from uncontrollable natural forces such as infectious disease.

Although they diverge so profoundly, both impulses share the fact that they regard the earth with mistrust and fear. Both serve to entrench our alienation from our bodily home, pitting ourselves against it as if it threatens our integrity, rather than recognising it to be a primal source of integrity, wholeness and belonging. Both point clearly to the mistaken direction we've been heading in too long and that we must reverse if we are to survive this crisis of the whole earth. If we don't even feel we belong here and can entrust ourselves to the planet, can we be expected to feel responsible for its ongoing welfare? Especially if it is either nothing much more than inert matter to be arranged to greatest human advantage, or God's business only, for him to decide the nature and timing of its fate?

Although in hoping for a deep change of heart we must take some pause from this, we can take consolation from the footnote nature offered to the years of the Black Death endured by Europe in the fourteenth century. It has been found from carbon-dating trees and correlating both maps and records of wild animal sightings that in the fifty years in which plague decimated Europe's population and wiped countless settlements from the map, the forests of Europe rebounded with startling speed from their greatly reduced state. With them came an equally strong and rapid rebound in the populations of wild animals and birds, especially the larger predators such as wolves and bears, which had been close to extinction.

Of course the people repopulated too, in time, and gradually pushed things back to where they'd been, and more. Always more. But the heartening or cautioning note, depending on your viewpoint, was sounded: we are ultimately incidental to this planet's deep urge towards generous life.

Biodiversity as a *practice* for human beings

It is now obvious that it is in our hands either to save or miserably squander the earth's gift of life, revealed to us as an intricate weave of amazingly diverse life forms in an ecological harmonic that beggars—even while it *creates*—the imagination. Biodiversity is not just a quantitative inventory of species. Far beyond that, it is the revelatory communion event of life on the earth—the ecological principle that each life form implies both the whole *and* all the other lives being lived alongside it.

The human part of that communion involves the fact that a large proportion of the millions of life forms blossoming on the tree of life have been individually *recognised* and indeed named by us; that they then flower all over again in the minutely branching 'tree' of the human brainstem and cerebellum; and that these forms and styles of sentience are intimately observed, absorbed, embodied in mimicry, committed to memory. Which is simply what fascination and love demand in a human being.

To successfully defend this miracle of biodiversity from our own limitless predation, we have to recover personal awareness of the full nature of mind. To fail to make this effort of knowing our own mind is to agree to fail as a species, and to fail the particular call of the earth upon us as individuals and as a species. We alone among the species can catastrophically rip down the weave. And we alone can literally *mind*—hold in mind and consciously care for—this delicate, animated web of numberless relationships, and discover in its mysterious nature the self-same essential nature of our selves.

Such a conscious, disciplined, inquiring use of the mind is called a *practice*.

It's called that because you have to keep doing it to discover it, and all the time it's discovering you. It's called that because it doesn't ask you to take as a given a single thing that does not arise out of your own experience. It's called a practice because the theory is to constantly test the nature of your self by working into it; there are guidelines provided only so that you may set out into the unknown with some likelihood of getting past your preconceptions. It is a practice of deeper awareness, a constant, conscious choice to live that way. It sees life itself as a practice of awareness, one that can either be unconscious and disordered, as if it is something that just happens, or can become a continuing series of conscious choices. Oddly, this power to choose your mental state grows out of a practice of choiceless awareness, paying close attention to what appears but withholding judgment.

To understand and practise such an awareness of mind, and to live from that ground of paying close and open attention, is not only a means of enriching intellectual understanding of a problem as vitally important as massive loss of biodiversity. It is actually to practise embracing biodiversity as our *selves*, our true nature, and to begin to want to actualise *that* mind. Not only does each of us, in our human consciousness, 'contain multitudes', as Walt Whitman put it, the practice of the mind of biodiversity recognises how greatly *we* are diminished, in person, with every species loss. A practice of such a mind means ceasing to live as if nature were a difficult, threatening force always somewhere out there, and starting to bloom into the awareness that knows nature and the earth to be inseparable from the very nature of mind.

How is this so? What have the vagaries and challenges of possessing human consciousness got to do with the collapse of biodiversity?

Empty of the sense of self

My perspective is founded in the way Zen sees the problem or gift of mind. Zen is the self-erasing, theory-erasing practice of breaking through the habits of mind to experience reality directly—and finding that immediacy to be the most natural state of mind, sometimes called 'ordinary mind'. But to make clear that it is not a special state of mind is not to say it finds anything to be ordinary. Nor that it is always easily accessed without conscious practice. Zen finds that in those great moments that are *empty* of all of the suppositions mind can generate, then our own mind is discovered to have an exact fit with the reality or nature of this universe.

'Empty' can seem an alarming word; saying that 'self' has no enduring substance or boundary may sound like being sentenced to the death of all meaning and a meaningless death. But the *experience* of 'no-self'—or the experience of liberation and broadening of what the self is, when freed from the delusion of a fixed self—is radically different to this. It is an overwhelming recognition of the perfect equality of everything in every direction, of everything seamlessly connected and exactly in place, and not separable from who we really are—including the more customary and limited sense of self, which is now seen as a highly persuasive and useful but momentary and ever-changing construction, constituted by memories and slow-evolving ideas of itself, rather than actually existing as a fixed fact. In other words, in radical departure from Descartes, who established that he existed because he could think it, the experience of Zen is that we are literally *not what we think*. Its path leads insistently away from the abstracting attitude and habit of mind, back to the wholeness of reality and the particularity of each thing.

The earth's extravagant web of biodiversity, upon which everything that lives depends, is the vividly detailed face of this reality, an overflowing plenum that is fundamentally empty of all boundary or separation, and this is also what composes us. The Buddha called this 'dependent co-arising', which is to say that nothing exists intrinsically, for everything arises and is conditioned by everything else in a network of relations. And so our centre of gravity shifts from seeing our true nature as a small sovereign sense of personal self, to discovering it to be inextricable from the vast interdependent, self-organising structure of reality itself. In other words, our true nature is 'to be part of one another', as Joanna Macy puts it. Impossible, then, to treat nature as a mere 'standing reserve' of energies and materials passively awaiting our pleasure.

The individual sense of self is a vital matter; lacking it, we are profoundly disabled as social beings. There is good reason to see its relative nature, but no reason to declare war upon it. The experience of Zen practice is to catch a transforming glimpse beyond the confines of this sense of self, where it does not disappear but is no longer sustainable as an absolute reference point of experience. This is a shift away from a mind that establishes all meaning on a ground of duality—of *this* as opposed to *that*. The self can be wondrously realised as inseparable from all that is.

In a genuine opening of this realisation, everything is seen to participate in one essential nature empty of separation because it is overflowing with *relationship*; within this one nature, an infinite number and variety of distinct entities manifests, as both themselves *and* the unbroken whole, which is expressed in the interconnectedness that makes each particular life form and distinct individual possible. Each aspect constitutes the other. Metaphors of a web or net of relations are of considerable help in trying to convey the ineffable nature of non-duality, but even the shimmering metaphor of the Net of Indra falls short of the subtle and dynamic *experience* of wholeness perceived in diversity, and of diversity lit up by wholeness.

So Zen practice is most simply described as the study of the nature of your own mind, and with that, of the nature of reality. To bring mind and heart to rest in reality involves a practice of paying unqualified attention to each moment and each thing presented to awareness. It is impossible to do so without deepening and transforming your relationship with the earth, which not only formed us and ceaselessly sustains and informs our lives, but also has the power to wake us up. At this point in time, a human being cannot wake up on any other planet. We wake up to this earth.

To practise knowing mind this way is to come to a sense of wholeness of identity unconfined by concerns about 'my life and my death and my place in the world', whilst fully embracing life and death.

It is to this dimension of mind, this essential nature that we all share completely, that I now turn.

PART IV

MINDING THE EARTH

CHAPTER NINE

Medicine and sickness heal each other

Medicine and sickness heal each other. The whole world is medicine. Where do you find your self?

Zen master Yunmen

Once Zen Master Thich Nhat Hanh had what he called a deep conversation with nature about global warming. Meditating, he asked, 'Do you think we can rely on you?' The answer from nature came back as a question. 'Can I rely on *you*?' After a while he found himself replying, 'Yes, you can mostly rely on me.' Nature responded, 'Yes, and you can mostly rely on me.'

The Buddha—whose name means 'awakened', and whose teaching or *dharma* has been called the 'medicine' that heals the 'sickness' of our human condition of fundamental unsatisfactoriness and inability to rest completely in our lives—famously said, 'We live in a house on fire.'

He wasn't anticipating global warming a good 2500 years ago, but pointing to the fact that we live in—and as—pure change. The mortal body that houses this mind and self is temporary; it burns with impermanence, or constant transformation from one state to another. Luckily, for without that, no child would ever grow up, no adult would ever mature. We cannot step out of the universal fact of being one thing continually becoming another. Waking up is a joyous fall into the realisation of being *precariousness itself*, and finding what is precious and indestructible in that very fact. Until then, we can *feel* very precarious, subject to hostile forces beyond our control that will duly weaken and kill us and take everything from us.

The tiger's very particular form of 'kindness' is found right here in the nature of reality that we discover to be also our nature, when we stop being scared of it. You can trust yourself, and rely entirely on that wild kindness, to the extent you can stay steady and in touch with reality without withdrawing in fear. Nature can rely on us to exactly that extent.

To see ourselves and reality so clearly is the business of dharma, a multifaceted jewel of a word that actually means several things at once: Dharma is the fundamental *law* or nature of reality itself— the mysterious dance of form and emptiness at the heart of the cosmos. But dharma also refers to every single momentary *form* this 'no-thing-ness' constantly draws into being. That's you and me and everything down to the last pebble and twig—all dharmas, which is to say, all embodiments of the fundamental law of the universe. And finally, dharma refers to the body of *teachings* of the Buddha that point the way to knowing yourself this way. The teachings are of great value; it is often said that it is rare to be privileged with a human birth, and rarer still to be privileged by stumbling upon this profound body of wisdom. But the teachings are merely prompts towards reality, which can only be encountered in person. As the old Zen saying goes, 'Don't mistake the pointing finger for the moon (of enlightenment).' And as the Buddha cautioned on his deathbed, 'The things I've told you are no more than a handful of fallen leaves from the whole forest. Don't take a single thing as dogma. Test it for yourself, realise it for yourself. Only then have I succeeded in imparting anything of value.' Or words to that effect.

And so in this universe—rather than the one that an overly fearful human being might design—life implies death, and being here now implies disappearing later. The distress our species seems to experience in embracing this shows itself most plainly in the distressed state of our planetary life-support system. The death sentence we make of life is now being forced upon the whole earth. When we can embrace this reality more fearlessly just the way it is, we find it fits us perfectly well—always has. The way opens, the sky does not fall in, the ocean confides its songs, each drop of dew forms in exactly the right time and place in the grass. Pain and discomfort are just part of this whole, not always easy to welcome, but not a personal assault. 'Thank you very much, I have no complaints whatsoever' becomes not a ridiculous statement at all but—as with every koan—resonant with all that is.

Perfect days

The 'yes' spoken to us by reality is constant and requires no mental contortion to pick it up. Instead, it takes gently and persistently relaxing into the way things are—something entirely natural and simple, but that is not quite the same as easy. Relaxing body and mind back to a more natural state needs to be practised with genuine commitment if it is to become instinctive and restored to being second nature. But while we may be constitutionally prone to self-interruption and all too easily drawn away to easier things, still the whole world never stops calling, singing that natural mind back up.

Today the rain has lifted after a week of heavy downpour and the birds are back in evidence, diving for insects in air as clean as a whistle. Life teems, every puddle reveals a tiny empire. Steam rising, mist dissolving, creek garrulous with floodwater, creepers almost visibly creeping, mountains resolving sharp in the sunlight. Everything sentient *together*.

Every day is the perfect day for seeing it clearly, the fundamental equality and wonder in all things that makes boredom impossible—though admittedly some days will feel more perfect than others to hazy human consciousness.

We have never exited the fundamental reality of the natural world, even if we have partly 'technologised' ourselves out of intuiting our place in it. Every breath we take confirms it, every morsel of food we swallow, every sip of water, every moment of walking about or lying down in weariness to sleep. No material component of any tool or artefact ever created by human beings can come into existence independent of its animal, mineral or vegetable origins in the earth—with the sole exception of some rare item fashioned from meteorite material. Material and social culture is an abstraction we often oppose to another abstraction we call nature. After all, a steel, rubber and plastic car does not look too much like rock, tree and oil any more; a house is expected to exclude uncomfortable impact from 'the elements'; medicine is geared to defeating or delaying many of the natural causes of death; agricultural chemicals are intended to overcome pests or soil infertility. But no one ever stepped outside of nature, not even into a sealed spaceship, or medical unit with laminar airflow, because it is your wild human body, 70% water, intricately shaped by the nature of the earth, that takes the step.

Even to say 'nature' creates a cultural artefact that makes a cut in something that is seamless. This essential nature of reality expressed in every form found in the universe is sometimes called 'the *thusness* of things', which recognises the unrepeatable nature of, say, the thornbill dipping its beak into a flower, while reaching past the impulse to divide thornbill from flower, or intense energy hit of nectar from whirring wings, or wings from gravity, or gravity from the sudden thrill of song.

'Thusness' sees all categories and all things as empty of differentiation while embracing the exact way things are in their momentary arrangements of matter and energy, as well as the infinite intersecting *patterns* of matter and energy that bring them into existence and hold them in interconnected relationship. But 'thusness' also expresses full awareness of the empty, equal state of fullness pervading each thing in its unrepeatable existence.

In the deepest sense, we can't fall out of relationship with nature since we are nothing but a momentary knot in its infinite net of relationships in the first place. But it does seem that we can disturb that net of relationships pretty thoroughly when we approach it with a carefully narrowed consciousness. That disjointed consciousness is still capable of perceiving the dissonant state of things and how far it is putting at risk our likelihood of flourishing as a species. But as we have seen, that degree of awareness still does not seem to be enough to urge us to recover our senses and unleash the huge creative forces of repair and loving restoration that is latent, I believe, in all sentient human beings. Something remains asleep in us, leaving us oddly dead to the world.

Solidarity

Arne Næss, the leading philosopher of 'deep ecology'—the branch of ecology that insists on seeking the *spiritual* depth of ecological systems in gauging the consequences of disrupting them—described a moment of staring through a microscope at the meeting of two drops of different acids, when a flea, jumping at random, landed in the reacting chemicals. He couldn't save the flea. It took many minutes to die, during which time 'its movements were dreadfully expressive'. He grew acutely aware of his own reaction—compassion and empathy were there, but he noticed that the empathy was a process of complete identification. He saw himself in the flea. If he had been unable to intuitively see anything resembling himself, he would have regarded the death struggle with cool indifference. Næss concludes that without identification there is no true compassion and little chance of solidarity, between human beings and between human beings and other species.

Zen Master Ryokan understood such solidarity without

qualification. He went so far as to carefully leave one leg out of his covers at night for the sake of the mosquitoes. My own sense of solidarity has trouble reaching to creatures who intend to suck my blood. Ticks, leeches, mosquitoes and fleas can get short shrift when they bite me. On the other hand, I once drew close in solidarity with a large cockroach that had taken refuge inside the rubbish bin I was bringing in from the street. When I picked up the bin, disturbing him, he ran a rapid single lap of the bottom of the bin, out from the pie wrapper someone had dropped into it, right around and back in under the paper. I shook the bin again, experimentally. Out he ran once more with alacrity, a complete circuit round the bottom and then back under his private wrapper. He duly completed each of the laps I required of him with unflagging vigour, until I began to feel mean and released him to the home comforts of a nearby drain. I really liked him by then. We kind of waved feelers before parting. Someone has suggested that if cockroaches were not the colour of human excrement, but came in a whole array of brilliant colours, and were called perhaps something like 'attenboroughs', people would proudly point out the jewel-like attenboroughs scurrying in and out of their kitchen cupboards right in front of their admiring dinner guests.

If we cannot form a sense of at least a wary, working solidarity with the crawling, the invertebrate, the scaly, the many-legged, and even the blood-sucking creatures with whom we share the whole, and drop our chemical warfare approach to them, we seriously compromise the wholeness of mind that can heal an ailing planet. Not to mention the biosphere, and our own bodies. Think of the disastrous 'silent spring' Rachel Carson alerted us to, when the unrestrained spraying of DDT to eliminate pesky insects all but eliminated the birds and bees as well, upon whom rests not only so much beauty but food crop fertility. DDT made its way through the food chain into human breastmilk all over the earth, and was found even in the tissue of Inuit women living in latitudes far beyond the Arctic Circle and all possibility of cropping agriculture. It is a sombre footnote that Rachel Carson herself died young from breast cancer, some time before the carcinogenic properties of DDT in human tissue had become fully recognised.

The bone-knowing need for such solidarity—that this world is *us*; that these creatures matter in the way we do and are deeply implicated in what we are; that the prodigious creativity of the earth is not here to passively serve us, but for us to actively discover ourselves within—has been muted and dimmed. I've already searched some of the most powerfully shaping stories of our culture and seen how they reflect our severance and retreat from nature. I have also explored the potential of the great story of the unfolding universe to arouse in us the energy and imagination to seek reconciliation with the earth, and to help us handle our challenging new reality with some skill. But is this enough?

A narrative of this order can give us a possible cultural foothold in an Ecozoic future. But what can reawaken in us an intuitive responsiveness able to really meet this blazing reality in which we find ourselves? How do we mend the fault line that seems to separate us from the immediacy of this reality? And how can we set about in person to recover our misplaced *natural* human mind, which by its very nature bends towards minding the earth?

Just mend it

The finest Korean maker of wooden pots once had a visitor who noticed with astonishment he was using timber so green that resin was flying in his face. Shocked, they asked, 'Why use wood so green and unseasoned? When it dries out this beautiful bowl will surely crack. What will you do then?'

'Just mend it,' was the uncomplicated reply. Excellent advice for a throwaway world that has meticulously forgotten all such arts as mending and frugal care for things in favour of a frantic churn of consumption and waste.

Mending, frugality, composting—and knowing and caring for not just the things but for the life *story* of the things we own, from the point of their creation down to now—how rare all these ideas are now, how ripe and ready to return to a world that so deeply needs *minding*. Have you noticed how even inanimate things seem to respond to being minded in this way?

Our confidence seems strangely intrinsic to the cooperative wholeness of things. Confidence arises when we know ourselves to be confided in, held in intimate confidence or trust by others. And even more deeply, confided in by a sense of the whole world.

The Korean potter had an untroubled confidence in his relationship with even the greenest, freshest and most volatile of the woods he was working with. He welcomed any difficulty they would present him as an opening, an artistic opportunity.

Later the visitor examined the artist's wooden bowls and cups and conceded that their great character gained much from the random patterns of lovingly mended fissures. He realised that 'just mend it' disclosed an intimate agreement between the potter and the way things are, and far from being a mere solution to a 'problem', 'just mend it' was an entire creative strategy of working with the unexpected.

That is *not* saying we can afford to be complacent or cavalier towards the damage we do to the earth. Rather, that a humble readiness to 'just mend' any harm we do might be an interesting and beautiful matter in its own right, with its own fund of human genius to disclose.

'Just mending' always has something a little miraculous about it, though nature thinks nothing of it but simply sets about it, undeterred by difficulty or the possibility of failure. Mending and healing what is ruptured blossoms directly out of the untraceable net of relationships that we call nature. A cut finger heals. A snapped tree trunk will attempt to form a new main trunk from a minor branch. A tear in the canopy is soon filled by new saplings powering up to the light, seizing their chance. The Black Death that devastated Europe greened the continent once more, and the return of the forests brought wild animal populations back with a roar.

The fossil record shows that any great extinction event on this life-prone world will be followed before long (in geological time that means some hundreds or thousands of years) by an explosion of new or opportunistic species. Unless pushed over a threshold of overheating that proves too hostile for life—which is not beyond the realm of the possible—earth will always 'just mend' the tears in the fabric of life, without special reference to the human species.

The step beyond 'me'

The first step out of the claustrophobically limited frame of reference of *me*, is learning how to just be, minus the opinions about it. It takes persistent practice in consciously using the mind to gently doubt or actively 'not know' every supposition our thoughts will always keep providing, about what seems to be going on, and how reality might be improved upon—for *me*. There's no need to drive suppositions away, it's just a matter of being openly and insistently curious to open a space in which to genuinely wonder, 'Is that so?' instead of immediately knowing, 'That's so!' In time, the state of willing questioning becomes a little more like second nature, displacing know-all mind from the driver's seat. And in this way, 'me' and 'mine' gradually lose priority seating, which proves to be something of a relief, making room for something far more interesting.

This state of mind, as well as sometimes being called 'ordinary mind' because it has no tickets on itself, is also known as 'heart-mind', because experiencing it makes compassionate response hard to refuse. Whatever you choose to call it, it's simply the mind that is given a chance to recognise its own essential nature clearly and to repeatedly choose to live in that light.

This practice and its discoveries are entirely personal, and yet plumbing the human heart-mind with meditation and koans is curiously clear of the personal as well, for the more we fathom our own hearts, the more we find every other being and the whole world itself right at the core of what we are, intimately present. To master this is to become what Zen calls a 'true person', which means knowing yourself well enough to rely on what is truly happening rather than your dream of what would be preferable and less demanding.

Meditation can take many forms but in Zen it means settling into stillness with an upright spine while becoming softly, willingly, keenly aware of your own mind just doing its thing. To focus lightly on each breath in and out often helps to give you enough reprieve from the usual insistent pressure of thought to begin to see that the mind and its thoughts—you and your thoughts—are actually not identical. You are asked to favour a gentle persistence—not so much in trying to control the mind, or despising it in any state, as in letting all thoughts soften, while maintaining a foreground awareness of the whole body breathing, hearing, feeling, resting. Just the feeling of one hand resting in the other, your weight on the chair or floor, any unbidden sounds, sensations and feelings passing through, are taken to be just right, and just enough. You offer 'just what is' your complete confidence, and rest your mind in it.

All of these keep the mind poised and attending in the present, more alert to its frequent tendency to stray from what you have set as your wide and simple but highly focused field of attention, learning to catch that straying as it occurs, gently declining all propositions about what is happening, over and over, until such thinking loses its grip on you and your body and mind together finally begin to just be here.

There's no need to fear failure You were always here anyway, whether you noticed it or not. Failure is nothing but another useful prompt to the learning process, and in fact as Zen Master Sheng-yen said, 'If you have never failed, you have never tried.' When effortfulness drops away from the process, what is more natural can appear in it, and success and failure no longer trouble you. 'Natural' means already closer to your true nature. And as self-consciousness begins to soften its grip, a sense of who you really are becomes harder to tell apart from whatever you are encountering breath by breath, more and more intimately. How interesting, that 'going beyond me' can only find less and less that is 'not me'. The discovery is also quietly consoling, for it is hard to fear the end of an existence that doesn't appear to have any beginning or end anywhere you look!

To this practice of concentrating the mind back to a greater wholeness and seeing through the self, Zen adds the practice of introspection upon koans, which offer a unique way to mend the splits we create in the mind. Once your 'koan mind' begins to turn mind habits upside down, koans begin to appear everywhere. Not only is every great spiritual tradition discovered to be full of them, but they pop up all the time in the most ordinary of places. For example, a fine koan overheard recently on a country train: 'Well who do you think you are!' Yunmen would approve.

Koans mend the divided mind by drawing us back to the ground of the whole mind, and the mind 'mended' to its original wholeness is *always* a more beautiful and capacious vessel—more serviceable, much more fun to use, and far more adept with the unexpected, rather like the whole world itself. Some move of mending yourself back to wholeness, and resuming a greater accord with your natural mind, is latent in every koan.

So the mending—of mind and world together—can take place in a way that lies immediately to hand in every human being right where they are right now, as I explore in the final part of the book. What might 'just mend it' mean at the level of the questions I started out with? Not only, 'Where and what is the thinking that did not create the problem?' but also, 'How can we wrap our minds and hearts around something so vast as the destruction of the biosphere, and instead of going mad, grow alert and very interested?'

A deliberate *practice* of mind

The mind has thoughts the way the ocean has fish, seaweed, waves and bubbles. Out of nowhere swim images and propositions about what is wanted and what is unwanted, what feels threatening, welcoming, irritating, pleasing, right, wrong, just, unjust . . . the list has no end. Some of this content is little more than a slight surge towards verbal thought, but also whole sentences form, conversations are rehearsed, feelings about something are emphatically reiterated, sometimes to a maddening degree.

Much of this is as fleeting as clouds forming and dissolving in the sky, but to the extent that we give substance to our thoughts as reliable accounts of reality, a whole thought pattern can slowly form like a kind of weather system, with the power to colour the mind for days, weeks, years, whole stretches of a life, and to shape thoughts and outlook in an internally consistent way that feels very solid and resistant to alternatives. The fact that it may be completely inconsistent with external reality can become harder and harder to access.

Yet moments of finely aware non-thought visit us endlessly too—whether for fleeting lucky seconds or, with awareness, for many sustained minutes. Just sitting with a cup of tea in hand and gazing at the leaves or the clouds, doing nothing, wanting nothing; stepping into the shower and completely entering the fact of warm water on glad skin; catching sight of your child's face and small body as they step from the school bus; sliding into cold sea or river on a white-hot day.

These moments of reprieve from the constant churn of self-important bulletins from the Ministry of Misinformation become, with practice, more noticed and more interesting. They offer a taste of the mind in its most natural state, which is relaxed, poised, open, awake—seeing clearly whatever lies in its field of awareness, unclouded by any kind of fear, trusting in itself and the original nature of things. You will find how entirely of a piece this state of non-thought is with the call of the birds, the sound of footsteps, the movement of the wind in the grass. Entirely here and entirely at home.

The key difference between the mind roaming at large, and such a deliberate, disciplined practice of mind, lies in the word *relationship*. A steady, sustained practice of becoming curious and impartial towards your thoughts rather than immediately being persuaded by them gradually lets you back into a reasonably awake relationship between your mind and its thoughts, fears and hopes. Instead of instantly identifying with your thoughts as they arise in reaction to something, as though they are what *you* are, a layer of mind that is deeper and quite different to 'I think and that is what I am' becomes available. It turns out that with practice your mind can watch its flow of thoughts and feelings with quiet calm and unmoved interest, and begin to be aware of their pattern and nature, as well as their forming and insubstantial dissolving.

With practice this more tolerant and flexible relationship to your own mind just as it is can open, both by slow and sudden degree, to a wide, receptive state of mind that is less confined and disturbed by the content of thought. It appears to want nothing and have no edges. The old name for the mind at vibrant rest is 'samadhi'—an all-pervading sense of there being nothing missing, lacking or needed, a state deeper even than contentment. In this state of mind, all that is feels reassuringly alive, intimate and present, and unconcerned with being either 'better' or 'worse' than some other set of circumstances.

Curiously enough, it is this willingly and lovingly *dispassionate* state of mind that is most ready and able to come up with useful and creative responses to any emergency. And we certainly have one of those on our hands at this moment in history.

The whole mind is medicine

This unconfined state of mind is roomy, alert, responsive and at ease. There is a deep sense of being free and unburdened. Using drugs to lift the burden of mind bears only the most superficial resemblance to this state. Unlike the practised mind, the medicated mind is dependent on something chemical to be brought in from 'outside', whereas the open state I am describing can find nothing truly *outside* itself. Moreover, the medicated mind defaults to a place of high anxiety about intolerable feelings, from which it can be freed for a time only by the drug. By comparison, the practised mind constantly learns new ways to trust itself and to find the many subtle steps of freeing itself by its own means; it gains new insight into *mind* itself every time it meets (and does not turn away from) difficulty. It becomes less easily drawn to the idea of an easy fix, because it keeps discovering the unforeseeable uses of difficulty. In fact it learns that meeting difficulty right where it arises is actually less exhausting and more rewarding than following the vast detours imposed by trying to elude it.

Medicated mind does not build any such resilience and skill; in a way, it all but skips *you*, the subject, altogether and seeks relief from the boring, the frightening or the wearisome as though 'you' were a mere footnote to the transaction. A drug or addictive pattern can have the uncanny feeling of being an entity seeking only itself and stripping the intermediary of much of their humanity in the process.

In passing, the analogy with the highly addictive behaviour of our civilisation towards the 'intermediary' of the planet that supports it, in our rapacious hunger for the quick fix of dense energy offered by coal, oil and uranium, is all too plain, and all too painful.

There are many forms of medicated mind beside the obvious one of mind-altering substances. The constant feed of social media and virtual reality, the entire 'too-muchness' of our consumerist culture, inoculates against the threat of the reality that might invade and touch us if we went quiet. The medication is its own disease. But equally, Yunmen declares that medicine and sickness heal each other. The whole mind heals the gap between itself and all that it perceives. When we see the world whole, we see reality itself as powerful medicine, even including all that we must acknowledge to be broken, damaged and endangered.

So what is it like, to see the world whole?

Not presuming anything
The mind that practises fitting the whole world is impartially friendly and curious towards its circumstances. If you consciously

don't 'know' that something is boring, frightening or wearisome, it has an excellent chance of being none of the above. 'Not knowing' is not the blankness of being clueless. It is a highly intelligent, concentrated and liberating way to use your mind—to remain open and enquiring while not presuming anything is the active way to encounter the circumstances in which you find yourself. And in that rather fearless and yet humble condition an intelligent response becomes a real possibility.

Tolerance is often taken to mean not caring overly about something, but in fact it is a matter of becoming able to sit patiently with your discomfort in a difficult situation. There is always a degree of hardship involved in discovering the nature of one's own mind, but the hardship endured in any act of mastery, including self-mastery, is exactly what assures its genuine quality and keeps opening new horizons of skill. Consider the disciplined hardship of learning to play a musical instrument, for example, and the rewards that come only with taking a firm position *beyond* your own procrastination, doubts and resistance.

However, I am not suggesting crushing the mind with austerities but something far more interesting, subtle and enjoyable, which is practising *harmonising* the mind, with itself and with all of its circumstances, and thus with the nature of the world.

In describing the mind of the hunter, philosopher Ortega y Gasset inadvertently supplied a very fine account of the intentional practice of awareness I have been describing—still, alert and relaxed, intently observing the flow of what is happening, while at every point making an impartial kind of peace with that flow, and with itself. The technical Zen name for this practice of mind is *shikantaza*, a disciplined state of actively resting in the most natural state of mind. Let's look at his description once more in the light of what I have said about meditation:

The hunter does not look tranquilly in one determined direction sure beforehand that the game will pass in front of him.

215

The hunter *knows that he does not know* what is going to happen. Thus he needs to prepare *an attention which does not consist in riveting itself on the presumed,* but consists precisely in *not presuming anything* and in *avoiding inattentiveness.* It is a *'universal'* attention, which does not inscribe itself at any point, and *tries to be on all points* (my italics).

Knowing how much you do *not* know about what is going to happen is a first step towards being at ease in not presuming anything, while remaining sufficiently alert (consciously 'avoiding inattentiveness') to be ready for what in fact *does* happen.

'Preparing an attention' in this fashion is a continuing discipline or practice. It is nothing like edgy vigilance. Oddly enough, instead a kind of active contentment is its basis, in the sense of seeing quite clearly what is here, including any clamour the mind might make for things to be different. It's like someone finally turning off the loud music and letting you hear the world. When you manage to sustain such attention, you find contentment quietly present under everything. I think of the Sufi poet Rumi's description of this most delicately enduring tone of the world that finally reaches the still mind resting:

> All day and night, music
> a quiet, bright
> reedsong. If it
> fades, we fade.

Wanting nothing

So an unusual yet deeply familiar contentment can be uncovered inside that steady relaxed capacity to remain untroubled and neutral towards desire for alternatives, while finding possible ways to enjoy what is actually here. Even objectively boring, irritating or painful circumstances are perfectly interesting to a non-resistant frame of mind. If you don't object to what's going on, it has a hard time becoming objectionable. And whenever we succeed in the quite difficult practice of not judging things to be good or bad for us, everything seems more able to freshen and come back alive, in even the most banal circumstances. Waiting for a bus (having just missed the last one) on a street whizzing with traffic that flattens even the weeds growing in the cracks of the pavement. But there are fingers of late sun creeping orange over the concrete. There's a small plastic bag pirouetting in the jet stream of each passing truck. There's a pigeon growing curious about you, and the exquisite copper sheen cast by the late light upon its many subtle colourings is so absorbing you almost miss the next bus.

Michael Leunig gives us a telling glimpse of this entirely ordinary state of mind in a cartoon that shows a man, hands in lap, bent over in a chair just gazing peacefully at his floor. The cartoonist assures us that he gazes at the floor brightly, as if reading a good book or looking at a painting, though his eyes, fascinated and contented, are simply fixed on bare boards. The floor reveals itself completely, holding nothing back. It is superior even to the new media, says the cartoon, for it is where he can find the truth. We are witnessing a man caught in the act of discovering what Leunig chooses to call the integrity of the floor, finding it reliable, free, enchanting and, above all, everywhere. Substitute the word 'reality' for the word' floor' throughout, and you may begin to understand why Leunig leaves the man in the final frame at peace, absorbed in fresh ideas, alive with wonderful feelings, 'his eyes sparkling and alert'.

Any meditator—or artist—will smile with recognition at this image of a man gazing with enjoyment at a floor, a situation entirely understandable if you have ever truly allowed yourself to enter an unknowing, receptive state towards something so everyday and right under your own nose, just as if you were burdened with no preconceptions about it whatsoever. And so had begun to *see* it, for the first time on earth. As Emily Dickinson says, speaking about dwelling in this wide-open state of mind: 'Life is so astonishing; it leaves little time for anything else!' A floor, the subtly shifting light and shadow falling on it, your own mind quietly absorbed, can be everything a person needs for a good long stretch of time that is free from all sense of time.

And not *pushing* anything

The Chinese understanding, stemming from Taoism and Chan Buddhism, gathered up in the term *'wu-wei'* is rich in this regard. *Wu-wei* occupies the far side of the moon from all forms of acquisitive or driven behaviour, and yet gets everything done. Nelson Foster comments that it 'literally means inaction or non-doing and holds connotations of not scheming, not pursuing, not controlling, not manipulating, not forcing things, yet it doesn't equate to sitting on your hands either'. He quotes the Taoist master, Chuang-tzu: 'Each thing minds its business and all grow up out of inaction . . . Heaven and earth do nothing and there is nothing that is not done.'

How do we get hold of this creative, generative power of least resistance that comes right along with the mind at ease? Well, it is already everywhere apparent in all things of the earth—including your own body and mind. Consider the repose of mountains, flow of rivers, growth of trees, song of birds, flexing of muscle with the surge of an idea, steady arrival of the next breath, and then the next . . . Who is *doing* any of that? And yet it all gets done.

And how wonderfully well everything is using this inconceivable power already. Heaven and earth with no effort at all are the complete expression of doing nothing—nothing that has clear beginning or end or can ever be isolated from anything else and all that is happening. The complete efficacy of the natural world is pushed by no effort and moved by no practical purpose but simply to be. That branch curves up entirely of its own accord and holds up hundreds of leaves to the glittering light as a breeze arrives. Where is effort in that, or the 'practical' as opposed to 'impractical'? At every moment the earth openly sets an impeccable example of not scheming, not pursuing, not controlling, not manipulating, not forcing things—and yet unendingly achieving completeness. And yet we can push right past this, frowning with effort and concentration to get the next important thing on our list 'done', just as if we were not privy to this marvellous open secret that is everywhere displayed.

In a world of one thing constantly becoming another, what can ever be said to be 'done'?

How funny we are, in all our self-important belief that we can, indeed *must* control and engineer things for ever-improved 'outcomes'. Exactly what is the planned 'outcome'—or room for improvement—of a river, a mountain, or a breaking wave? The systems of the earth that support life (at least up to now) seem uncommitted to the idea of 'having done' something that underlies so much of what we obsess about. Even a tiny bird that must daily eat ten times its weight in insects to survive is intent and ready rather than driven.

The nineteenth-century Zen hermit and poet, Ryokan, who never had anything so important on his mind that he lacked time to join the village children in their games, knows the contentment of *wu-wei* inside out. His manifest contentment comes all the way down to the delicious sovereignty we all enjoy if we turn towards it, so long as we are still able-bodied enough and not suffering unbearable privation:

My whole life, never troubling to get ahead,
I've just ambled along, leaving things to the stars.
In my sack I've got three measures of rice,
by the hearth, one bundle of firewood.
Why ask about enlightenment and delusion?
What truck have I with fame and fortune?
Here in my hut I tilt my ear to the night rain
and stretch out my two legs just as I please.

The ever-moving creek I can hear as I write has much the same mind as Ryokan, leaving all its plans to the wind and stars and rain.

Between rains it makes quiet unceasing music, never troubling itself in the process; in a deluge it roars with tumbling boulders and remakes all its beaches and banks anew, sometimes choosing to pile them high with water-sculpted driftwood, other times scouring them fiercely clean; its impressive power is effortless, its work both always done yet never completed. I hear it as one long prayer of agreement with just exactly what is happening. That's the one thing always available, so contentment is guaranteed.

The mind of peace intently practises this art of mental *not-doing*. As Foster points out, though it may sometimes yield a pleasurable 'peace of mind', practising the mind of peace involves much more than entering a restful state. *Not*-doing takes focused and sustained attention. It is intent upon not missing a single thing, seeing and appreciating things as they are in their natural limits, while responding—with all the resources that come from a good fit with actual circumstances, including a healthy measure of self-deprecating humour—to *what needs doing*. But that response will be guided in its aim by a steady awareness that is as clear of wishful thinking as a human being can get it to be.

So there is no invitation in *wu-wei* to inertia or passivity, for its contentment is not complacency but a guide to action. A state of contentment that is not wishful about its circumstances but has developed alongside a willingness to meet the real limits of a situation leaves us informed and alert, ready to respond to what may endanger the conditions that provide for a fundamental contentment. A durable contentment ultimately comes down to what life needs to live, and live with enjoyment: clean air, clear stars, fresh water, good food with vivid taste, intimate contact with the natural world, reliable seasons, productive soil, living oceans, prolific variety of human and non-human life, equitable sharing of the resources that support it, a good fit within the ecology of our circumstances . . . All of these can be protected and passed on to the coming generations *only* with a wide-awake, collective, indignant refusal to continue consuming the life of the world.

What if the indicator of a society's rate of growth was gauged not in levels of production and consumption of goods and services, but in deep satisfaction with the sheer fact of a day of life? What if it was calculated instead by a measurable increase in substantive knowledge; in levels of health and nutrition; in the percentage of accomplished artists, thinkers, writers, mentors, brilliant educators and spiritual teachers in the population? In restoration of waterways and forests; in successful understanding and rehabilitation of delicate ecologies that support endangered species, fish nurseries, plant biodiversity; in the healing of bioregions ripped apart by mining or desecrated by chemical spills? In the amount of time people get to make and listen to live music, dance, walk, lie on the grass and watch clouds? In the degree of productive sharing behaviour that a society achieves in a given year; in its ability to meet natural emergencies in a collaborative way, to restore habitats quickly, and to mitigate habitat damage? And in the degree of decarbonising and 'greening' of industry achieved in that year?

To the extent that we subscribe to a way of life with little or no connection to the most fundamental indices of wellbeing, we are in danger of being here on the earth only under duress, awaiting our deaths, perpetually sacrificing the moments of our lives for—for what? The economic bottom line?

Meditation cultivates a mind that begins to find such attrition to the basic grounds of contentment in life ever harder to accommodate. The fruits of meditation include: a tolerance for what is actually happening, unclouded by preferences for what would be more acceptable to the self; a resulting depth of contentment and pleasure in what is simply and already at hand; a conscious relaxation of any impulse to try to force reality to conform with the many dreams born of a drama called 'self versus world'; and a heightened sensitivity towards genuine danger, harm and injustice, with far greater skills of responding in good time.

So we live in a house that's on fire, and when we discover that fact it is difficult not to panic and struggle for 'safety', and to constantly fight the fire. But all the time, we aren't *in* a fire, we *are* the fire, composed of the very precariousness we have been fighting. When we know we are the fire that runs through all things, then we can begin to fight a great fire, like the one that is threatening our world right now, *with* fire—more fearlessly, and so with greater personal and collective conviction and efficacy.

For in the end we practise being aware, not for our 'enlightenment', but to ease the existence of all the beings who happen to be with us in the ark of the world, as well as all those coming ahead of us, in gratitude to all that led the way to being here. That fire leaves nothing out: medicine is not distinguishable from sickness in that fire, suffering and joy are found inside each other. And when harmony with the nature of things reappears, then both medicine and sickness disappear.

And this is where we really find our selves.

The whole world is medicine

I came to realise clearly that mind is no other than mountains and rivers and the great wide earth, the sun and the moon and the stars.

Zen master Dogen Kigen

At the deepest level, nothing is wrong. The whole earth is medicine. And at the same time, it will be facing a dramatically more unstable and difficult world by 2060, even if we could stop right now and add not another jot of greenhouse gas emissions to the atmosphere. So much is badly wrong and we are the only ones who can respond.

Medicine and sickness heal each other. The potentially dire planetary emergency beginning right now in our lifetimes is in its way an unprecedented offer, the one that cannot be refused if we can only remember how to trust life enough to wake up and fight for it.

The old Zen expression for a woken-up human being is 'the true person of no rank'. 'No rank' means free of all burdens of comparison, ordinary, equal. This is not describing a saint, though true people are rather roomy individuals to be around, and the sense in which they are 'ordinary' is unusually natural and at ease, rather than commonplace and lacking in special interest. Waiting for human beings to reach sainthood seems a luxury we cannot afford when there is a world to be saved from ourselves. 'Just imagine, even relieving my bladder and I have to do it in person,' an old master replied when asked about his special powers. For better and for worse, we're entirely human.

Purity and perfection in any case are most uncertain virtues in human beings. How many purges, inquisitions, ethnic cleansings and persecutions have been sponsored in their name? How much careful editing of the fullness of being human, cutting away whole races, religions, sexual preferences, even genders? Perhaps the earth can see us more clearly when we come forth just as we are, fully human, unmarred by ideals of perfection.

One time when I was helping Uncle Max in a ceremony I asked why I also needed to have ochre markings on my face and shoulders, and he explained that without it the spirits would have a bit of trouble recognising me. An earth spirit said to be dwelling in the grounds of ninth-century Zen Master Dongshan's monastery had a similar problem. He had no trouble at all watching the rest of the monks coming and going, as he liked to do, but try as he might he could never catch sight of the famous Dongshan. One day, however, Dongshan saw a monk throwing out some leftover rice and chastised him angrily for not being more frugal. The earth spirit was delighted—in that flash of anger he caught sight of Dongshan at last.

Highly self-disciplined and awake to himself—all of that and human too! How reassuring. A human path is one we all can walk.

Human, humus, humble, humour—all stem from the same root meaning 'the earth'. And 'human' itself until relatively recently implied what we now gesture towards with the word 'humane': having or showing benevolence and compassion; making sure that our actions inflict a minimum of pain upon others; as well as the branches of higher learning that are intended to have a civilising effect on people—literature, theology, philosophy, art, music, history, languages, classics . . . In other words, the humanities, all of them in recent times, strategically underfunded as having nothing to contribute to the economic bottom line—nothing but a depth of knowledge of the nature and history of civilisation, and an ability to think and judge ideas with acuity. In other words, a true human being was understood to be an accomplishment rather than a given. Being human was a life-long cultivation and refinement of awareness, to be won with whatever effort and self-sacrifice was required of you in response to the amazing opportunity of being granted a human existence.

I think it fair to say that it takes a discipline of mind to see right into all the possibilities of being fully human. Saints may inspire us to touch our greatest heights and depths, but a practice of awareness is realistic in temperament because when we meet reality face to face we find it empty of the distinctions upon which idealism depends. And it is impossible to maintain a genuine practice of any kind without humour, as it builds a most robust sense of our own limitations.

It is a sick world indeed right now. And yet, though you search to the end of time, you cannot find a better one: the rain from a brief shower drips from the roof gutter in twos and threes, the cat stretches by the fire, a cow bellows in the distance, and the moon appears pale in the late afternoon sky. When you glimpse its seamless whole in any single one of its marvellous details, does it not begin to make plain that the medicine we seek to cure this sickness is the nature of this earth itself?

'The whole world is medicine' reveals the true nature of the self to *likewise* be a field of relationships, an ecology, a self-correcting, self-healing system of meaning and energy, a richly distinctive being that is mysteriously more than the sum of its past experience and its ceaseless flow of ideas and emotions. There is no person without such a world as this, and indeed, no whole world without such a self-aware and unself-conscious person.

Walt Whitman famously said, 'I contain multitudes.' When you take your seat of meditation in order to take up this mind, know that it contains multitudes. All beings sit in solidarity with you. Not only do we sit with all beings, we sit as ordinary human beings. The Buddha declined sainthood and deification and effectively said about his own awakening, 'You're a human being. So you can do this too if you really care to.'

CHAPTER TEN

Where do you find your *self?*

We are here to awaken from the illusion of our separateness.

Thich Nhat Hanh

When the Handless Maiden of the old fairytale by that name sees her beloved infant fall into a well, the dire exigency of her situation sees her instantly grow a new pair of hands to reach and catch the baby. A most vivid demonstration of 'just mend it' that can only happen right here, right now.

Seeing into a koan and finding the radical alternatives already right at hand that can mend the destructive way things have been going in the world have much in common.

Great work if you can get it

Koans became part of Zen training during Song dynasty China, especially around the time of Yuanwu (compiler of the magisterial collection of one hundred koans titled *The Blue Cliff Record*) when the records of exchanges between recognised Chan Buddhist masters and often anonymous student monks of the Tang and

Song dynasties began to be taken up as '*gong-an*' (Japanese 'koan'), or 'public cases' to be clarified by practitioners. 'Clarifying' does not mean 'explaining' or 'answering', but rather becoming able to directly present and embody the koan point, which means discovering in yourself the mind of the master whose words or actions yielded the koan. The practice continues in Rinzai (Linji) schools of Zen down to the present day and formed the backbone of my own training path of more than 1700 koans.

Koans are that strange class of miniature stories, questions, images or even single words, which turn out to be holographic towards reality. Just as every particle of holographic light contains the image projected by the entire hologram, every koan directly answers to reality in such a way as to contain and convey the nature of the whole—of mind, heartbeat, world, galaxy, universe.

So every koan in a particular way mends a tear in our relationship with reality, helps reverse our fear-based withdrawal from it, which has cruelled our own lives and been so violently damaging to our world, and takes a decisive step clear of the thinking that created the problem. Koans invite us to share the mind of someone who can see whole.

Since they always strip away what we use to hide from original mind, koans are a special kind of origin story in their way—extremely portable ones, small enough to be held in the palm of one hand, and never lacking a playful power to overturn rusted-on thinking. They are origin stories because they share with creation or cosmology stories a fundamental interest in the source of all that is. But with the vital difference that they do not try to explain it—not even metaphorically—but instead just point it out steadily and directly, never limiting it with a name or explanation. You can think of them as tiny, potent detonators to reopen entry to reality lying in wait for us right under our very eyes and noses, in the most ordinary details of the world including words themselves.

Koans are traditionally close to the oral tradition in its participatory, improvisatory freshness. They are drawn mainly from live encounters, were traditionally offered in a somewhat ceremonial face-to-face encounter between teacher and student, and the response (rather than 'answer') that they evoke is offered, when it ripens, in direct presentation rather than explanatory form.

By their very nature koans are literally *not* what you think. They are instead what you cannot fail to realise when you strip away all your suppositions.

Their great virtue is that you simply cannot use ordinary conceptual means to resolve the offence they seem to offer to ordinary ways of making sense. Instead they oblige you to look in a radically fresh way, and immediately the misunderstanding that there *was* a problem dissolves. Or to put that another way, koans reveal, by sudden means, that the real problem was that we were blocking our own access to the fresh wholeness of reality.

The thinking that divides the seamless world, thinking that generally originates in the proposition 'me', just won't work for a koan. Whenever we resort to the usual categories (always relative to an insular sense of 'me' or, at best, a partisan 'us') to try to approach a koan, we will always find it impossible to put Humpty Dumpty's original egg back together again. Grasping after reality in the form of opposable fragments only persists in creating the problem.

So every koan requires that we find our way to resume the original undivided state of mind, which turns out to be as natural and at ease as the rain falling and the earth getting wet. Until we do, the koan won't stop bothering us. When we do, it brings us back to our senses and to what and where we actually are—which is oddly familiar, intimately at home, yet bigger, more roomy, and in touch with a remarkably interesting energy.

It's like drawing your chair out from its place at the kitchen table, to sit down full of the hugeness and weight of 'so much is wrong with the world', and finding that to be suddenly inseparable from a seamless fullness and vast contentment, the overwhelming sense that Julian of Norwich spoke of when she had no choice but to say, 'All things shall be well, and all manner of things shall be well . . .' Or what Leunig's man lost in looking at the floor with an open mind discovered, or what the shadows of the trees stretching now in long rhythmic lines across the winter grass explain directly to my eyes and heart whenever I glance up. The mind of peace draws enlivening solace from intimate detail in the world.

Practising getting back into this natural mind is quite properly tough work, and not just because there's so much distracting blather in the mind and in the world. It is tough because it accepts hardship (our resistance) as its reality and enters there. And is prepared to do this over and over, the way a concert pianist must play a recalcitrant phrase over and over until it discloses its architecture fully and has become second nature to the bones and sinews of the hand.

Basho also had a word to say about hardship in many of his poems from his long pilgrimages into 'the Deep North', the uncushioned natural world. The word, effectively, was, 'What hardship is that?' Whether he is launching into the cold autumn rain with no wide straw rain hat, or lying at night in flea-ridden straw next to horses and the sounds of their pissing, his mind is at peace in a tolerant open curiosity and enjoyment of what is, not made uncomfortable by ideas of discomfort, not bothering to be troubled by pointless preferences.

That is the true 'Deep North'. And it may be the strongest and finest place to go seeking the strength to face the time we're in, as the natural world falters in its resilience and ability to bounce back from our relentless pressure upon it. Accepting hardship can open reality to us in a form no longer distorted by fear of hardship. And then the fun can begin.

To follow nature and return to nature
Koans are a reality project, not a self-improvement project. Koans can find nothing to improve in the true nature of the self we are all born with. Martin Buber recounts the deathbed scene of the eighteenth-century Hasidic rabbi Zusya. Very close to death, he roused himself

just enough to say to his followers crowding and leaning in for his last words: 'You know, when I get there, they will not ask me, "Why were you not Moses?" They will ask me, "Why were you not Zusya?"'

How strange that we seem to find it easier to struggle all our lives to inhabit some notionally acceptable self, and easier to bear the inevitable failure of such a project, than to let ourselves be who we discover we are when all notions of who we are have dropped away and left us in peace. Those few who manage to live and act in genuine and untroubled relationship with that for the whole of a lifetime are actually the lucky ones, however difficult their life circumstances. A truly lucky life is not the cushioned one of undisturbed consumer dreaming; it's the one that has no reason whatsoever to shrink from the crowning question of a lifetime: 'Why were you not (*insert your own name here*)?'

Our culture seems haunted by fugitive awareness of how far it falls short of daring any of us to inhabit who we really are and to live the life that follows from that. Yet this is all that has ever actually been asked of us, and the only thing that ever really satisfies a human heart.

In the same spirit, a koan is not asking you to impress as someone great or special, or to solve a devilish riddle, or enter a cabal of esoteric learning. It is interested in allowing a kind of healing crisis of mind and heart that will yield a genuinely liberating glimpse of who you are and what reality is, minus all opinions about it. After that, there's a chance to live more true to that unbounded and straightforward sense of self, to live up to it, go deeper into it. Profound changes in how we want to act in the world follow on from that stance quite naturally, and if we remain honest with ourselves, become a matter of no choice.

The poet Basho, when asked for his advice to poets, said simply, 'Cultivate a mind to follow Nature and return to Nature.' Koans likewise invite us to follow and return to our original nature. Human beings become natural meditators and poets and ecologists when they follow this indigenous (meaning 'born here') way of practising being aware. It is a state of mind and a leaning of the heart older than any religion. In a way, it is earlier than human consciousness, or at least was already latent in the trickle of water over stones, the response of clouds and pterodactyls to rising thermals. The earth's meditation has been going on a very long time and will not stop for us. But it will always let us back in.

Two year olds and adolescents are notoriously sure they are the centre of the universe, and spend considerable time colliding, painfully all round, with the fact that not everyone shares their view. I sometimes feel our civilisation has not yet got past the two-year-old or at best adolescent phase. While there is a great liveable truth to be uncovered in the proposition that each of us is indeed at the very centre of the universe, paradoxically that truth has far more to do with giving yourself away than grabbing all you can get. Our maturity as a species, if we get there, will be one of consciously contributing to the unfolding of the world while living intentionally within the means of the earth and in accord with its terms.

Everything that is flows from being to non-being. Rejoining this mind lets us learn how to be at rest in the vast, all-inclusive and impartial reality in which we find ourselves, open to it in all directions.

A koan is a means to prising open a door we hadn't noticed ourselves closing, liberating us from the thinking that learns to divide reality in order to handle and manipulate it cleverly, but leaves us caught painfully locked outside the whole. We may be in possession of a marvellously skilful thinking mind—the ultimate tool, thus far, in becoming dominant among the warm-blooded species—but it leaves us unaware of how narrowly aimed it can be, how stiff and confined in its relationship with all that is. Every koan opens to the same 'one mind' that enjoys reality directly and is unrestricted by living and dying, but each does so from a different angle.

The ecology of *not-knowing*

The troubling presence of a koan first draws a natural attempt to solve it—like wanting to solve the koan of global warming with a measure like 'engineering the sky to repel solar radiation'. A measure that is largely a shallow fear reaction, completely unwilling to look at why we think we have the right to be even considering such a thing, and where we have gone so wrong to produce such an emergency.

It is surely already plain that a koan, like an ecology, does not respond to the approach of a mind wanting to think in parts. A koan is a whole ecology of unending relationships that opens your mind to reality the moment *you* turn fully towards it, empty-handed. And to do that you must place what you think you are in jeopardy, by means of an unusual form of doubt.

For the next thing that happens in keeping close company with a koan is that a testing, productive kind of doubt sets in. There is no right answer. At first, the feeling in response to that fact is ordinary doubt directed at the koan itself and the idea that it can be of any value. But when you turn the doubt not away but back upon the very methods by which you usually arrive at the answer, it begins to grow into a rich form of *self*-doubt that is also an ability to be a little more comfortable with not knowing. This is the kind of doubt called 'great doubt'. Pregnant women were once said to be 'great with child', and great doubt can feel rather like being pregnant with an unknown capacity for new understanding.

To sustain great doubt, great faith must rise to meet it. Instead of doubt being weak in the presence of faith, or confidence, in Zen practice, the greater the doubt, the greater the faith. They are both energies of the mind stirring towards awakening.

You can have faith in something external to you—the example set by the Buddha's awakening, for example, which has influenced thousands of millions of other human beings to proceed along the path he walked. But looking more closely and inwardly, allowing great doubt to grow and gradually soften your usual cognitive means of saving yourself from the unknown, gives access to a surprising store of trust in something hard to name, neither inside nor outside you, reinforced by the sun lighting up the dew on the grass, the air on your face, the creak of a floorboard. With that comes the will to continue on in the dark, where the usual operations of mind seem to come to an end and drop away, leaving you curious but without any of the usual assumptions left in place.

There is nothing left to do at this point but wait, first allowing and then actively rather enjoying the company of the unknown. This state of mind, with so few recognisable features, is in fact a promising and oddly familiar one. The self is slowly being emptied of all of the old ideas about there being any kind of separate or fully independent being. It is a state of being sufficiently open and still that you do not quite know where you begin or end, liable to be tipped over by the smallest thing into an overflowing state of empty fullness, the experience known as awakening.

At this moment you can't find a will or a way to distinguish yourself from the cry of the kookaburra or the light on the floor. But thankfully this is not the feeling of the self vanishing piously into unworldliness, but rather a delightfully free and unburdened sense of your self stepping right into the world just as it is, finally home in reality and ready to help. Waking up is discovering ordinary mortal life in the ordinary human world in the radiant light of no distinction between self and other. However, seeing things like this is wonderful but has to be lived out in the complexities of life and turned to humble use in the minding of the world, else it may turn into 'trying to be Moses'. 'Being Zusya', that's the gold standard here.

Your true self turns out to be essentially no-self, but opening your eyes to this does not annihilate the 'you' that memory and experience has shaped, a sentient being who acts in the world in a characteristic way. Rather, it is a radical rediscovery of that 'you' in the world seen whole. Ralph Waldo Emerson called our rich body of gathered memory and experience 'the thread on which the beads of man are strung, making the personal identity which is necessary to moral action'. 'You' are indeed indispensable.

And so 'breaking back into the conventional world' with an

understanding of no-self brings personal identity and moral awareness more sharply together. Character grows more, not less, distinct. Instead of straining to be Moses, Zusya plain and simple can emerge, self-aware, at home in this life which can never be longer or shorter than this moment, and not unduly threatened by a looming death. A greater generosity of being can arise with this, an aptitude for resting in the grace of the world, and being free. A natural subduing of the demands of 'me and mine' through increased sensitivity to the 'other' and to a world no longer possible to entirely sever from the sense of self.

Realisation passes over from 'something special' into 'seeing things just as they are—and then helping them be the best they can be,' as Shunryu Suzuki put the whole matter of Zen—thereby humbly describing every genuinely great life that has ever been lived.

A word about words

Koans are made of words—spoken words, originally not written. Spoken words retain a vibrant physical existence—made of breath, and the warmth of our bodies, they are exchanged in air and pass into the bloodstream of the listener and ripple out into the world through further talk and actions that may follow. Take care. Words are powerful. They create human realities that can be hard to unpick.

A koan is an 'unpicker' of words even as it makes use of them.

Written words can be especially hard to unpick. They can draw us out of direct participation and immersion in the natural flow of the world, diverting us into a parallel purely human world that we've seen grow increasingly unchecked in its sense of self-entitlement and alienation from nature. Philosopher David Abram has argued that the pre-literate cultures of tribal peoples form a continuum with the more-than-human (not 'non-human') natural world. This fully participatory sensibility has been dismissed since the Enlightenment, so-called, as non-rational animism. But Abram notes that even the way that letters 'speak' to us on a printed page is a form of animism, one that seems to make the stones and trees fall silent, and the animals turn dumb, when 'our senses transfer their animating magic to the printed word'.

In Genesis, God gave naming rights to Adam over all the creatures—a distinctly co-creative gesture that goes so easily wrong without a corresponding measure of self-aware self-discipline. A name establishes the evocative link between consciousness and the thing named. Literally, it calls the thing up—both into and out from reality. Names are mysterious powers in their own right, both carving things out from the whole and ordering them into a human scale of utility, exchange and understanding in the world. So they re-establish living tissue between consciousness and the things it can identify, while papering over a crack in that continuum, the very crack that they helped create.

Something strange and interesting happens to names and words in koans. While the koan rests in words and names, it is unconfined by them. A koan invites you to step beyond confinement in the reality words habitually circumscribe, to let a word become a door that swings open into the reality of the whole that no words can ever circumscribe. It is simply empty of that possibility.

And looking even further, words themselves are admitted back into this wholeness of reality. They belong too. The habit of mind from mid childhood onwards is to immediately jump onto a familiar verbal track that generalises and predigests raw experience, stranding us in a realm of suppositions, just shy of what is really happening. Nevertheless, words, too, have no choice but to bring the whole universe with them, just as much as the sudden whiplash of that bird-call from the scrub does, or the liquid syllables of the creek, the soughing of the wind, your own heartbeat, a distant droning plane . . . Words jump in so fast to replace experience with a notion of that experience, almost as if to save us from the trouble of being here at all. We can whiz past a great river and think 'river', if we notice it at all; or turn briefly from a magazine to glance through the aircraft window and think 'clouds'. Likewise, 'trees' in all their immense character and variety are thought to be dealt with by that word, while in fact they are simply disappearing into it, right in front of us. But in koans, no word is hobbled to a notional meaning in this way. You have to take each one as it confronts you, believing nothing about it in advance. Any word can turn upside down, or suddenly open to a night of turning stars. If you can trust yourself enough to let go of who you think you are, koans have it in them to make such openings even out of the very words that compose them.

Words move us into literacy, and there they gain another kind of authority. We often take it to be an authority we possess over our world, and that's partly true, but words simultaneously create an authority over us, and the world that we can have. Literacy, even more than spoken words, can further arrogate 'reality' to purely human utility and distance us from the living continuum. And yet it can create the way back to its immediate, unforsaken embrace as well. Think poetry, for example! And when you think poetry, you can think koan as well, because both speak to what cannot be said. And both expect language to be strong enough to *mend* the interrupted continuum between consciousness and what is real and whole. Restoring us to the state of becoming its living connective tissue once again.

If this sounds complicated or mind-bending, rest assured that once you manage to let a koan bend your mind a little, things actually feel oddly more straightforward. Think of it as a wonderful form of adult play with the strictures of consciousness. It's like Keith Johnstone's 'impro' game in which you rush around the room loudly calling out wrong names for things. People report that after five or six minutes of ardently misnaming the world, everything and everybody looks brighter, bigger, more present.

Names and words are seriously powerful. Nature writer Barry Lopez once talked with Japanese novelist Kazumasa Hirai about how to behave as a writer and storyteller who cares about the world. In conversation about this with Bill Moyers, Lopez said Kazumasa told him to look after the 'spiritual interior' (*kotodama*) of the language. That each word is a vessel carrying something ineffable, and that when you use words you become the caretaker for that. Koans are caretakers in that spirit.

The brilliance of a koan is that when we lose ourselves in the right way, it can return to us—and return us to—the spiritual interior of words, the inconceivable secreted in every word spoken.

Lost and found in the best way

If 'losing your self' sounds rather abstract or daunting, the experience is not even slightly so. The sense of self dramatically spills free from all understood boundaries into all that can be perceived, finding no seams or edges, no beginnings or ends, each thing bright and particular, entirely itself and at the same moment blessedly emptied of any limited identity—flowing with sheer being instead of solid with fixed identity. Every single thing brings the whole of creation with it, astonishing yet deeply familiar.

This experience in sharp form can feel like a sudden breaking free into an amazed self with no beginning or end, released from the laughably small place in which you had confined yourself for reasons unknown. There is nothing that is not also you and so, in truth, nothing to fear. This is known as beginner's mind because it is so fresh and open, not 'knowing' like an expert but rippling with the creative vitality children enjoy, yet with full adult awareness brought to bear on the playfulness.

Of course as the experience fades, the more familiar 'you' will gradually resume taking centre stage of consciousness. You need a confident sense of yourself to navigate a complex human world, but you can never entirely forget the undivided reality that the intuitive aspect of consciousness has glimpsed and, in glimpsing, confirmed. You can't forget your true self any more than an animal can forget what it is and how to be itself. For when you see yourself clearly, the whole world is radically revised by that seeing. It has found out how to be whole in you again.

However, the practice of mind needs to be kept up, never taken for granted. What unfolds is a fascinating exploratory, an open-ended relationship with reality. It resumes any time you grow quiet enough to look in on how things are, rather than how you'd like them to be. It is a habit of being attentive, willing and resilient within the flow of all things in constant change, including the mind itself.

You really can't step into the same river twice, as Heraclitus said, not only because it never stops flowing but also because you can't step into the same *you* twice, if you really look closely.

Fresh access to a flexible, non-fixated, creative and playful state of mind, born as the whole earth and, like it, at home in an open-ended, unfinished universe—this is what every koan calls up.

The fight for the restoration of a whole earth demands nothing less.

PART V

A MEDICINE BUNDLE OF KOANS

Chapter Eleven

On opening the bundle

Long life, honey in the heart, no evil, and thirteen thankyous.

Old Mayan blessing

A 'medicine bundle' is a kind of tool-kit for shifting consciousness back in the direction of wholeness.

It is traditionally a miscellaneous collection of odd items—say, animal hair, a pine cone, seeds, resin, small carvings, arrowheads, beads, tobacco, teeth or claws, feathers, stones—things deemed to be of spiritual value in healing and transforming consciousness. Each of them might seem ordinary and incidental at a quick glance, but once in the field of a medicine bundle they grow more strange and begin to relate efficaciously to each other and to the world they interact with. In fact, they seem to have the power to bring the whole world with them. A resinous pine cone, half-opened, its beautifully formed structure revealed in a state of becoming, is a revelation of the nature of this world. As is the hand that holds it. Medicine bundles can look quite odd when you first unfold them. But that's okay. You look quite odd too at first, as you break back into reality. Their other virtue is their size—they are small, and can be easily carried with you as you go.

In this case it is a small bundle of portable koans.

I will do what I can to tap on the words and help break them open a little, perhaps enough to let the koan begin to take an interest in you. Your job is to enter the world of the koan the way a story invites you in, and to let it inhabit you freely, keeping company with you the way a song might, letting it nudge or prod your habitual way of thinking into getting out of the way for a moment.

You can make yourself available to a koan in a number of ways, all of them valuable. For example, you can say the koan out loud to yourself, quite loudly, possibly a number of times, allowing the words to grow a little strange the way words tend to do when you repeat them. The more outlandish it sounds the better. Take your cue here from Alice in Wonderland when she protested to the Red Queen that 'One can't believe impossible things!' The Red Queen told her she simply hadn't had enough practice. 'Why, sometimes I've believed as many as six impossible things before breakfast!' she briskly told Alice. Feel free to sing the words, shout them, whisper them, or even act or dance them out. The important thing is to let the koan into you almost bodily, before thought or self-consciousness steps in and starts finding fault. With any koan, you have nothing to lose but your dignity, and that's a small price for your mind, whole.

An equally fine way to take up a koan is to sit quietly and read or speak it to yourself before meditating for half an hour or so—not so much upon the koan as in its resonant company. Keep company with the koan not just while meditating, but in all kinds of circumstances. On a bus full of strangers, or alone on a windswept beach, if you are keeping company with 'What is my original face?' then you will carry that in your chest and belly as you sit or walk, heart and senses open, not so much looking to find an 'answer', as seeing what the koan wants to do with you.

And in the finest spirit of koan introspection, experiment! For example, if you are keeping company with 'Shakyamuni touches the earth', you might want to do what Aboriginal elder Aunty Maureen Smith taught a number of us to do on a women's retreat: walk until you find the place that seems to want you to sit down there on the ground. Take a few quiet breaths and then touch the ground with your fingertips, easing them a little way into the earth itself, and say aloud, 'Hello, mother, this is your (daughter/son) saying hello to you,' giving your name. Wait for the response.

Every koan yields not so much answers to a question as responses from some deeper part of you that resolve the tension the koan had created. Trust every honest response that has a little bit of a shock of something new about it. Share the process with others, take up a koan in company with others and pool your findings. If you can meet in the classical dialogue situation of a Zen teacher and student, you can take this process much further, but in any case, no koan sincerely accepted as an offer ever stops opening. It shares that character with the universe itself.

My hope is that you will let each one find you exactly where you are, and in letting them engage you, help you back to your share of the playful confidence of human being in shape-shifting form: enlarged, at home on the planet, free to move in unexpected ways, willing even to be ridiculous and to fail. For each of these koans can call you back into what it is to be fully human, and how that might serve the great work of minding the earth. They may look rather slight and unlikely, but in a medicine bundle, everything relates, and that is what brings the whole back to life.

The thirteen koans are drawn from Zen and other places and chosen for their mutual power to return us to the mind of the earth, which is not only friendly to your life but has never been apart from it. Each of these koans is a matter to be resolved, or made clear. Once I woke from a dream with the words, 'Dreams are real till it rains.' *Realising* a koan is real rain falling right through waking up the dream. And 'making it clear' is becoming unable to respond except completely as yourself.

Every koan is a free gift, ripe to be remembered and passed along. When on earth, do as the earth does. As Walt Whitman said:

> The earth does not withhold, it is generous enough.
> The truths of the earth continually wait,
> They are not concealed, either—
> They are calm, untransmissible by print,
> They are imbued through all things,
> Conveying themselves willingly . . .

Fourteen koans, then—a baker's dozen, free for the taking, and an extra one for good luck.

Unnumbered. The koan *mu*

Explanatory note: You'll meet Zhaozhou more formally, below. With this koan, no explanatory note will ever stick.

The koan: **A monk asked Zhaozhou, 'Does a dog have Buddha nature, or not?' Zhaozhou replied, '*Mu*.'**

'*Mu*' is the Japanese way of rendering the Chinese character '*Wu*', which can be taken to mean 'No' or, even less than that, something like the prefix 'un-'. In the context of the monk asking whether a dog has Buddha nature or not, '*mu*' is saying, 'No, it does not have nor not have Buddha nature.' So *mu* marks the spot where you begin to dig for the fundamental self-nature that you (or a dog) can neither have nor not have. Can you either have or not have the universe?

The word is less a word than a greatly truncated expression of the whole universe and your own self-nature. It is the tiny and immense turning word that is often the first koan ever taken up by a person following the Zen path.

A turning word is some form of verbal provocation that spins you around 180 degrees to face yourself directly, if you let it. *Mu* is called 'the gateless gate', because while it lets us back into the fullness of reality that we had somehow locked ourselves out from, the moment that lock-out gate is open it becomes perfectly plain that it never existed.

It is a 'no-gate'.

Your job is to resolve not a question about dogs but the obvious and impossible question, implied here, which is 'What is *mu*?' Every great existential question is caught up in your search. What is reality? Who are you? What is this? And every minor non-existential one, too. Why is this so uncomfortable? When is this annoying koan going to leave me in peace? (The answer is, 'It's not.')

Mu throws you back into beginner's mind. It lets you approach and touch the really big question as something as close and personal as your innermost self. But the way *mu* works is by cutting you off at every pass, just saying 'no' to every idea you try to have about it. Thus you can approach and touch it only in terms of what is *not* the case, and for which you have *no* words. It makes you tongue-tied. Nothing, but nothing, sticks to *mu*. Finding your way into great doubt and not-knowing becomes the only relief from ordinary doubt (this is hopeless, makes no sense; I am hopeless, make no sense; this is just a nasty little torture trap for the mind; I can't do anything with this).

When you truly can't do anything with *mu*, you are actually finally getting somewhere quite interesting.

At some point, this state of being implacably blocked by *mu* becomes oddly freeing. You go about putting *mu* like a joyful torch to everything you experience. You let the no-dog into the house to gulp down his no-breakfast. You walk down the no-street and look into all the suddenly mysterious no-faces of other people. You notice you are feeling a touch of no-blues today. You look in the mirror and see for the first time no-you.

You start to see the spaces between things, the place where things are not, as charged with presence. What if nothing is what you had thought? The barriers are falling.

When *mu* 'breaks open', as we say, because the feeling of release and an overwhelming 'yes' is immense, it is everywhere and in plain view to all the senses and the entire body and mind, no more hidden than the air ever was. How did it pass unnoticed right under our noses for so long—the medicine bundle of this whole universe? Nothing but *mu*.

Enough said about *mu*. In any case there is neither a koan anywhere that is not also the koan *mu*, nor a thing or being anywhere that does not already fully disclose its nature.

Basho:
> Cold autumn rain
> no rain hat ~
> so?

1. Shakyamuni touches the earth

Explanatory note: Shakyamuni was the historical Buddha, who walked the earth 2500 years ago. No god, but a human being who woke up from the dream of himself and proceeded to live pretty much as one awake. In the course of this waking-up it is said that Mara visited repeatedly, trying to tempt him to abandon his quest and stay asleep. 'Mara' means variously delusion, destruction, death—you've probably noticed how these all work rather closely together. Even seen simply as our own resistance to waking up, Mara can certainly be persistent.

The koan: **When Shakyamuni meditated beneath the Bodhi Tree, Mara pointed to the place where he sat and demanded, 'Who witnesses and confirms your right to the seat of enlightenment?' Shakyamuni reached down and touched the ground with his fingertip. 'I call the earth as my witness,' he replied.**

The story goes on to say that with this, the earth shook, flowers rained down, the earth goddess herself emerged half from the ground (after all, earth cannot ever fully 'emerge' from what she already is), attesting to and sanctioning the right of the Buddha— of any one of us!—to enlightenment.

But you don't need to get fancy for this koan to set you on a path of minding the earth. Stay for a moment with this powerful image of contact, the touch of human finger pointing to and meeting with the fully responsive earth. A fingertip is highly sensitive body and consciousness combined. Explore the *charge* in that. Michelangelo's image of the moment of creation of human beings has the fingertip of God reaching down to touch the extended fingertip of Adam. There's a two-way flow there—Adam reaches towards God in mirror image, though one is above, one below.

In this koan, Shakyamuni asserts that the ground and source of his being is not separate from the earth, and that the ground of his being, earth itself *is* his waking up. Earth and fingertip—touch and confirmation—are interchangeable. Who can finally say who reaches out to whom, and whether earth confirms the waking-up, or waking-up confirms the earth?

Look all the way into this trusting, tender, fearless touch of human flesh-and-bone re-igniting full contact with the responsive earth. How badly this needs to be restored to the understanding of what it is to be human, and sharing the address Planet Earth, Solar System, Milky Way, The Universe, Mind of God . . .

Meditate on your own hands and feet of flesh and bone as a miracle of the earth. Where did they come from? Do you understand the full marvel of such business as 'sitting on the earth', 'sitting under a tree', or 'walking on the earth'? In walking meditation, some say a flower grows under every footstep that touches the earth as if for the first time, feeling into it with every one of the twenty-six bones of the foot, presuming nothing. The earth returns the favour in full—exactly meeting the foot or fingertip, fully returning the intimate contact, with an equal touch addressed to the awareness of the human being.

If we write off this affinity and mutuality as 'mere' gravity, that simply renames the mystery. Dante wisely named the force that sculpts all form and maintains the dynamic holding patterns of the universe, 'the Love that moves the stars and the other planets'.

It's the earth that gives us ourselves, and the earth that gives us back ourselves—by which I mean *wakes* us—when we can reduce our human noise enough to stop drowning out the signal. And at that moment of such deep response, it seems the earth has always been calling to us. Such generosity deserves to be returned. It's good to ask—does this action I might take, or situation I am in, meet with the terms and suit the spirit of the earth, or not? Does it 'cultivate a mind to follow Nature, and return to Nature', as Basho recommended?

Waking up certainly does so! Waking up goes as far as sharing one mind with the earth—literally *minding* the earth.

Walt Whitman understood what the Buddha, alone under the

Bodhi Tree, confirmed when he called on the unparalleled generosity of the earth to help him break free from a too-small dream of himself:

> Whoever you are! You are he or she for whom
> the earth is solid and liquid,
> You are he or she for whom
> the sun and moon hang in the sky,
> For none more than you are the present and the past . . .
> No one can acquire it for another—not one;
> No one can grow for another—not one.

Basho:
> Field of cotton ~
> as if the moon
> had flowered.

2. Asan's rooster

Explanatory note: Asan was an enlightened laywoman in Shinano who, late in life, encountered the towering Zen teacher, Hakuin. Hakuin greeted her simply by silently holding up one hand. Asan immediately responded, 'Even better than hearing Hakuin's sound of one hand, let's clap both hands and do some real business!' Hakuin was delighted to accede.

The koan: **Asan was a laywoman who studied Zen with Master Tetsumon, unremitting in her devotion to practice. One day during her morning sitting she heard the crow of the rooster and her mind suddenly opened. She spoke a verse in response:**

'The fields, the mountains, the flowers and my body too
are the voice of the bird—
what is left that can be said to hear?'
Master Tetsumon acknowledged her enlightenment.

As one always blessed by not one but *two* roosters in my morning sit, I can understand Asan losing track of everything she thought she was with the help of a rooster. We did have three, but a fox snapped up the exceedingly handsome Jubal Farnsworth when he rushed to defend two of his hens deep in meditation upon their eggs.

That left young Pericles, *not* a hen after all but very beautiful, and his pal, Shadrach, who makes up for stumpy tail plumes with a pompous way of walking. There's no choice at six in the morning but to enjoy their cries that claim the whole world—repeatedly. But the creek music flows right through, the wind, too. At best there's no irritated person left to hear; at worst, handy reminders to get out of my own way.

To meet Asan where she is, you have to discover what 'unremitting' and repeated practice might be like. And then the chance of discovering what she meant by 'no one left to hear' becomes distinctly possible.

Repetition can be useful—the word 'practice' already implies something about that. But roosters take it further. They know what an acoustician like Murray Schafer knows, which is that there is no harm whatsoever in repeating a good sound.

After all, no natural sound ever comes again: each appearance in the world is its own freely accepted extinction.

'Repetition never analyses but merely insists,' says Schafer (also on behalf of roosters). 'Repetition makes the listener participate not by comprehending it but by *knowing* it.' When we find the centre, this whole body becomes an ear, and with no impediment of thought, sounds can at last bring the world whole, *knowing* it.

And it is the *whole* world that finds out the true person.

Not only roosters can deliver this lucky break but the creak of a floorboard, the clink of china, somebody's sneeze in the early morning—any sound that finds little or nothing left of you to stir and follow after it but just fills you completely can let you in directly to the shocking open secret: 'What is left that can be said to hear?'

For the Zen Master Ikkyu it was not roosters but a crow calling in the early morning as he lay in a rowboat on Lake Biwa: KARRRHHHHH!!!! How generously they give themselves away, holding nothing back, these wondrous forms of 'nothing left to hear'. Always at hand to ease us back completely into 'fields, the mountains, the flowers and my body too'. What is that body, at such a moment?

And how patiently they wait for us, the cries of the world, always ready to meet us when we suddenly let ourselves back in. Calling out repeatedly, just to let us hear what love sounds like when there is nothing attached to it. Like the girl in the old Chinese folksong, who knew her lover was somewhere out there in the dark, so she called time and again for no good reason to her maid, just so her lover could hear her voice. 'Little Jade! Little Jade!'

AURrroockkkauurrrocckkkarrrrhooooooooOOOOOOooo!!!

No-one. No-thing. No-rooster. No-me. Not even fields, mountains, flowers; waves gently slapping the sides of a wooden boat; though they're here, too.

But look, it's not just about lying back and having the whole world advance and confirm your utterly unexpected self as the cry of a bird. It's what you do next. When the mind suddenly opens, the cries of the world grow no less acute. Ask Kuanyin, goddess of mercy, who hears all the cries of the world with no picking and choosing, no barrier in her heart.

The hen, it is said in Chinese lore, listens with her heart to hatch her eggs: a useful pointer to the ripening of a practice. And listen well, says the hen. We don't know when we will be snatched by one fox or another.

In a world on the brink of crumbling in mass extinctions, how will you actualise the cry of the rooster with this whole great body and mind, of fields, mountains and flowers? As Zen Master Linji said, 'When you know who you are then you can be of some use.'

You won't be alone. Asan will be there, and one or two roosters, in fact we're *all* in this together. The helpful ongoing cry of the world. How vast it is. How important to tune in. And how interesting 'you' turn out to be!

Basho:
> Sparrows in eaves
> mice in ceiling ~
> celestial music.

3. Welcome

The koan: **A student asked, 'When times of great difficulty visit us, how should we meet them?' The master replied, 'Welcome.'**

At the end of his masterful story, 'The Dead', James Joyce has the famous passage that begins, '. . . Snow was general all over Ireland.' It goes on to follow the snow falling softly everywhere, into the little waves of the Liffey, onto the pickets of fences, deep into the hollows of graves . . . Somehow we know this to be mercy, falling softly and equally on the just and the unjust, without distinction. A general amnesty.

Likewise in the koan: 'Welcome' is extended without discriminating worthy from unworthy. First it welcomes the question which itself, whether consciously or not, receives and extends the welcome that is everywhere too. How should we meet the crowding difficulties on our earth? May welcoming them be our only choice, if recoiling from them is the invitation for planetary emergency to become planetary disaster?

'Welcome' is a bold use of consciousness rather than a way of being polite. To commit to a practice of mind begins to return the *welcome* that is already apparent in your sheer existence. When you practise 'Welcome' you can try breathing it into every out breath, regardless of any preferences about what is currently happening. When you extend that impartial welcome, preferences start to seem like small change. Just bits and pieces of little value that will rattle about and weigh you down.

And if you relax your thoughts, grow still and look closely, the 'Welcome' offered with each breath starts to *discover* welcome, picking it up everywhere—in the way the skittish breeze picks up the leaves and has them take off across the grass, delighting the pup. It finds the welcome freely available in just what is.

Difficult times are surely visiting us. Polar bears would agree. Cool-climate species clambering in hasty retreat up warming mountainsides would agree. Islands of plastic swirling in the middle of the ocean would seem to bear it out too. Even in difficulty, the koan tells us, maybe especially then: extend the welcome. And not just because there's nothing much to admire about running from it. Big-heartedness and fearlessness come in together across the welcome mat. Which, if you look, both welcomes whatever comes visiting *and* equally welcomes you back into the world, every time you step out from closed habits of mind.

The koan seems to think that even in difficulty you are free to not just offer but to *find* the welcome. 'Welcome' means don't protect your self from what's true. Akira Kurosawa tells of his mentor, film director Kajiro Yamamoto, chastising him for covering a moment of ignorance by pretending to know the meaning of two characters on a sign, a minor detail on the film set. "'You must not say irresponsible things. If you don't know, say you don't know." I had no reply,' Kurosawa wrote in his autobiography. 'These words have stayed with me. Even today I can't forget them.'

The welcome offered to what is true keeps us honest, alert, less likely to cut ourselves out of it. 'I don't know' is an open door to exploring the welcome. The alternative quietly clicks shut and locks us in.

Many teachers suggest you take your own inventory. Not a bad thing to do in the dark sometimes, while also softly knowing you are breathing in and breathing out. Look back at your day— what motivated you in this moment or that one? Kindness? Fear? Indifference? When did you feel yourself stepping outside the welcome? What were those brief moments of feeling perfectly at rights, entirely welcome here? Could it just be feeling water running over your skin and needing nothing more, gazing from the window for a few moments of wanting nothing. In every open moment, the welcome slips in.

'Welcome' can test and demand patience, but a peaceable mind is a crowning advantage when times of great difficulty visit. It's not immediately easy to accept insult and injury without becoming injured and insulted. But if you can truly sense that you are welcome here without qualification, there may be no great need to be insulted or injured. Then the way to be and act is unconstricted.

Most human insults will be nothing in a hundred years, but our collective insult to the earth threatens to mean even more in a hundred years than now, delivered to the generations who follow us. We're choosing the world our descendants will have to bear. What must 'Welcome' grow to encompass in this powerful light? If we don't rouse ourselves to recover our manners as a species and rediscover how to extend the welcome to the earth and all who share it with us, the welcome that the earth extends to us, how will we live with ourselves?

Death may be the final welcome we need to find in this bodily life. But even then, 'final' is hard to find. Think of the resolution of the 1972 Stockholm Conference, precursor to the 1997 Kyoto Accord: 'Life holds to one central truth: that all matter and energy needed for life moves in great closed circles from which nothing escapes . . . moved through vast chains of plants and animals and back again to the beginning.'

The earth hides nothing about how to live with it, with our mortality, and with each other—and so even with our selves! When we know ourselves we know the earth—*that's* the fullness of the welcome. Walt Whitman once more:

> The earth does not argue,
> is not pathetic, has no arrangements,
> does not scream, haste, persuade, threaten, promise,
> makes no discriminations, has no conceivable failures,
> closes nothing, refuses nothing, shuts none out.

But in the face of the depth of insult offered to the earth by *our* arguments, arrangements, screams, haste, threats, promises, discriminations and failures, the form that its resilience takes this time may not fit inside human plans at all. The 'Welcome' will go on, but we may not be here to return it. Better start to return it now.

Basho:

    Coolness of the melons
    mud flecked
    in morning dew

4. All over the body, hands and eyes

Explanatory note: Yunyan (780–841) and Daowu (769–835) were both Tang dynasty Zen masters of great note. In Buddhism, Kuanyin, the Bodhisattva of Great Mercy, embodies compassion as the wisdom of non-separation. She is said to hear all the cries of the world, and is often depicted with many (read 'countless') arms reaching out to alleviate suffering, each furnished with an *eye* in the palm of the hand. Awake and free of self-consciousness, responding without hesitation to the cries of the world direct and in person—that's compassion.

The koan: **Yunyan asked Daowu, 'How does Kuanyin use those many hands and eyes?' Daowu answered, 'It's like someone in the middle of the night reaching behind her head for a pillow.' Pressed to explain his understanding he said, 'All over the body are hands and eyes.'**

In the Song of Solomon comes the beautiful line, 'I sleep, but my heart wakes . . .'

Waking up happens when the sense of self finally drops off to sleep. Exactly as that subsides, an entirely natural ease and immediacy begins to open in the heart. 'Like reaching for a pillow in the middle of the night'—how simple and natural real help is, not straining to do good or disturb anybody, just helping everything be more at home and at ease. Kindness, like ripeness, is all.

What if the powerful correction needed to avert calamity in the course of post-industrial human life were also as simple and natural as this? Is it possible? How can we get all the way back down to that level of sanity and coherence? The koan suggests how: 'All over the body are hands and eyes.' Where's the 'doing' then?

Zen teacher Katsuki Sekida gives a glimpse into 'where' when describing an old priest close to the end of his life. The man, who lived by himself, had been ill, and was mostly just sitting quietly and basking in the winter sun by the window, occasionally composing a haiku. In the course of his conversation with Sekida, he pointed to a pine grove in front of the temple and said, 'You know the Zen question, "The Bodhisattva of Great Mercy has a thousand hands and a thousand eyes; which is the true eye?" I could not understand this for a long time. But the other day when I looked at the pine trees bending before the cold blasts from the mountain, I suddenly realised the meaning. You see, all the boughs, branches, twigs, and leaves simultaneously bend to the wind with tremendous vigour.' He made some quiet, earnest bodily gesture as he spoke and Sekita could see his intimacy with the pine trees. Sekita saw that he was in the evening glow of his life. He died a few weeks after that meeting.

As a child I recall lots of moments when I did not really know for sure where I stopped and the grass or mud or sky began—didn't you? This *body* covered in hands and eyes is very big. It turns out to be so much bigger than my skin and bones or yours, yet does not leave me or you out. Every leaf in the wind is included, along with the scatter of red hens on the green grass, and the mountain looking on. Everything moves together, and when that is so, in a deep sense nothing moves. An ecology in its state of balance is like that.

So, too, the sensitivity of the body in meditation is like that. Helpful hands and awake eyes all over the body and right throughout as well.

When looking for a way out of paralysing fear and confusion at the immensity of the problem we are facing now, much can be entrusted to the hands and eyes all over the body of the earth, for we too are made of this responding even before thought of responding arrives. The 'tremendous vigour' the old priest saw in the soughing branches of the pines, bending as one in the wind, comes back to each of us when the sense of 'I' begins to relax away from resisting reality so hard ('I sleep . . .').

When this happens ('. . . but my heart wakes . . .'), we find ourselves right at home with our fellow beings in the vast net of life, all in it together. And this 'it' has no beginning or end, front or back, up or down. Just looking at us, all so different, you'd never know we're family. Just joining us, it's very plain.

Kuanyin could easily be mistaken for our singular blue-green planet swimming in space, blooming with life, the most vivid expression of interdependency yet found in the universe. Now, how will you align your mind with a mind like that?

Tim DeChristopher, in his inspiring speech to the court when sentenced to two years in federal prison and a $10,000 fine for the crime of disrupting a Utah Bureau of Land Management auction in 2008 in order to preserve a fragile ecology from destruction of oil and gas exploration leases on public lands, shows what 'hands and eyes all over the body' might look like in these later days:

Those who are inspired to follow my actions are those who understand that we are on a path toward catastrophic consequences of climate change. They know their future, and the future of their loved ones, is on the line. And they know we are running out of time to turn things around. The closer we get to that point where it's too late, the less people have to lose by fighting back. The power of the Justice Department is based on its ability to take things away from people. The more that people feel that they have nothing to lose, the more that power begins to shrivel. The people who are committed to fighting for a liveable future will not be discouraged or intimidated by anything that happens here today.

And neither will I. I will continue to confront the system that threatens our future. Given the destruction of our democratic institutions that once gave citizens access to power, my future will likely involve civil disobedience. Nothing that happens here today will change that. I don't mean that in any sort of disrespectful way at all, but you don't have that authority. You have authority over my life, but not my principles. Those are mine alone . . . At this point of unimaginable threats on the horizon, this is what hope looks like. In these times of a morally bankrupt government that has sold out its principles, this is what patriotism looks like. With countless lives on the line, this is what love looks like, and it will only grow. The choice you are making today is what side are you on.

Writer and former Zen monk, Clark Strand, pictures each species as a flame handed down, 'from deep time to deep future' by one individual to the next. The flame is protected from extinction by being passed candle to candle. It is not about protecting the self—that merely protects the candle. To protect the flame, we must protect *the other*. Everything moves together.

Life depends upon this fundamental sacrifice of self. The only way to keep any great gift is to give it away. But in full intimacy with the other, nothing can be lost. Perhaps the only way to fully restore the ancient welcome of the earth, so long ignored and trampled, is to *personally* welcome the earth's demanding difficulty right now as our own, and as vital news from home about intimacy with the other.

Basho:

Deep autumn ~
my neighbour
how's he going, I wonder

5. Your own original face

The koan: **What is your original face that was yours before even your parents were born?**

I once heard an account of a treaty signing, high above the snow-line, between a party of Indians and a party of soldiers. The soldiers arrived on horseback, muffled in greatcoats, scarves and fur hats against the bitter wind off deep snow, whereas the Indians, also on horseback, arrived bare-armed, with just pieces of fur slung across their bodies.

The soldiers were impressed despite themselves. 'How do you stand the cold?' the general managed to convey through his Indian interpreter. In reply, the chief of the Indian party pointed to the soldiers' bare faces. 'You do not cover face.' The general and his men were about to protest how that was different, faces being less subject to cold, when the Indian chief waved them to silence. 'Indians—all *face*,' he said.

Only the wind had anything further to say.

The *face* bears our most intimate image of ourself. It's mysterious how acutely and comprehensively we can recognise an individual from such a tiny set of features—eyes and mouth horizontal, ears and nose vertical, with minutely different shapes and distances between—and read them for subtle signs of character and telling shifts in emotional states. How together such a small set of variables can generate seven billion utterly distinct and memorable visages that matter so much and will never be seen on earth again.

The Indian chief wasn't talking about self-presentation, ego cover or saving face. 'Face' in his world evoked something very different, and long neglected in these times: a shaping of the self through years of hard and willing discipline of mind and body, in a way of life *not* carved out as far as humanly possible from 'nature' as though nature were something threatening or inhuman.

'Face' then implied the contrary—a deep accord that had been won with nature, a trust or confidence that felt somewhat mutual and returned, a quality of being calmly face to face with reality. The dignity and fearlessness of that strong presence of *face* silenced a victorious general.

'Indian, all face.' On the strength of such evidence of mutuality, could we dare to wonder 'Nature, all face', too?

The original face of you and me—what could be more personal than that? And yet what could be more public, too, always the place to which our eyes go first to know *the person*? And yet, the koan says *this* face preceded even our parents who formed it, which means we must look right into the disappearing point and final darkness of the word 'original'. The darkness in it suggests we try abandoning presupposing anything, while keeping eyes, ears, skin, heart peeled, as we proceed on in. Meditation, the practice of open awareness, is like this.

Clues to your original face will not be found in family trees—though the tree of life may be another story. However many updated photos of yourself appear on your Facebook wall, searching there will make it even harder to spot—though in truth there's nowhere it can hide from view. And while the story of your past does nothing to hide it, looking for it there will lead you astray. For that story is a question, too. The story that shores up your sense of self may identify your parents, as well as the one who must pay taxes in your name and remember to put out the garbage bins on the correct night, but your original face is not restricted in any such ways.

Seeking it is the very opposite of self-absorption. *That* mania, currently taking star billing in the world of boundless consumption, has probably always had more than enough time on the stage of the human mind. The disconnect from reality inside self-absorption can be very powerful; it seems reality can always be put aside in its favour.

But ignorance and a walled-off mind offer no amnesty from reality. Opening to reality *is* the amnesty. A breeze stirs the trees in early sunlight, dissolving last night's touch of frost into a brief glittering shimmer of leaves. Face to face, you cannot turn away.

Seeing through that disconnect is not so much a matter of self-effacement, or dwindling in scale before the immensity of nature, as recognising with simple amazement that your entire being cannot be told apart from it. Then you start to catch confirming glimpses of the original face—entirely yours—in the flashing mirror of twigs, wombat scat, droplets on bracken, washing pegged out in the breeze . . .

So take a bold look, for your original face has nowhere to hide. When you know who you *are*, then the question, 'What on earth can I do to help?' grows far less arduous and tortuous, remote. Earth's grandeur is not outside you, earth's cries are right in your own chest, earth's hand and feet are not other than your own.

'What to do' just follows on naturally from here.

Basho:

> Pine mushroom ~
> a leaf of some kind
> sticking to it

6. One treasure hidden in the body

Explanatory note: Yunmen (864–949) is the great master towering over the end of the Tang period of Zen. His brief words, struck like sparks from a flint, carried immense force, often reducing people to powerful silence. 'The whole world is medicine' are his words that initiate the entire impulse of this book.

The koan: **Yunmen said to the assembly, 'Within heaven and earth, in the midst of the cosmos, there is one treasure, hidden in the body. Holding a lantern, it goes toward the Buddha hall. It brings the great triple gate and puts it on the lantern.'**

That's *your* own body that hides the treasure (although that's not quite the end of the story). Equipped with heart and lungs working intricately together in a way that beggars the imagination; elbows that do not turn backwards; toenails that can grow unruly; limbs that fray strangely (if you think about it) into things called 'hands' and 'feet'; twenty-six separate bones in the foot; that heavy, warm, wet, foamy jelly inside the skull called 'brain', which carries the infinitely subtle touch of thought in its cells; possibly hair growing out of that head, possibly not . . .

The body in itself begins to sound like quite a treasure! With miraculous powers. For that body can sit still and quietly breathe and come to peace, inclining the mind to follow suit. It can carry a lantern and put it on the gate. The hidden, the mysterious, the essential side of everything begins to come clear right out in the open, when this kind of thing happens.

The Buddha sat his body down under the Bodhi Tree for seven days and nights, vowing not to get up until he had unearthed the treasure and come clear—radiantly so. One story says it wasn't just the human being called Shakyamuni who came brilliantly clear when he happened to glance up and see the radiant Morning Star hanging low in the sky, finally recognising himself beyond all doubt. That one treasure within heaven and earth, in the midst of the cosmos, which body was it hidden in? Buddha? Star?

Yunmen assures us there is just one treasure hidden and discoverable in this unlikely human form. What *is* this one treasure that seems to take every variation in its stride and make no distinction whatsoever? It cannot even seem to tell stars from human beings. But its powers are such that it can take the great triple gate, the elaborate set of gateways at the entrance to a temple complex, and set it down upon a fragile lantern. Now that needs looking into!

But in fact, even 'body' needs looking into. How is your body or mine finally distinct from, say, the grass that raised the cow that gave the milk that made the cheese you ate for breakfast? Or from the rain and soil that grew the grass, or from the rivers, glaciers, winds, rot, worms that made the soil? Or before that, the vulcanism that poured lava into mountains of intricate mineral composition? Or the infinite lineage of ancestors living and dying, and the thousands of marvellous errors and inventions that shaped the genomes that led all the way down to you, me, cow, earthworm . . .? Or the supernova that exploded to give birth to the sun and Planet Earth? What final distinctions can survive the scrutiny of the heart and mind looking into what lies 'hidden' in plain view?

Butterflies are not left out of you any more than the sound of creek water rushing smoothly over its rocks. Not with this in mind but with *this mind*, the one treasure is disclosed to your heart. Four blue and purple king parrots just flashed from one green branch to another. Four gorgeous parrots, one treasure. Now our handsome Sussex rooster, Pericles, arrives importantly beside me on the verandah, friendly in his shyly offhand way. Five birds then, and me. One treasure. Or even less than one.

Everything that is comes out of nothing and goes back in again. Not one thing exists without all the others. And these 'others' are finally hard to find. When you really look, and turn all its pockets inside out, this whole great body of form turns out to be marvellously empty of defendable distinctions. That's so even given the fact that your fingerprints have never been seen on earth before, and never will again.

Is this strange set of circumstances the real source of the efficacy and accomplishment displayed by everything? Take the miracle of walking on the earth, placing one foot, lifting the other and then placing that one, shifting your weight forward, falling and not falling with every step. Once you bring your attention to it, like anything else, it grows astonishing—leaving you little time for anything else.

This effortless power of knowing how to move your hands and feet: where does it come from? And how wonderfully well we are constantly using it.

Sometimes, for no reason, you can suddenly see that to be as compelling as it really is. Once, towards the end of a road trip, still under the light trance of a long drive, I slowed at an intersection and saw two people coming to a halt as they waited to cross. They were gently—but suddenly mysteriously—still *swinging* their arms slightly as they talked. Have you ever tripped over how strange, beautiful and unlikely *swinging* is? Involving *arms*, whatever they really are? I found tears in my eyes. What they were doing, and how wonderfully well they were doing it with no thought of doing anything at all. Astonishing.

This one treasure hidden in the body—it is remarkable over and over again.

The natural world endows everything with this original efficacy, and when we go with it we find everything using it impeccably. So rising to the occasion of the long emergency may not seem so impossible once we stop supposing anything and meet it, together with our selves, straight on.

And it's some occasion! In the ancient image of the jewelled net of the Indian god Indra, reality is an infinite net holding everything that is, holding vast emptiness, with a uniquely faceted gem set into every knot in the net. Each of these treasures (each being) reflects in every one of its dazzling facets every other jewel in the net. And each jewel is the exact centre of the entire net that radiates from it in every direction without end.

It doesn't get much better than this. My seven-year-old self knew this completely. Yours too.

So the one treasure hidden in the body: What if you can use it forever but never exhaust the sheer joy and unlikelihood of its magical powers? Children's dreams are made of such stuff. Adult reality is the business of making excellent use of it.

One treasure, and all seven billion of us possess it from the beginning. No need to be stingy, then, in rising to the occasion.

Basho:

> I don't know
> which tree it's coming from ~
> that fragrance!

7. You'll never single it out

Explanatory note: Zhaozhou (778–897) was one of the great figures of Tang dynasty (618–905) China, which witnessed the 'golden age' of Zen (in Chinese: 'Chan'). It was said that a light played about his lips as Zhaozhou spoke. He lived to the ripe age of one hundred and twenty, and certainly took his time agreeing to teach, finally no longer refusing that role at the age of eighty.

The koan: **A monk asked Zhaozhou, 'What is the fact for which I must accept responsibility?' Zhaozhou replied, 'Though you search to the ends of time, you'll never single it out.'**

How reassuring, old Zhaozhou. Oh, boy, but also how demanding!

Is he telling us that only if I can legitimately find the beginning or end to 'me', will I ever be able to find a beginning or end to that which I must accept as 'my responsibility'?

Take old school photos. You scan the dim line of tiny faces for the one you love (but did not meet for several more decades), or for your brother, sister, best friend, and—from the generalising blur of the past suddenly out leaps that irreplaceable being, stamped and charged with unrepeatable life. Even if the one you look for now is dead, no difference. What responsibility that must be accepted comes with this potent charge of possessing a singular life?

Sharon Olds wrote a poem about seeing her child off to summer camp. The child disappears into the tinted gloom of the bus with all the other identikit teenagers, and yet of *course* she can instantly tell the exact line of jawbone, slant of hair, tilt of nose, tip of ear, that surfaces dimly at one of the dark-tinted windows as the bus makes off with her fledgling.

That lurch of a parent's heart. What a vast responsibility it is.

When my beautiful cat succumbed to a paralysis tick, I felt stricken for weeks, and not just by the piercing loss of her arrival onto my legs at night with a thud, the warm drugged weight of her curled dead centre in our bed, her silver-tabby markings and startling blue eyes so cool in the ermine luxury of her fur, and that one endearing split ear-tip earned in a street fight back in feisty young-cat days . . . A whole year later I still feel the drag of my failure to find the tick in time, to catch her safely in the net of my love, and never ever let her slip away to so terrible a premature death. Responsibility hurts like love.

When the whole exquisitely wrought balance of our astounding blue-green world begins to crumble before our eyes under the weight of so many billions of us straining to live so far beyond the physical means of the earth, then 'the fact for which I must accept responsibility' is so vast that it either threatens to become the final shame from which there can be no recovery, or else offers to be the making of me as a human being.

But what if we fail? In the spirit of the earth, the jury is never quite in on 'success' or 'failure'. Earth herself is by nature unfinished, and besides, the time frame of this matter exceeds (by many magnitudes) a human lifetime.

In any case, can there be failure if the undertaking is to let this crisis be the making of us? Maybe the only failure possible is not turning up to claim life while it is still on offer.

Seven billion of us now, and yet even if you search to the end of time you can never single one of us out. This is the natural source of all generosity. In one of the Hassidic stories, a teacher asked, 'How do you know when night has ended and the day has begun?' Someone ventured, 'Is it that moment when you can't tell the morning mist from the clouds?' 'No, it is not that moment,' said the teacher. 'Is it when each tree begins to step out from the hillside, distinct?' The teacher did not accept that either. 'Then how *do* you know when night has ended and the day has begun?' they asked at last. 'It is that moment when you look into the face of another and can recognise yourself,' said the teacher. 'Until then, the night is still with us.'

The first and most comprehensive of the eight *paramitas* (literally 'perfections' or completions) of enlightened behaviour in Buddhism is *dana*, or mutual generosity. *Dana* comes down to the principle that if you have something that could benefit another who needs it, giving it away benefits all. Life is lived entirely as such a gift. All life is lived courtesy only of other beings, eating and being eaten. Everything and everyone fully used up by living fully.

Lending yourself consciously to the generosity of life and death hurts far less in the end than resisting it. And resisting it hurts all life—look around at the state of the biosphere, as humanity seeks to make a quick killing from the earth rather than share ourselves with it in mutual generosity. For even if you search to the end of time, you'll never single it out.

Now is the real end point of time, though when you look for it, as with the end of the rainbow and its promised pot of gold, it constantly escapes you. Searching for our responsibility is the preoccupation of this book, and I think it properly troubles every human heart that allows itself to hurt with awareness of how we have been living.

Searching for it may be different to what we think. A few timely postcards from the future would be a great help in discovering how we get there from here. But as the old joke goes, if you ask a country bumpkin for directions to a nearby city, he'll tell you sagely, 'You can't get there from here.' He's right. We can't get anywhere sane with the thinking that has created the problem. 'Here' and 'there' are simply not on the same map.

Consider the way a dog proceeds from here to there, nose to the ground, imagination on fire, intently haphazard, *dancing* the trail of a scent, disdaining nothing on the way, as Denise Levertov describes it in her poem 'Overland to the Islands'. Proceeding in this way is a kind of joy, 'every step an arrival', and every arrival a fresh suggestion about a possible way to the next. One step (leap, pounce, twirl) at a time is surely the only way to get anywhere.

Basho:
> When I look carefully ~
> shepherd's purse in flower
> beneath the hedge!

8. Do you mean now?

Explanatory note: Once you've seen through one thing all the way to the end, koans come to be found everywhere. Two small kids talking in the lane beside me at the swimming pool gave me one not long ago. 'I can't see with these goggles!' complained one. 'They can see you but!' said the other, just like that. Yogi Berra was a legendary generator of accidental koans. How accidental, no one quite knows. 'I didn't really say everything I said,' he once explained. A major baseball player for the New York Yankees, possibly the greatest catcher of all times, he advised, 'When you come to a fork in the road, take it.' So, let's take it.

The koan: **When Yogi Berra was asked, 'What time is it?' he asked, 'Do you mean now?' It's a good question, though it made everyone laugh at the time.**

The vast majority of climate scientists concur that we have prevaricated dangerously for the past two decades and, yes, the planet does mean *now*! There is no more time to kill. Though that does not mean there is no time for human laughter too, and fun.

But what does 'now' mean? If the planet means now, and in an increasingly forthright way, could we look into Yogi Berra's question a little further and see that it equally asks, 'Does now mean *you*?'

Zen Master Dogen wrote an astonishing, mind-bending fascicle on time in thirteenth-century Japan called 'Being Time', sometimes translated as 'Time Being'. Essentially, it asks: can you drop free of a divided mind in which time is an external force that wears away all things and makes life unbearably precarious? Can you then sense how you are neither actually 'in time' nor 'subject to time'? Rather, when you look without certainty strapped onto your wrist like a tiny implacable god, can you see how time cannot be other than you; and you cannot be other than one thing continually becoming another? Which means there is no time but you. And you are now.

'Impermanence' sounds like the opposite of permanence, but—take a close look!—it *has* no opposite, there is nothing to oppose. That all things are passing through and nothing is fixed is the revelation of this universe in every one of its details. When you take to heart that you cannot step outside the ceaseless movement of one thing into another, the strange thing is that suddenly you free yourself within it. A tremendous fight with your very nature can finally be put down.

To put it another way, when you can dare explore and inhabit your own precariousness without reserve, you become precariousness itself—and can find nothing lacking there, nothing to oppose or fear. How freeing!

In Russell Hoban's wonderful *La Corona and the Tin Frog*, much loved by the adults who read it to their children, a collection of discarded childhood treasures long ago relegated to a forgotten La Corona cigar box come to life at midnight. One of them, good friend of the Literary Dormouse who publishes a quarterly literary journal, is the little Night Watchman, who (when activated) puffs out small clouds of smoke as he calls the hour. His moment of realisation comes when, instead of announcing 'Eleven o'clock', 'Twelve o'clock', he proclaims with joy, '*Now* is the only time there is!' The Literary Dormouse, caught up in the revelation, immediately realises that 'Quarterly is not enough!' From now on, she's going monthly.

And the Night Watchman is right. Without short-changing the karmic weight of history even for a moment, all time is present in a real moment of peace. Try losing yourself for a while in just the watching of your own breath in, breath out—keep it up for some time and the very nature of a moment changes quality. No longer fleeting, it is neither quick nor slow to pass; it is edgeless, and edgeless is surprisingly roomy.

Like Doctor Who's tardis, the tiny moment of this breath now might look small, ordinary and predictable from the outside, but move inside it unreservedly with the whole of your sustained focus for a time and it turns out to be a very different sized space: This moment is the only time there is; it has no walls and no discernible edge of past or present. It is hard to say how small or big that is. Or how unexpectedly joyful to discover what can be here when you can find no time at all.

Practice means now, which is where life lives. Realisation happens only *now*. So does any action that helps things be the best they can be. For that matter, so does any breath.

In terms of responding to the crisis we're in, it is already pressingly late, and the appropriate sense of urgency keeps getting buried under 24/7 blather. Two and a half thousand years ago, the Taoist master Lao-tzu posed this question to his own much slower time, 'Do you have the patience to wait until your mud settles, and the water is clear? Can you remain unmoving until the right action arises by itself?'

That's not easy when it seems the sky is falling in—just ask Henny Penny!

Any crisis is an exceptional and unprecedented learning opportunity but usually we first rush for all the known and well-worn views that come to hand or are most loudly peddled. It's not easy to go into the darkness of *that which is not yet clear*, for it calls for some patience and serious mental effort—and yet it is likely to be the only fruitful place to look.

In an old story a man searches frantically for a lost key under a lamp post. A kind passer-by joins the search but no key turns up. 'Are you sure you dropped it here?' they ask. 'Oh no, it was way over there,' the man replies, pointing off into the darkness. 'Then why aren't we looking for it over there?' asks the passer-by, exasperated. The man is greatly surprised by the question. 'Because it's far too dark to see anything over there!' he explains.

When we don't know where to look for easy answers, when we agree to live right on the edge of the not yet fully known, we're far more open in all directions. Remember the hunter's mind, at peace with not knowing, while being able to stay intently aware. 'Can you remain unmoving until the right action arises by itself?' asks Lao-tzu of our age of perpetual motion and limitless ambition. 'Unmoving' does *not* mean passive—on the contrary, it means not easily tempted into presuming too much, and that can take considerable effort! Countless subtle movements of understanding go on under the surface of alert, patient waiting for the fresh intuition to arise in the mind by itself.

Another koan challenges us to 'Take up the plough with empty hands'. Is this a clue to the way that 'you' can mean 'now'? That exceptionally productive writer, Jean-Claude Carrière, once reflected that he probably gets so much accomplished only by doing each thing very, very slowly—which means as if it were the most important thing in the world and he had all the time in the world. But you can only have that when there is some contact with the coherent mind of steadiness and focus, and the trusting patience to let it resume itself. 'Unmoving' means drawing on that practised mind, while taking all due care.

Now is never too late. Plant wondrously slow-growing trees even in old age. Because now is you, the outcome luckily is not about you but the nature of the whole shebang—without which there's no you in any case, and in which you can rediscover your unlimited self ever more richly.

Basho:

Not long to live
you'd never know it ~
cicada's cry!

9. No axle, no wheels

Explanatory note: Yuean (dates unknown) was a twelfth-century Song dynasty master principally known for composing this koan. Xizhong was the legendary cartwheel maker who made hundred-spoke cartwheels—a technical feat that is simply unimaginable, clearly surpassing world's best practice and heading for best in universe. There is a faint drift here of the great wheel of the dharma with its countless spokes, turned by every wise teaching, by any beneficent action—indeed by every night sky of turning stars.

The koan: **The priest Yuean said to a monk, 'Xizhong made a hundred-spoke wheel cart. If you take off both wheels and the axle, what would be vividly apparent?'**

Some wonderful cart! Sounds like a ruin. That wouldn't get you far! How would the wheels turn when they have been removed and the axle has gone? Is this just more of the unmoving?

And yet at the very centre of a turning wheel—or universe—is indeed the utterly still point. The entire movement of the whole depends on this 'nothing happening', or from another point of view, comes down to it. In the very nature of the whole, there is nothing happening, and nowhere to go.

The verse traditionally attached to this case says, 'Where the wheel revolves even a master cannot follow it.' In order to 'follow' the movement of the spinning earth, 'the master' must first find some way to be separate from it. And at the very centre of the spinning nothing moves and there is nothing whatsoever to follow. A master cart builder depends entirely on this fact that lies at the core of his great skill, and lets everything happen from there.

But still a cart with no wheels goes nowhere fast. Actually, that sounds quite a restful, restorative antidote for a world 'engineered' into an out-of-control juggernaut with no easily locatable brakes.

This tiny word 'no' is not unlike the still point of the turning wheel. Nothing to it, and everything depending on it.

Zhaozhou, who we met a little earlier, famously said 'No' when a monk asked if a dog has Buddha nature or not. That 'no'—*mu* in Japanese—is not a categorical answer. As we have seen, it is an injunction to step past all thought of having or not having, of dog, monk, master. Even Buddha nature, the entire goal of realisation, disappears into the undivided mind of Zhaozhou.

Sometimes it is called 'vast emptiness', this experience of mind in its original freedom; other times, simply 'equality'—all-pervading, deeply felt equality that appears clearly in all things, empty of distinctions, when the walls in the mind fall away. 'No' releases everything from its mind cage and ensures that, though you searched to the end of time, you'd never single this mind out from all that is.

The dream of one thing separate from another fades away and instead of searching for release you find you've always been swimming in it.

A koan is direct transmission of the nature of reality from mind to mind. The finest made cart in the world, with wheels and the axle removed—what becomes vividly apparent then? Ecology, nature, reality—now *there's* a cart with no wheels, no axle, no separate parts, completely unmoving while so vigorously unfolding. A mind that has discovered itself in the light of the strange, unexpected sanity and wholeness of 'no'—finding there is no-self, no-me, no-dog, no-mind—is likewise unmoving and unimpeded.

Have you ever stroked a no-dog? It's worlds away from stroking a dog. It is you and the dog lost completely in sheer touch, dissolved barriers, warmth of heart, groan of pleasure, nearby hillside floating with cloud shadow, mare's-tail cloud, rough grateful lick of wet tongue, the thump, thump of a tail.

'No' can take away that which is never finished with carving up the world to fit what we think we know; 'no' can help us get back closer to the real nature of what is happening. It is a curious shape, that word, for the gateway back home.

The earth does not argue with what we think we know; it silently offers itself without opinions. While it suffers from our actions, only we can dispel our strange thought worlds that lead to so much damage. We have to do it all ourselves and in person—return to the natural terms of the earth, and the generosity inside those limits.

Once in a dream it became apparent there was a tiger outside the house in which I lived with my children, deep in the Russian woods, many miles from anywhere, and with numberless frail doors and windows that had to be quickly, frantically bolted and secured. At last the final bolt slid home—a painfully slender barricade against the massive force of tiger will. Outside, somewhere, unseen, *tiger* breathed and roamed at will. But I had made us safe. I had time to breathe again. And then, the realisation slowly dawned. I had made myself not perfectly safe but perfectly imprisoned, entombed. We never really left Eden, just fell into a dream that we are separate and that safety and security can flow from that. We're not, and it doesn't.

So 'no wheels' is prowess of a completely different kind to 'Look Ma, no hands!' A well-functioning ecology doesn't engineer a single thing, or make use of effort in the inconceivable concatenation of interrelated circumstances that sustain the whole. Can we let this prodigious 'no-thing' and 'no-action', evident everywhere in the natural world wherever we have not yet disrupted it, ease back in under our skins? Where it may provoke us to skilful response to the crisis of the planet, in greater accord with its deep ways?

The world comes whole again with the mysterious barrier-dissolving power of this tiny word 'no'. The journey from juggernaut complete with wheels, bells, whistles, the whole kit and caboodle, to finest cart in the history of the world complete with no-wheels, no-axle, is minute, a journey less than a hair's-breadth in size. It is the shift from where we think we are, to where we really are—which is the journey also from ruinous end of the Cenozoic era to actualisation of the Ecozoic era.

A tiny journey like this is hard to see only until you travel the distance (repeatedly) and become the difference. But old habits die hard, and it takes real practice to train the mind to recall its true home under all circumstances. Mahatma Gandhi trained his heart and mind to live reflexively close to Ram, the Hindu god who reminded him of his own deepest self-nature. To call on the name of Ram was to instantly return home to that understanding. When his assassin stood before him with a gun and fired its bullet, Gandhi died crying out 'Ram!' Building the practice of minding and never forgetting the earth is the journey of a lifetime. 'No!' is the shout that can call up the courage exactly equal to a crisis.

No wheels, no axles, no walls up in the mind—no walls at all, and therefore, oddly enough, no fear.

Basho:
> Cicada shell ~
> just sang itself
> completely away

10. How can we avoid cold and heat?

Explanatory note: Dongshan (807–869) was the luminary recognised as one of the founders of the Caodong (Soto) line of Zen. Together with the Linji (Rinzai) line, it is one of the two remaining Zen schools that began in China during the Tang dynasty.

The koan: **A monk asked Dongshan, 'When cold and heat visit us, how should we avoid them?' Dongshan said, 'Why not go where there is neither cold nor heat?' The monk asked, 'Where is that?' Dongshan said, 'When it is cold, kill yourself with cold. When it is hot, kill yourself with heat.'**

Thomas Berry said, 'This is not an abandoned world', and I think he is right so long as we dare to live our predicament with the same no-fear as the earth.

The fundamental vow of Buddhism is to ease suffering, protect life and save the many beings. So what is this 'killing' of the self? Some kind of merciful end to all the complaining?

In a warming world, the monk's question of how to avoid difficult climatic extremes is timely, even if it is more than a thousand years old. But is this remarkable old Zen master speaking just of climatic extremes?

If he is, then what's wrong with putting on warmer or cooler clothes—or just turning on the reverse-cycle airconditioner plugged into the coal-fired electricity grid? Is he really asking that we suffer more?

Dealing with the extremes of 'temperature' in human minds may actually be the most pressing and immediate concern in mitigating the approach of climate collapse. I mean hot states like anger, rage, shame; cold states like fear and denial. Maybe 'killing yourself' with these difficult states is a way of saying: why not try using them as a chance to see through yourself when they visit in overwhelming form?

The Buddha once asked an assembly, 'What is wisdom?' And

when nobody could reply he said, 'It is the ability to perfectly understand and patiently accept the truth of suffering.' The *truth* of suffering—that's surely a matter to look into for a lifetime or two. But what might 'looking into it' look like?

Many forms of fear seem to be paralysing us in the face of so much mounting damage—including the fear that far too few of us seem ready to admit that damage and take its consequences to heart. The one thing that may be equal to the utter hopelessness the situation can induce is the shortest prayer there is—a powerful and surprising one, once you dare embrace it: *'Fear not!'*

So, how to embrace unbearably hot and cold states without fear?

It's strong medicine to look honestly at our overwhelming predicament, care very deeply, never abandon that caring and be not afraid. A practice of mind as I have been describing it helps access a calmer, steadier sense of self that can be more at ease even in difficult circumstances because it can be strong and clear enough to remember 'I am not my thoughts and feelings'. Have a look: is the awareness of coldness, *cold*, or of heat, *hot*?

When we stumble on the fact that the awareness of anger is not angry, of confusion is not confused, of fear is not fearful, something in us is freed up.

So when calmed by an unmoving, friendly awareness, all the hot and cold states that make it hard to see clearly and act wisely reveal a surprising reservoir of energy and clarity exactly equal in strength to the predicament we're in. The intensity of our fear, anger, shame or grief about a situation is a gauge of intense caring that has been locked down, alienated from reach, waiting to be released.

Reaching this awareness, it is hard to find enduring hot or cold.

Anger can mask unexpressed fear, which in turn can mask unnameable grief. Self-justification arises and reports for duty split seconds after anger bursts its banks. It's usually wise to be sceptical about the highly detailed case that hot anger will present. The Dalai Lama, when asked why he does not appear filled with rage at

China's brutal occupation of his homeland, asked in reply, 'Should I let China rob me of my mind as well?'

If 'Fear not' can be the way to avoid 'cold', the saving grace for 'heat' may be 'Judge not'. Which is to say, don't move to declare judgment until the energy of anger has had time to bring some slightly more judicious thought to light—which might include checking on how far you can genuinely distinguish your own actions from the ones so greatly at fault. Whose fault exactly is it?

'Judge not' never means 'See nothing, discern nothing'. It points more in the direction of the famous Zen virtue of 'Not picking and choosing'—not 'avoiding' heat and cold in the sense of wanting things to be different, but working from the way things really are, unobscured by preferences.

The indignation and grief that can cry out, *'This must stop!'* to those pillaging the earth and laying waste to lives and life itself is immensely valuable, but it must first come clear enough to recognise itself in the face of the other. The self disappears into that clarity. Then the truth it speaks can be ruthlessly merciful and direct.

Long life is measured not in years but in ease with circumstances, which in any life will entail a fair acquaintance with suffering. The birthing, suffering, withering, dying of things, even the horrific, unthinkable destruction inflicted on people, fellow creatures and this astonishing planet, prises open our hearts and minds like nothing else can. Dongshan's recommendation to welcome the difficulties of heat and cold when they take the trouble to visit us implies that the *truth* of suffering is to be won again and again, in circumstances not usually described as relaxed and comfortable. The truth of suffering makes us true, and can draw a human being so deeply into life they end up willing to substitute the word 'acceptance', if not 'joy', for much of what was once deemed 'suffering'.

If that is hard to understand, then let me ask you what joy would be without that surprising taste of sorrow and tears—the welcome grief of *caring* so deeply—running through it. Would it be joy? Would it be complete? Would it be even recognisable?

And by the way, when it is time to hole up and draw breath, put your feet up and enjoy the moon rising, raise a glass of wine with people you love, walk in the evening as the dew forms, play with a child . . . Why not lose yourself completely in *that*?

Basho:
How cool ~
noonday nap
feet planted on the wall!

11. It is only for your benefit

Explanatory note: We meet Dongshan again with another monk. 'Acharya' is an honorific title, like saying 'Wise One'. So he's addressing the wisest part of us and trusting its response when he speaks to the monk. 'It' is a word in Zen that always needs caution. Don't leap to conclude that 'it' refers simply to suffering. And it is valuable to know that what Zen calls the heart-mind is so wide, it no longer finds it so easy to distinguish curse from blessing.

The koan: **Dongshan and a monk were down by a creek washing their bowls when two birds flew down and tore apart a frog sitting on a stone, right in front of them. The monk asked, 'Why does it come to this?' Dongshan replied, 'It is only for your benefit, Acharya.'**

Why does it come to this? There it is, the age-old anguish, growing sharper every minute as we watch the world casually risk an unthinkable future.

Why is the earth being torn apart by the ferocity of human greed, hatred and ignorance? Why must life always come to the moments of tearing and pain, accidents and grief, sickness and old age, death and loss? Why do we lose every single thing we love (while possibly failing to notice how generously we are given every single thing we love in the first place)? And why must we give it all back, give back even ourselves?

That monk by the old creek is staring at our world too. All this that we are threatened by is 'only for our benefit'? What!

Dongshan's 'It is only for your benefit' is remote from someone telling you, 'No pain no gain', or 'You can't expect to be relaxed and comfortable all the time'. (Though they're right.) When 'it' occurs in a Zen koan, always reach for your whole mind, which means undivided reality. 'It' *includes* suffering, of course—it includes everything, but does so without picking and choosing, not singling out anything at all on which we could try to hang an accusation or a dream of saving ourselves from life, nature, reality.

This *benefit* Dongshan extends is quite severe. Most great blessings are. It asks that we rigorously give up any dream of the self as separate from the rest of life and exempt from unavoidable suffering. But in reply it gives us back the whole world, an inconceivable grace—able to include both suffering and joy, torn frogs, and two at least half-satisfied birds, without a hint of self-pity.

All things are passing through the mysterious interchange from not being, to being, to not being. The universe itself shares this self-nature with us. That which we are, we will not be; that which we have, we will lose. We eat now but later we will be eaten; prevail now, but later will yield. The way one thing insists on continually becoming another is beyond judgment: it is just the way things are in an ongoing creation event that, for reasons undeclared, brings all things into being from nowhere, and releases them back there again.

Moment by moment we are born into this and we die into that, on and on until you cannot precisely tell the one from the other. The *entirety* of this, says Dongshan, is its benevolence. 'It is only for your benefit' implies an open response to suffering, an openness that is exactly a readiness to be of help.

Gary Snyder, poet and essayist, evokes that same generous courage: 'The Bodhisattva must live by the sufferer's standard . . . to be effective in giving aid to those who suffer.' A Bodhisattva is one committed to helping all beings become at ease in their own self-nature, which means freed from all avoidable suffering. When you know who you are, then you can help others. Enlightenment *is* helping others in need, and into enlightenment. By helping others we help ourselves to enlightenment. We're all in this together. That is the great benefit.

So why stand apart and leave yourself out of the benefit? To be effective in giving aid to those who suffer, give yourself freely away. That's the Bodhisattva way of clapping hands and doing business.

Must we live by 'the sufferer's standard'? With sentience, as the Buddha noted in the First Noble Truth, comes suffering. It hurts to live. We're born covered in blood and it unfolds from there in all its joy and pain. So in one sense we have no choice in the matter. But maybe there's a positive reason too.

We can't know and respond to the pain of others until we have felt pain, and, going further, *borne* pain. 'To suffer', in the light of its root meaning, means 'to bear', 'to allow' and 'to support'—to provide or ripen a capacity to hold such experience. So 'to live by the sufferer's standard' implies living open towards our own and other's suffering, letting that temper and make us tender.

To live by the sufferer's standard is not a passive submission to pain but a *standard* to live by—actively seeking the truth of suffering so as to be of some use to a suffering world. In the Grail legend, the truth of suffering is borne through the feast hall with great ceremony as the sacred chalice, and belongs—*instantly*—to the first who is moved to ask the guardian of the Grail (the mortally wounded Fisher King), 'What are you going through? How can I help?'

The natural rising of concern for the other *is* the Grail, the thing of supreme value. 'Only for your benefit' ripples out in mysterious, ever-widening circles. Moved to help someone, it turns out to be *you* who are so greatly helped.

To seek no escape from the reality of suffering while taking the risk to keep your heart receptive and open—does that actually hurt more than it heals hurt? Remarkable how courage can spring up so powerfully when things are disastrous. The frog, the child, the town, torn apart in front of our eyes. When disasters happen, great things can appear in human beings. The need and painfulness of the suffering of others can grow fresh hands and hearts in people.

So, in order to meet what is shaping as a massive, slow-moving disaster for our planet, can you risk uncovering and ripening a bravely open heart? Perhaps the even better question is, can you risk *not* doing so? Can you live with that?

The current of connection that is compassion shapes all of life and holds it together. In all that is so wrong with the world it would be wrong to forget the altruism of the most fundamental bonds between people. It is easy to focus on their shortcomings and miss the fact that other people are here, they're alive, they are breathing, they are in front of us, feeling love and pain, usually doing their best.

When we meet people who have found their way to ease the suffering of those around them in a profound way, by mastering ease with their own suffering, we can't turn away from it. The relinquishment of self that we see in front of us is beautiful instruction. They have let their circumstances take them away completely. It doesn't mean they are not present, by the way—they are *very* present. But they are, themselves, not *in* the way. There is no noteworthy 'I' straining their presence. And no mosquito whine of self-pity marring their generosity.

We live as best we can, we tough yet fragile beings, frogs and humans, all so briefly here. We swim in timelessness at every point of joy and suffering when we look at what is happening with clear eyes, place our feet firmly on the earth and find the courage to love the whole of it.

'It', the whole shebang, is only for our benefit in a most personal sense. It is our light, inseparable from the natural 'no you no me' that rises in us in the presence of another torn by suffering, unbidden and immediate, with no thought even of needing to help.

Unless we know this 'it', are we actually *alive*? When we know it, the benefit is precisely what we are—and impossible in the end to tell apart from the tearing. A man awaiting open-heart surgery for replacement of his entire descending aorta writes, 'In my "medical Sesshin" (or seven day silent meditation retreat) the bells are now beeps, my cushion an electric bed, and I meet new companions daily. My teachers are many. All caring hearts are one. Not exactly a silent retreat though! . . . I am thrilled to be here and desire to be nowhere else. It is where my feet are.'

And the threat of climate crash hanging over a smallish blue-green planet in a remote corner of the Milky Way finally begins to wake up its large, clever, but often oblivious two-legged population to the fact of where their feet actually are.

With the beautiful tearing shock of discovering we really *are* all in it together.

Basho:
> Departing spring!
> birds cry out,
> tears in the eyes of fish

12. I have already become like this

Explanatory note: Tongan Daopi (date, uncertain) was a tenth-century Song dynasty master. Monastic forms of practice customarily renounce or relinquish 'the world', meaning desires for worldly things.

The koan: **A monk asked Daopi, 'An ancient master said, "I do not love what worldly people love." I wonder—what does your Reverence love?' Daopi replied, 'I have already become like this.'**

Renunciation is actually not so much rejecting something as choosing to keep resolving *not* to give way to a weakness, a choice renewed on every occasion the pull is felt. 'All face', for example, in that party of Indian warriors, may be understood in part as strong fidelity to something discovered to be actually far more interesting than 'I want', 'I need', 'I should have' . . .

Such mana holds itself in check and communicates itself by doing very little or nothing at all. Consider the mana contained in the sight of a powerful mountain face. Just being itself and holding up the light seems to be enough to help the many beings in sight of it.

This monk in the koan would also have renounced worldly things to enter a monastic life, but would be no less prone than anyone else to wanting things. Perhaps more so, since he has risked becoming fully conscious of the wanting. Now he asks about what his teacher loves.

A psychologist may have some useful things to say about love, but Zen master Robert Aitken said in all seriousness that a Zen teacher no more resembles a psychologist than a persimmon resembles a banana. That a flea bears a closer, clearer resemblance, or a mountain, perhaps, or cool breeze.

'I have already become like this,' is all that Tongan says.

'Love' is a word that this koan looks into. So, of course, is 'this'—'like this'. 'Love' is a word routinely emptied of its meaning a thousand times over, on Academy Awards night alone. No one can keep track of its ongoing abuse in greetings cards, self-help books, love songs, SMS texts (where nothing more than x marks the spot of its disappearance).

It's also a word mistrusted as 'desire', 'attachment' or 'the flesh' by religions that fear life and pit longing for God against some parts of the reality in which such longing is born. Just as though some parts of creation should—or could—be thrown out of the universe. When all along the universe shows nothing but the power of inclusion. No part of it is possible without the rest of the whole. Persimmon, banana, flea, cool breeze, mountain, distant rooster crow . . . Each one, the face of the whole. Becoming 'like this' is free interchange with each thing just as it is. Is that inclusiveness not love?

'Becoming like this' is a position as modest as river stones lying deep in the stream; giving way to so much flow rounds them greatly. Tolerance is not being comfortable with what is happening but the willingness to be *un*comfortable with it.

'Becoming like this' and renouncing preferences can be a joyful, playful business with considerable creative payoff. Zen Master Banzan showed how. Or rather, a butcher showed him how, quite by accident, when Banzan overheard him talking to a bossy customer. The customer demanded, 'Show me your best cuts of meat. I want only the best meat in your shop!' The butcher protested proudly, 'But everything in my shop is best! There's no piece of meat in my shop that is not the best!' Banzan was struck by collateral lightning, you might say. *'Everything is best!'* hit him with such force that he could never quite shrink the world back to his own small terms again.

In some parts this is called 'enlightenment'. But really, it's just consistently dropping the resistance in your mind while doing all you can to be of some help. After a while, it will be hard to tell *you* from a cool breeze passing right through.

This *best* has no room in it for better or worse; in fact it has trouble separating you from me, or valuing this leaf on the tree while finding that one hard to like. That threadbare leaf on the ground, is it not as completely itself and in place as a shining one still intact on the tree? 'Everything is best' sees right through preferences to the reality of infinite relationship in which everything counts and is completely worthy of awareness and care. 'This' is a word for it in the present koan. 'Become *like this*.'

It's actually not so hard to try it out. Watch waves rolling to shore or breaking onto rocks for an hour or so and try to find a single one you can't admire. Or a patch of grass with one blade of grass that fails to be the best.

Another Zen troublemaker, Linji, was heard famously to say, 'There is nothing I dislike.' This did not make him a pushover, just a bit more fluid, responsive and in the right place at every moment, the way the creek flows, the mountain stands its ground, the clouds dissolve and form. What makes such relaxed readiness possible is having no constant interruption from a self that needs to say, 'But what about me. I deserve the best!'

We all deserve the best, it's just a matter of seeing how you already have it. When you can see in all directions nothing but the best doing its best, we're freed up to be of some use. Until then, the sense that so much is wrong, and it has grown too late to fix it may defeat even the best of us.

Nothing is held back in the natural world, neither life nor death, and by this unparalleled generosity we continually test our limits. Giving away what we are, and have, until life goes back in to the mysterious place it came from—that's the only way to hold the gift of being here. Our limits are transparent, with no final state. They don't need to hold us back, so we just go beyond them. That's 'becoming like this' too, a more fearless generosity that knows that uncontrived reality is the only safe place from which to act.

So 'I have already become like this' cedes a lot—everything, to be exact—to the way things are, and the generosity hidden in that is easy to appreciate because it embodies love that leaves nothing out. This 'already' quietly contains a lifetime of rigorous practice of awareness.

It takes all you are to know yourself this way. But that's love, and it keeps us entirely on our toes and in the world.

Basho:

Spring!
a nameless hill
swims in the haze

13. Reconcile with *this!*

Explanatory note: Uncle Max Harrison, Dulumunmun, is an Aboriginal elder from Yuin country (south coast of New South Wales) who has been right through initiation into blackfella law. He was born in the 1930s, and was still classed under an antique law as 'fauna'. Since the 1980s, whitefella concern about past and present wrongs became the Reconciliation movement, supported by government to draw both mobs together. Blackfellas were invited to sit down with whitefellas to talk about the impact of past and present government policy and share their life stories, law and culture.

The koan: **Uncle Max said, 'I don't hold with this talk of reconciliation.' The people listening were shocked. He continued, 'How can you have *reconciliation* where there's never been a relationship in the first place?' He knelt and cupped a handful of dirt from the ground. 'I just tell both mobs, "Reconcile with this!" and you won't need any "reconciliation" after that.'**

'Become like this', 'Reconcile with this'—what's the difference?

The cartoonist Michael Leunig once remarked that the best thing about talking with a duck is that you have to get down on the earth on your hands and knees, usually in mud. Gary Snyder pointed out the virtues of going *crawling* when fire has made the Sierra manzanita grow back too thick to walk through. You lose all dignity in the best possible way—in exchange for fern dew on your face, intimate meetings with exceptionally shy animals never seen in the open, and literally sniffing your way to where the most delicious Boletus mushrooms are growing. And that interesting thirteenth-century Zen monk, Myoe, was fond of digging a hole in the ground and talking into it. In fact, he was doubtful of the worth of really getting to know anyone who found this unusual, or who could not understand the reason to talk with trees, and he regularly meditated seated high in the branches of his favourite tree.

Myoe once had his monks deliver a letter he had written to an island well known to him as a child and greatly missed as an adult. He referred to his island as 'truly an interesting and enjoyable friend', and his famous letter says in part:

> Even as I speak to you in this way, tears fill my eyes . . . I am filled with a great longing for you in my heart, and take no delight in passing time without having the time to see you. And then there is the large cherry tree that I remember so fondly. There are times when I so want to send a letter to the tree to ask how it is doing, but I am afraid that people will say that I am crazy to send a letter to a tree that cannot speak. Though I think of doing it, I refrain in deference to the custom of this irrational world . . .

His monks dutifully got ready to depart with the letter to the island—a virtual set of whole earth *reconciliation* instructions for the very monks who carried it—but then they faltered, a bit embarrassed by the whole thing, to ask to whom they should actually deliver the letter. Myoe told them to simply stand in the middle of the island, shout in a loud voice, 'This is a letter from Myoe of Tonganoo!', deliver the letter into the hands of the wind, then return.

Which they did. It is not recorded what the island wind had to say in reply.

'Truly an enjoyable and interesting friend.' How many think to treat and speak of the world this way? As Uncle Max makes uncomfortably clear, reconciliation can't begin without mutual relationship. The instincts that tend good friendship would tend the whole world very nicely. But friends need to be able to sit down together and chew the fat—exchange ideas and emotions.

Sometimes I think of good meditation like that. Meditating out in the open, under a tree—even *in* a tree—often goes very differently to sitting inside a room full of human energies. You can touch the earth with your fingers and reintroduce yourself. The earth never ever holds back in returning the greeting. The intelligence of feeling passes surprisingly freely between you both.

Uncle Max has remarkable grace of character for a person who was technically a non-person until more than halfway through his life. In the fringe camp of Wallaga Lake, provision of formal schooling for Aboriginal children was scanty. Yet his education was immense because his mother held a lot of important law, and so he was taken comprehensively through law—by five remarkable elders he calls 'those old scientists'. One was his grandfather, who rode broncos in country rodeos into his nineties. Not purely for fun, by the way. It was the only way available for him to make a living.

He doesn't trouble to hold a lot of blame or anger for the injustices of his life, seeing integrity resting in taking your own inventory, not someone else's. 'It comes down only on us,' he says—another excellent koan for our times.

At one point of being taken through law, he was required to spend ten days alone in difficult country with no water. A stone saved him—by sucking on a stone he never became overwhelmingly thirsty. He had to endure and just *be*, testing his wits and depending on the strength of his spiritual practice. The trick was accepting hardship without doing a runner either physically or mentally. 'If I didn't succumb,' he says, 'I could come to know my body, mind and spirit.' He found this harsh experience no imposition but the biggest gift of all from those old scientists.

'If I hadn't learned, I would have been punishing myself,' he says. Every time we squander the offer that comes inside hardship and difficult times, and fall back into the ultimately tedious dramas of the small self, we punish ourselves. The punishment is that the chance is wasted.

Living as if we were the only show on earth is clearly living in dangerous ignorance of the very terms of life on earth. In reality, the interdependency that *is* this very life goes so deep that in the end you cannot entirely say where you and another begin or end. Acting in ignorance of this tears the web on which each life depends, and can only be tolerated for so long. The time comes—the sooner the better, actually—when you have to tell an out-of-control two year old to *stop.*

Shaman and activist-poet Martin Prechtel insists 'The next revolution is composting.' Nothing wasted, and everything that is used yielded back to the growth of the soil. Human life organised around not the endless take but the ancient principle of the gift cycle, everywhere apparent in the web of life. My life becomes your life. As Uncle Max puts it, 'The only way to keep any gift is to keep giving it away.'

Our world is excruciatingly split along a thousand fracture lines, the loving act of mending long overdue. It begins with the split in our minds between the world and our selves and goes on from there. The slow-motion collapse of the biosphere. The yawning gulf between rich and poor. The less than fully human status of any perceived 'inferior' in terms of race, religion, gender, sexual preference. And on its goes, the cut that keeps on cutting . . .

Zen Master Nanchuan is infamous in Zen circles for having cleaved a cat in two. He found the monks of the Eastern Hall and the monks of the Western Hall arguing over a cat. No one knows now if it was a metaphysical dispute or just that the cat was a damned good mouser and both mobs wanted it guarding their storehouse. And anyway, how quickly we can get such things confused!

Nanchuan picked up a knife and held up the cat, saying, 'Monks! If one of you can say a turning word, I'll spare the cat!' No one could say a word, so Nanchuan cut the cat in two, right before their startled and appalled eyes.

Who can defend such actions of a mad Zen monk? But equally, who is left by his action unaware that one cut cuts all? 'I' and 'you' are cuts. 'Good' and 'bad' are cuts. 'Put down that knife!' and 'This must stop!' are mends. His action brings us down to rock bottom. Reaching rock bottom may be all that will finally goad us into minding and mending the earth. Nothing could more clearly show how to practise that mind than the earth itself.

For what holds up original undividedness more clearly than its loss—in climate collapse, ecological and biodiversity collapse, toxic chemicals and radioactivity entering groundwater and biosphere, desertification of the oceans, decapitation of mountains, destruction of rainforests, oil spills, genetic mutation, a once blue sky engineered to iron brown?

But equally, one mending mends all. That one mending—it comes down only on us.

'I have already become like this' is the inward, personal stage of the outward, shared revolution of mending the earth. 'Reconcile with this!' is its call to arms. Arms that entirely embrace difference.

Like Eretz Shalom (Land of Peace), which is a small group of West Bank settlers who have become *unsettlers* of the Israeli settlers' movement narrative that so ruthlessly dispossesses Palestinians from land, creating a wake of mutual hatred. Eretz Shalom sees the group's mission as changing awareness and consciousness in relation to the land from a claim of attachment to a sense of belonging. *Belonging* to the land means you are part of the land, which then makes it impossible to ignore how strongly the belonging of others makes them equally part of the land. 'Reconcile with *this*.'

Consequently Eretz Shalom members are engaging as allies in the daily human rights struggles of their Palestinian neighbours, setting up economic cooperatives, exploring ecologically sound practices, and learning to speak Arabic. They support the notion of a Palestinian state within which they would hope to continue living as a trusted Jewish minority. They are attempting to carve out a new story that emphasises the reality of two peoples who feel an equally strong and justifiable sense of belonging to the land, and who must learn to accept and care for each other as equal tenants and stewards of this beloved place. To reconcile with the earth is a work of profound social healing, in which establishing peace is inseparable from establishing empathic understanding of the needs of the other.

If we do manage to reconcile collectively with this great earth, the contesting differences between all the various mobs that make up humanity will have had to do a mighty lot of composting of differences along the road. Achieving the transition to the Ecozoic era will have healed *us* as much as the biosphere.

'This' is the great matter that addresses each of us, intimately, now, and in person—while requiring that we take nothing personally, least of all our selves.

Basho:
> Harvest moon ~
> the rising tide
> edges to my door

The country after the burn

Be joyful though you have considered all the facts.

Wendell Berry

*At this time in history we are to take nothing personally, least of
all ourselves, for the moment we do our spiritual growth comes
to a halt. The time of the wolf is over, gather yourselves, banish
the word 'struggle' from your attitude and your vocabulary, all
that we do now must be in sacred manner. And in celebration,
for we are the ones we have been waiting for.*

Prophecy issued by a Hopi elder, 8 June 2000

In 1994, not long after savage summer bushfires had ringed Sydney
and blackened a swathe of bushland right up to my own house, I
set out on my favourite walk for the first time after the blaze. The
path makes its way beside a little musical creek at the bottom of
the hill. The fire had raced up from the banks of the creek, where
a thirteen-year-old boy caught up in the frantic media drama of
'Sydney's burning!' had set it in motion with a box of matches and a

pile of old telephone directories. You could still smell fresh ash and charcoal all the way down to where the creek, which had taken the time—30,000 years or more—to carve an entire valley, could be heard calmly continuing on its way.

I knew every stone, tree and bush of this place by heart, so I felt tender walking into the scorched area. But the rains had come through since the fire, softening the mood from black, twisted and dead. Jets of new green were spurting from charred wood; seeds dependent on fire for germination were yawning wide open, tender shoots erupting through blackened remains of undergrowth. New life called urgently into being by fire.

I walked through untouched forest before coming to the place in the path where I stepped onto seared earth. The moment I did so a shockwave of feeling passed through me, leaving everything charged.

Abruptly, I was walking on sacred earth; each step hurt with this sharp awareness. An exquisite painful beauty flowed through everything, and through me. Is this how the *land* sees its violent visitations by fire? Every fragile thing was twisted into the shape of suffering, and yet something even more intense, something that lay beyond all harm, was now equally plain in their very contortions. Plain indeed, nothing was hidden—but what lay revealed was beyond the reach of speech.

It was impossible to move except incredibly slowly and barely breathing. I picked my way like someone fallen into a dream, tears on my face, to a place I'd never noticed before, though it was in no way hidden from sight, just across the creek on the unburnt side.

A beautiful angophora stood there, branching at hip height into four smooth-skinned pillars, creating a natural seat in the bole with a cushion of many layers of peeling bark. The four trunks—I felt them to be four sisters—rose straight and urgent before branching to twine sinuous arms around each other. I sat in that seat and let myself be carried even further away into the flowing state that had picked me up as a leaf in the stream. My loyal dog stayed close; she kept silent company with what was happening. When I was finally able to look about again, five tiny, stately, high-backed insects I'd never seen before were climbing the nearest trunk in calm procession just inches from my face, as plainly blessed as everything else in sight.

This grievous bodily joy in me seemed equally to belong to every detail—twigs, the odd percussive frog, softly moving shadows over subtle patterns of fallen leaves, late afternoon light, slow trickle of water over rocks; and in time the evening carolling of currawongs began to peal down from high in the trees.

It was a while before I could stand and move, and then just barely faster than before, to manage the feat of consciously moving back into the world and state of mind required for talking with my two children and preparing our evening meal. The transition was slow; I found I needed more time in the nearby park, to absorb the last sunlight turning the grass and flowers fluorescent, before I was finally released enough from the spell to walk the short distance home.

The old rule of wild medicines has long been, 'Where the danger grows, grows also that which heals.' But the country after the burn seemed to reveal something even subtler. In the danger itself, the healing is revealed. The healing that lies in waiting in the heavily impending threat of very great harm to the planet and ourselves may be more than we can see from here.

Signs of healing

Between the time I started to write and the time this book now draws to a close, many of the signs and portents have grown far more ominous. The slow burn continues, continues also to accelerate. The rate of release of carbon into the atmosphere has not slowed but sharply accelerated. And despite increasingly trenchant warnings from climate scientists, political reluctance to commit to the inevitable sharp change of course has mainly only deepened. Governments are pointedly ignoring the warning signs while caving in to the insistent demands of Big Oil and Big Coal, in what is now being called in some quarters a 'bought democracy'.

But at the same time, and partly in response to public loss of trust in compromised democratic institutions, the world began to see in 2011 a significant and growing horizontal or 'distributed' form of resistance. It manifested in the impressive mobilisations of 'people power' visible in the Arab Spring, Spanish Indignados, Chilean student revolt, Greek and Russian mass protests and, since 17 September 2011, the Occupy Wall Street movement and its many subsequent international formations.

This is beyond doubt the hour in which resistance to the 'time of the wolf' in financial, political and environmental matters has begun to become visible and audible, coupled with a vehement search for alternatives to top-down social and political organisation and decision-making. There are profound things to be considered, and at last a sense that turning to face them may be starting to happen in earnest—and in ways that model more ecological ways of relating.

To remain unmoved by evidence of so many millions of large and small people-power initiatives for change would be to insult the immensity of effort, humour and love that fuels them. Author Paul Hawken salutes them—us!—as the ever-growing tens of millions 'willing to confront despair, power, and incalculable odds in order to restore some semblance of grace, justice, and beauty to this world'. It would be as wrong to underestimate the scope of their transformative influence—which both gradually *and* suddenly is rippling and radiating into the shared public space through social networking and ordinary word of mouth—as it would be to underestimate the massively well-funded backlash that must be expected. But nothing can turn back a growing clarity in the world that climate damage and unbridled consumerism—and the deregulated corporate 'crony capitalism' that has driven both—can no longer be accepted, or addressed in isolation from each other.

Separately, these people-powered initiatives might be dismissed as inconsiderable; but regarded *together*, they comprise what Hawken has dubbed 'the Largest Movement in the World'— 'dispersed, inchoate, and fiercely independent', eschewing ready-made manifestoes, doctrines and authority figures, open to all, offering 'as many points of entry as there are human beings' alive on the earth.

Increasingly, people appear more willing to find ways to speak out and act against a predatory economic order and to prophesy radical change, refusing any longer to quietly capitulate to the destructive behaviour of powerful interests. This gradually coalescing globalised movement pointedly rejects traditional forms of protest that merely appeal to authorities to behave differently; instead they seek to harness energy in creative forms of social networking and passive-resistance displays of direct action. They— *we!*—refuse to pretend to have all the answers, but are ethically firm in refusal of the 'logic' of laying waste to the earth in order to massively profit a minute fraction of the world's population—less than 'the 1%' in fact; closer to 'the 0.1%'. To actively restore an inclusive sense of society and the shared common good, new forms of self-governance have emerged in such forms as leaderless 'general assembly' methods of evolving a genuinely shared consensus.

So there are real signs of a non-hierarchical, nonviolent, spontaneous revolution in thought beginning to happen, responding to the sense of emergency with both striking symbolic actions and a gradual suffusing of its alternative thinking and goals into what can be thought by existing institutions. This admittedly optimistic view must of course be balanced by staying alert to how quickly and efficiently corporate public relations will seek to defuse protest and immunise public opinion against any note of dissidence by smoothly co-opting the rhetoric of its critics, while smoothly pressing on with a destructive course of action. But this many-headed movement is not only beginning to provide enough small make-weights to truly start to shift the scale, it also seems to be contagious: an outbreak of resistance in one country has begun to spark resistance in another half a world away. The 2001 Argentinian revolution of general assemblies and *política afectiva* (the politics of affection) inspired similar tactics in the Spanish Indignado movement. The Egyptian uprising in Tahrir Square helped ignite the courage behind the Occupation of Wall Street several months later.

Nonviolent agency of change

Nonviolent direct action has become a hallmark of saying *No!* Direct action is the claim of a free person not to be captive to injustice. It involves a commitment to stand up for strong convictions and find unexpected ways to bring a message home to others, without violence, but with unmistakable withdrawal of respect for all forms of coercive violence by 'powers that be', including the violence of exploitation. It embodies another kind of power, one that refuses to be driven by fear and hatred.

Gandhi's symbolic public march in 1930 to the sea to freely harvest salt in defiance of British salt taxes—and by extension, British control of India—is a famous example. So, too, is the moment when, on 1 December 1955, Rosa Parks publicly refused the order of a white bus driver to surrender her seat to a white woman in Montgomery, Alabama, sparking the powerful Montgomery Bus Boycott that seeded the Civil Rights Movement. In the 1980s, Polish Solidarity supporters publicly pushed their television sets around in prams in mass 'evening strolls' during the time of nightly news broadcasts, to demonstrate their rejection of government-controlled and heavily censored news. There was no law in place saying that a television set could not be pushed in a baby stroller, no way the British could claim authority over the salt in the sea, nothing but customary force to the proposition that a white woman should not stand as long as a black woman sat. The loopholes of freedom are as wide as a human mind can manage to be when not closed down by fear.

And in 2011, squatting in Zuccotti Park became a potent symbolic act of proclaiming people power and reclaiming public rights against an overwhelming tide of privatised greed and power. Refusing to ask permission to peacefully assemble in a public space and occupy the public's own park was a striking way to begin to take back communal resources that have been openly appropriated. A functioning ecology might be taken as an instructive model of solidarity on behalf of all life. All these recent initiatives, whether consciously yet or not, display thinking and acting that is in closer accord with the example and terms set by the non-coercive, cooperative natural life systems of the earth, which by nature have no 'bosses'.

Writer Robert Korten calls it 'walking away from the king'—turning your back on vertical forms of power in this heavily brokered world, and rejecting the associated privilege of violence against others that power routinely takes for itself in such a world. The Latin word 'imperium' meant the all-too-familiar forms of authority imposed from above upon those deemed to be below. 'Auctoritas', by contrast, signified authority willingly accorded to another in recognition of some quality. Nonviolent protest refuses to be the mirror-image of imperium. It calls up auctoritas in the so-called 'powerless' 99%, and seeks to reawaken an inherent respect for life, which fear of imminent loss of power so readily subdues in the so-called 'powerful' 1%.

When people are seen responding in a calm and non-aggressive way while being brutalised by police, and even showing concern towards the ones using force, they win a powerful victory. To refuse to be brutalised already begins to neutralise the coercive power of violence. Nonviolent resistance can find ways to progress a cause that coercive forces are helpless to counter. The Occupy movement has not only shifted public discourse and forced it to acknowledge gross inequality and injustice that can no longer be considered acceptable, it has also shown how public disgust at police violence against non-resisting, unarmed protestors itself becomes a powerful force for change. The courage of a protest movement grows when the fear behind the coercion is unmasked and the moral failure of those who would use violence is laid bare, forcing power to disclose fear and weakness. A resort to violence by a state is a signal that all restraining public respect and tolerance of existing conditions has actually already been lost. After that, a continued use of force just further erodes a demonstrable loss of moral authority.

Martin Luther King made very clear that nonviolent resistance was not for cowards; what he called 'active nonviolent resistance to evil' is very different to passive non-resistance. Its refusal to be physically violent is a sign of being strongly active morally and spiritually. Instead of seeking to defeat or humiliate the opponent, nonviolent resistance aims to convert understanding on a large scale and awaken a sense of moral shame that will actually strengthen the sense of community, whereas the aftermath of communal violence is tragic bitterness.

Nonviolent resistance sets out to defeat what is harmful at the root, rather than to avenge harm. King adopted Gandhi's courageous stand that, 'Rivers of blood may have to flow before we gain our freedom but it must be *our* blood', seeing redemptive, educational and transformational potential in the example set by such suffering. Nonviolent resistance consciously chooses love over hatred, and faith over despair; that is its strength and the ground from which it commands attention and respect. The Occupy movement has attempted to publicly recover and demonstrate a civil, sharing society of individuals acting in aggregate rather than self-interested manner, displaying trust in one another. Similarly, the example of Martin Luther King was to act in trust that any action undertaken and suffered for justice and vital change *must* bear eventual fruit of love, peace and justice, even if—as his own violent death bears out—that may not be fully achieved in your own lifetime. This is the audacious choice of a free human being.

The action of love

Ideas and actions formed by love are as contagious as those driven by hate, but can seed far more enduring and more beneficial change than violent outbreaks of hatred and aggression ever can. The revolution in thinking that rises from clearly seeing great harm, but responding as far as humanly possible with creative, disciplined, non-aggressive resistance, resonates with what the poet, Robert Jensen, has called 'the work that allows one to live, joyously, while in a state of profound grief'. It is, as he says, the work of all the ages and the great work of our time.

Hope becomes a truly transformative force when it is fuelled by an unassailable energy of love that is not narrowed or fixated upon an idealised outcome. Just as an ecosystem persistently unfolds in the direction of maximum chance for life to flourish but with no final 'outcome' ever in sight, so too resistance to the array of destructive forces inside human beings and human institutions must strive to remain supple, persistent and process- rather than end-oriented, since this is bigger than our lifetimes, and a mere fragment of the great never-ending story. This way it may retain its potent creativity and avoid devolving into a zealotry that can grow lethal even while ostensibly serving the best of all possible motives.

The twinned violence of economic injustice and environmental destruction are now far more clearly recognised as two aspects of one life-threatening planetary disease that *must* be addressed for life to continue to flourish in any recognisable form. The evolution and collective fate of human beings are now inseparable from the evolution and fate of the planet. Never in human history have we ever been so clearly politically and physically implicated as a species with a common dilemma and common destiny. Our ways of steward-ing the life systems of the earth cannot now be separated from the evolution of the human world towards greater justice and equality. The minding of the earth and the mending of the world must arrive together, if either is to arrive at all. To meet this reality requires a radical re-imagining of the earth and our selves, in the artful pro-cess of reinventing a humanity that earth can better tolerate.

While most human beings on earth suffer violence primarily from each other and from powerful political forces that remain largely unchecked and immune from prosecution, the natural world also suffers our violence. It can offer only passive resistance to the brutalising effect of so much industrial-strength resource extraction. It needs—awaits—our passionate protest on its behalf.

In the Council for All Beings process, devised by John Seed and Joanna Macy, after working through exercises that open your imagination and empathy to the dazzling creativity and vulnerability of life in deep time through the ages of evolution and chance, you intentionally let some creature into your heart of hearts. It may be orang-utan, dugong, skink, dung beetle, blue-fin tuna. It may be a beleaguered waterway, a strip-mined mountain, an old-growth forest facing the loggers.

After spending some time allowing a creaturely fellowship to deepen in various ways, you come back to the circle of the Council for All Beings as 'your' chosen being, and when your time comes to speak, you give voice to the passion and eloquence of that being, lending your body, mind and heart to advocate for its needs, fears and desires. *'The tiger fears the human heart. The human fears the tiger's kindness.'* A tiger has much less to fear from a human heart in such an open condition, I sense. And a human, much less to fear in the tiger's kindness.

So the ones we have been waiting for turn out to be—*us*. Which may turn out to be our most surprising cause for celebration. For the healing of the planet proceeds by the healing of our painfully fractured human world.

∽

The three-thousand-year-old Taoist Chinese *Daodejing* says, 'The softest thing on earth overtakes the hardest thing on earth.' Composting and all forms of ripeness and decay creatively reveal this truth; time and inevitable change embody it; the life systems of the earth are composed entirely of its intelligence; watercourses carve it into stone. The way a human being explores this truth of suffering is by walking into the dark unknown of being, itself, just with love. There are no hard-edged 'knowings' here, no separate 'things' at all—nothing except the wholeness of reality.

The 'hardest thing' to be overcome, as we struggle to perceive and acknowledge our less noble inclinations that run so counter to the terms of the earth, will probably always be fear—of ourselves, of the other, of scarcity and discomfort, of loss and mortality. Fear compounded by shame at our own inaction. Unaddressed, such toxic fear makes us dangerous. It leaves us blind to the true face of reality, unable or unwilling to risk fully loving and trusting its large and mysterious forces. The greatest movements of human history are those that truly shape and give meaning to the world because they manage to reconnect us to the larger destinies of the universe. This crisis, which touches everyone on earth together and threatens our common survival, is our unparalleled opportunity to come into truer accord with the earth and the universe that gave us birth.

The overarching demand of *this* time is no less than 'to reinvent the human—at the species level, with critical reflection, within the community of life-systems', in the wise estimation of Thomas Berry. I deeply appreciate that man's humble, clear-eyed qualifier: 'with critical reflection'. 'Critical' literally means thought prepared to place itself in crisis—to fully accord with crisis in a state of awareness and coherence. The world is in unprecedented crisis. We will either gather all the means at our disposal to align our minds with that reality, or not survive it. 'Reflection' gradually becomes once more the deep conversation with the holy earth—humble, unhurried, and not cramped by self-concern.

The time of human beings wolfing down the resources of the world as if there was no tomorrow is definitively over, even if the most highly organised and powerful interests on earth cannot yet admit it. That time has not only exhausted itself, it has almost completely exhausted the planet. It has nowhere to go but to the wall of its own making. To decisively end this era of competitive predation and to help usher in the Ecozoic era that will admit us back into the company of all beings, means regathering ourselves at both the collective and personal level. The collective can be reawoken with a powerfully shared narrative—planet-sized, universe-sized—that can readmit us to reality and summon the imagination and daring to belong where actually we find ourselves. The personal is a matter of coming back to the open calm of our senses in meditation, prayer, conversation and art. Such a practice can gradually banish fear and perpetual struggle from the idea of being human, replacing it with the confidence to playfully and lovingly extend alert curiosity towards what is happening.

We have to do this knowing that the results of what we do will not be in our hands. What we must take our own stand against is great indeed, but as eco-feminist Vandana Shiva insists, using this fact as a means to continually discover and grow our own capacities is success already, providing fresh capacity and potential. She reminds us of the paradox that commitment is best sustained by consciously detaching ourselves from concern about where our efforts might finally succeed in taking us. An enduring commitment in any sphere of human life involves a strong ability to act in accord with that commitment while being able to rest in not knowing outcomes. And meanwhile, celebrating life and enjoying the ones who come along with us. A wise, informed and perceptive capacity for *not knowing* is what can keep fearlessness and joy alive even while we are facing catastrophic possibilities.

This is hope vested not in abstracted or ideal outcomes but in the continuing experience of the numberless creative ways in which life lost transforms into life found. That upwelling healing flow inside the country after the burn reveals the softest thing on earth at work inside the hardest. The *whole* world is finally the exacting 'medicine' that heals every 'sickness' of separation and isolation—from our selves, from each other, from reality. And the full reconsecration of the earth will be the reinvention of the human being.

To recover such a state of mind is already to proceed in a more sacred manner. With such awareness, every act becomes a ritual of coming to know yourself exactly where you are, and in what you are doing, and of discovering how to take generous responsibility for the way things are unfolding. Things quite naturally begin to proceed this way as fear subsides. Meditation, and all spontaneously arising prayer free of self-concern, is an inner form of service to the whole world; outer service in all its various forms can best be understood as meditation in action.

Who'd willingly miss out on the adventure of such a moment as this one? We're all in it anyway—why not be in it boots and all? While the world we choose chooses us, the choosing is in every step we take. No one's invincible, all vivid expression of life is also concession to the mystery of loss, and we may even lose the fight to become fully human as a species. But waking up is already the best possible use of this one human life anyway.

And an awake mind begins to see beyond winning and defeat. 'In the depths of winter, I finally learned that within me lay an invincible summer,' wrote Albert Camus. Call it what you will—the Beloved, the Tao, God, Nature, Buddha nature—it will always remain utterly unconfined by any names we lay upon it. If we follow it scrupulously and in close accord with its terms, all names fall away, and the whole world finally reaches our hearts.

'It is in this way that we must train ourselves: by the self through love. We will develop love, we will practise it, we will make it both a way and a basis, take our stand upon it, store it up, and thoroughly set it going.' The Buddha's words may be 2500 years old but still they lay down the challenge of this one and only time of our lives.

We now form the crisis point and creative moment in the further evolution of the planet. It comes down to us. So prophesy courage, have the imagination to break the silence, end the isolation, change the story. Concede to the ripeness of things as the great chance itself.

There are good reasons to be joyful—even after considering all the facts.

Further Reading

Abram, David
> *The Spell of the Sensuous: Perception and Language in a More-Than-Human World* (Vintage, 2007).
> *Becoming Animal: An Earthly Cosmology* (Pantheon, 2010).

Aitken, Robert
> *A Zen Wave: Basho's Haiku and Zen* (Weatherhill, 1978).
> *The Gateless Barrier: The Wu-men Kuan* (Northpoint, 1990).

Cullinan, Cormac
> *Wild Law: A Manifesto for Earth Justice* (Siber Ink & Green Books, 2002).

Christopher, Alexander
> *A Pattern Language* (Oxford UP, 1979).
> *The Nature of Order* (California Center for Environmental Structure, 2003).

Bateson, Gregory
> *Steps to an Ecology of Mind* (Ballantine Books, 1972).

Bell, Mike

'Thomas Berry and an Earth Jurisprudence: An Exploratory Essay' (The Trumpeter, 19, 2003).

Berry, Thomas

The Dream of the Earth (Sierra Club, 1988).

(with Brian Swimme) The Universe Story: From the Primordial Flaring Forth to the Ecozoic Era, A Celebration of the Unfolding of the Cosmos (Harper, 1994).

The Great Work: Our Way into the Future (Bell Tower/Random House, 1999).

Berry, Wendell

The Unsettling of America: Culture and Agriculture (Sierra Club, 1977).

Standing by Words (North Point, 1983).

Home Economics: Fourteen Essays (North Point, 1987).

What Are People For? (North Point, 1990).

Life is a Miracle (Counterpoint, 2000).

In the Presence of Fear: Three Essays for a Changed World (Orion, 2001).

Imagination in Place (Counterpoint, 2010).

Carson, Rachel

Silent Spring (Penguin, 1962).

Chuang Tzu

Chuang Tzu: Basic Writings (transl. by Burton Watson, Columbia UP, 1964).

De Chardin, Teilhard Pierre

Man's Place in Nature (Harper, 1966).

Human Energy (Harcourt Brace Jovanovich, 1971).

The Heart of Matter (Harcourt Brace Jovanovich, 1979).

De Christopher, Tim
'I Do Not Want Mercy, I Want You to Join Me' (Statement to the Court, www.americanswhotellthetruth.org).

Devall, Bill, and Sessions, George
Deep Ecology: Living as if Nature Mattered (Peregrine Smith Books, 1985).

Dillard, Annie
Pilgrim at Tinker Creek (Harper Perennial, 1974).
Teaching a Stone to Talk: Expeditions and Encounters (Harper Perennial, 1983).
An American Childhood (HarperCollins, 1987).

Eiseley, Loren
The Firmament of Time (Atheneum, 1960).
The Immense Journey (Random House, 1960).
The Unexpected Universe (Harcourt Brace Jovanovich, 1972).

Flannery, Tim
The Weather Makers (Atlantic Monthly Press, 2006).

Foster, Nelson
'Is There No Limit?: On Cultivating Contentment' (Wild Duck Review, 2000).

Hawken, Paul
The Ecology of Commerce: A Declaration of Sustainability (HarperCollins, 1993).
Blessed Unrest: How the Largest Movement in the World Came Into Being and Why No One Saw it Coming (Viking Press, 2007).

Kane, Sean
The Wisdom of the Myth Tellers (Broadview Press, 1994).

Kaza, Stephanie
The Attentive Heart: Conversations with Trees (Fawcett, 1993).
Mindfully Green: A Personal and Spiritual Guide to Whole Earth Thinking (Shambhala, 2008).

Korten, David
The Great Turning: From Empire to Earth Community (Barrett-Koehler, 2006).

Leopold, Aldo
A Sand County Almanac (Oxford UP, 1948).

Lovelock, J. E.
Gaia: A New Look at Life on Earth (Oxford UP, 1979).

Lopez, Barry
Of Wolves and Men (Charles Scribner's Sons, 1978).
Arctic Dreams: Imagination and Desire in a Northern Landscape (Charles Scribner's Sons, 1986).
Crossing Open Ground (Charles Scribner's Sons, 1988).
About This Life: Journeys on the Threshold of Memory (Knopf, 1998).

Loy, David
'Loving the World as Our Own Body: The Nondualist Ethics of Taoism, Buddhism and Deep Ecology' (Worldviews: Environment, Culture, Religion, 1997).
The World is Made of Stories (Wisdom Publications, 2010).

Macy, Joanna
Mutual Causality in Buddhism and General Systems Theory: The Dharma of Natural Systems (SUNY, 1991).
World as Lover, World as Self (Rider, 1993).

Margulis, Lynn and Schwartz, Karlene V.
Five Kingdoms: An Illustrated Guide to the Phyla of Life on Earth (Freeman, 1982).

Martin, Calvin Luther
In the Spirit of the Earth: Rethinking History and Time (The Johns Hopkins UP, 1992).
The Way of the Human Being (Yale UP, 1999).

Matthews, Freya
The Ecological Self (Routledge, 1991).

Merchant, Carolyn
The Death of Nature (Harper and Row, 1980).

Mollison, Bill
Permaculture: A Practical Guide for a Sustainable Future (Island Press, 1990).

Miura, Isshu
Zen Dust: The History of the Koan and Koan Study in Rinzai Zen (Zen Institute of America in Japan, 1966).
(with Ruth Fuller Sasaki) *The Zen Koan: Its History and Use in Rinzai Zen* (Harcourt, Brace & World, 1965).

Prechtel, Martin
Secrets of the Talking Jaguar (Jeremy P. Tarcher, 1998).
Long Life, Honey in the Heart (North Atlantic Books, 2004).

Schumaker, E. F.
Small is Beautiful (Harper and Row, 1973).

Shepard, Paul
> *The Tender Carnivore and the Sacred Game* (Scribners, 1973).
> *Thinking Animals: Animals and the Development of Human Intelligence* (Viking Press, 1978).
> *The Sacred Paw: The Bear in Nature, Myth, and Literature* (Viking Press, 1985).
> *Nature and Madness* (Sierra Club, 1992).
> *The Only World We've Got: A Paul Shepard Reader* (Sierra Club, 1996).
> *The Others: How Animals Made Us Human* (Island Press/Shearwater Books, 1996).

Gary Snyder
> *The Practice of the Wild* (North Point Press, 1990).
> *A Place in Space: Ethics, Aesthetics and Watersheds* (Counterpoint, 1995).
> *Mountains and Rivers Without End* (Counterpoint, 1996).
> *Back on the Fire: Essays* (Shoemaker and Hoard, 2007).

Swimme, Brian
> *The Universe is a Green Dragon: A Cosmic Creation Story* (Bear and Company, 1984).
> (with Thomas Berry) *The Universe Story: From the Primordial Flaring Forth to the Ecozoic Era: A Celebration of the Unfolding of the Cosmos* (Harper, 1992).
> *Canticle to the Cosmos and The Hidden Heart of the Cosmos* (video series).

Tanahashi, Kazuaki
> *Moon in a Dewdrop: Writings of Zen Master Dogen* (North Point Press, 1985).

Tarrant, John
   Bring Me the Rhinoceros: And Other Zen Koans to Save Your Life
   (Shambhala, 2008).

Van der Ryn, Sim and Cowan, Stuart
   Ecological Design (Island Press, 1996).

Varela, Francisco, Thompson, J. Evan and Rosch, Eleanor
   The Embodied Mind: Cognitive Science and Human Experience
   (MIT Press, 1991).

Wallace, David Rains
   Life in the Balance (Harcourt Brace Jovanovich, 1987).

Wilson, Edward O.
   Biophilia (Harvard UP, 1984).
   The Diversity of Life (Harvard UP, 1992).
   The Future of Life (Vintage, 2003).

Acknowledgements

My brother Michael, born naturalist, who set me decisively on the path of loving the earth.

My children, Jack and Maeve, and granddaughter Maya, who inspired this book from beginning to end without even trying.

John Tarrant, Ross Bolleter and Robert Aitken, who lit the way of Zen.

My students, Zen and otherwise, who have done their best to educate me – all remaining shortcomings being my own.

Thomas Berry, whose dream of the earth woke up my own.

David Abram, Martin Prechtel, Naomi Klein, Wendell Berry, Loren Eiseley, Matsuo Basho, Yunmen, Gary Snyder, James Thornton, Sean Kane, Clark Strand, Annie Dillard, Paul Shepard, Barry Lopez, Brian Swimme, among the many whose passion for this planet helped form a riverbed in which my thoughts could flow.

Uncle Max Harrison, Dulumunmun, who helped me understand old ways of living within the terms of the earth, in person.

Alexandra Craig, my publisher at Pan Macmillan, for so quickly seeing what this book might be, and Julia Stiles for being a most sensitive and astute editor.

And David Millikan, for always being here so completely – and always so exactly and entirely himself.

About the Author

Dr Susan Murphy is a writer, authorised Zen teacher and film-maker. Her last book, *Upside Down Zen*, was published in 2004. Film and television writing credits include *The Midas Touch*, *Secrets* (six one-off dramas) and in 1991, her own award-winning feature film as writer-director, *Breathing Under Water*. In 1997 Susan was awarded a five-year QEII Research Fellowship by the Australian Research Council in the social ecology of sense of place. She is a frequent freelance producer of feature radio works for ABC Radio National 360 Documentaries. She divides her time between Berry and Sydney.